ABLAZE
FOR
GOD

9/17/89

Compliments of

Bob & Topsy Plimpton

3711 Clair Drive

Carmichael CA 95608

916-944-0459

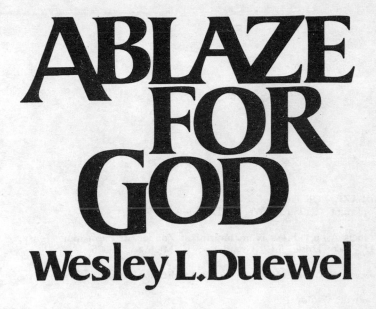

ABLAZE FOR GOD

Wesley L. Duewel

FRANCIS ASBURY PRESS
of Zondervan Publishing House

Grand Rapids. Michigan

ABLAZE FOR GOD
Copyright © 1989 by Wesley L. Duewel

Francis Asbury Press is an imprint of Zondervan Publishing House,
1415 Lake Drive, S.E., Grand Rapids, Michigan 49506.

Library of Congress Cataloging in Publication Data

Duewel, Wesley L.
    Ablaze for God / Wesley Duewel.
      p. cm.
    Bibliography: p.
    Includes index.
    ISBN 0-310-36181-8
    1. Christian leadership. 2. Holy Spirit.   I. Title.
  BV652. 1.D75 1989
  248.8'92—dc19   88-31429
                                        CIP

Printed in the United States of America

89 90 91 92 93 94 95 / DP / 10 9 8 7 6 5 4 3 2 1

Foreword

Ablaze for God is a book that speaks to the desperate need for spiritual leadership in the church. One does not have to be a theologian to recognize that persons prepared to minister in Christ's stead are in short supply today.

The necessary enduement for such service can come only through the enabling grace of the Holy Spirit. We may try to get by on less, but without His indwelling mastery we are noisy brass and tinkling cymbals.

Jesus made this clear to His followers before returning to heaven. Though credentialed as His witnesses and commissioned to disciple the nations, they were instructed to tarry until endued with power from on high. Nothing less than a baptism of consuming fire would suffice for the task to which they were appointed.

The pentecostal effusion of the Spirit marked the beginning of this new era of ministry. It was the culminating step of the descent of the divine into the human. Jesus as an external Presence now became the enthroned Sovereign in the allegiance of His people. His word became like fire within them, and with hearts burning with the love of God, they went on their way with gladness and singleness of desire, praising their Lord.

What the apostolic church experienced is the privilege of every believer. "The promise is unto you, and unto your children, and to all that are afar off" (Acts 2:39, KJV).

Dr. Wesley L. Duewel, eminent author and missionary statesman, brings this truth into focus in these pages. With keen sensitivity and deep humility, he sets forth qualities of life becoming Christian ministry. His treatment is simple and down-to-earth, and unfailingly reflects the mind of one who has sought to sit at the feet of Jesus.

Reading the book has been both a searching and uplifting exercise for me. I commend it to you with the expectation that it will be the same with you.

Robert E. Coleman

To You, My Reader

This is a book for every Christian leader—pastor, lay leader, Bible or Sunday school teacher, youth leader, missionary, or leader in God's cause at large. This is not a "how-to" book, although it is filled with practical suggestions for your leadership. It is a book on the spiritual dynamics of your leadership.

How can you be more of a person of God? How can you have more of God's seal and power on your leadership? God's radiance upon your life; God's anointing on your leadership; a burning love for Christ, the church, and the unsaved; your awesome accountability as a spiritual leader; your prayer life as a leader—these are all topics of ultimate significance to you. Read this from beginning to end. You will want to read from it again and again.

May this book challenge you and drive you to your knees as you read it, as it has me as I have written it. I have caught a vision of what God wants to do for you and me. I write—not as a master of all I seek to share with you—but as a fellow-pilgrim seeking God's highest and spiritual best.

You and I are not worthy to lead or teach God's people. Yet God has chosen us to represent Him. He waits to grant us all the adequacy we need. He longs so to fill us with His Spirit that we will be not just aflame, but ablaze for God.

Wesley L. Duewel

11

YOUR LIFE AFLAME

Chapter 1

You Can Be Ablaze!

Ablaze for God! Your personality so suffused with the presence and beauty of the Lord that others instinctively sense that God is with you! God's hand so clearly evident upon your life and leadership that a quiet holy power and authority seem to rest upon you! A repeated anointing of the Holy Spirit upon you in your daily responsibilities and leadership activities! Whether you are a minister or a lay person, God wants you as a leader to be truly ablaze with His Holy Spirit.

Have you been hungering for more of the touch of the Holy Spirit upon you? Have you longed for God to put His hand more powerfully upon you, His seal upon your leadership and your whole life? Have you felt that God must have more of the anointing of the Spirit available for you than you have normally experienced?

15

When you read the accounts of how mightily God used men like Wesley, Whitefield, Finney, and Moody, have you wished such divine workings were more common among Christian leaders today? Have you longed to have the fire of the Spirit more evident in you—to touch your lips as you speak, your heart as you pray, and to add the "extra" of God's blessing on your leadership? Rejoice! God gave you that desire.

He has a new dimension of divine enabling available for every Christian leader, including you. God is longing to prove to you that He is nearer to you than you realize. He has chosen you and led you for His own purpose. God wants to do new things through you and your ministry.

In a sense of which you undoubtedly feel totally unworthy, you are a person that God wants to use more and more for His glory. In yourself you know that you are not all that special. You would hardly consider yourself a "man of God" or a "woman of God." But God wants to use you in a special way. You are important to Him; He needs you. He wants to prove what He can do through your life and leadership. God wants you to be ablaze with His love, His Spirit, and His power. You can be ablaze for God!

God chose to use fire as a symbol of the Holy Spirit to help us understand what He longs to do for us. He wants His leaders to be ablaze for Him, ablaze with the manifest presence of the Holy Spirit, ablaze with His glory. He wants this sacred enabling to characterize you as one chosen and appointed by Him.

Much in this book can bless anyone hungry for more of God, hungry to be more used of God. It will be specially used for God to help you who are Christian leaders, whether in full-time service or leading Christian groups within your local church. Whatever your leadership role—pastor, elder, deacon, missionary, or leader of a Christian ministry—God wants you to be ablaze. Sunday school teacher, lay leader, prayer group leader—you too can be ablaze for God.

Christian leadership demands our spiritual best, and more. To our best must be added His supernatural enabling touch. We must offer our best; then we must look to God to add His holy fire. Our best is never enough. We constantly need God's extra touch. We need His fire.

In the service of God we need more than ability and skill. We need the manifest presence of God, the consciousness and evidence of God's special touch upon us. We rely, not on our knowledge, training, and experience, but on God's transforming addition to our highest and best. Spurgeon insisted, "It is extraordinary spiritual unction, not extraordinary intellectual power that we need."

We are not satisfied with being faithful; we deeply desire the special awareness of God's blessing upon our faithfulness. We are not satisfied to work hard; we look to God for His empowering upon our earnest efforts. We seek for something more than busyness; we seek the evidence that God uses us.

God created you to be filled with and anointed by His Spirit. That fullness makes your personality complete, enables you to be Christlike and radiant with God's presence, and your service to be Spirit-guided, Spirit-empowered, and used to capacity by God.

As a healthy Christian you can never be satisfied without that indwelling fullness, that divinely imparted Christlikeness, and that transforming enabling that makes you aware that God is using you for His purpose and glory. No Christian leader can be continuously and completely satisfied in his or her ministry without that divine enabling—the glow, the fire, and the power of the Spirit. It must be present in us and active through us.

It is beautiful and challenging to see a life ablaze for God and an inspiration to others. It gives them faith to believe for God's work in the lives of those they love and the situations about which they are concerned. It gives them confidence that God will answer prayer, and makes others want to draw near to God and obey God. A life ablaze is always a much greater blessing than the same life without the flame of the Spirit.

Of John the Baptist, Jesus said, "John was a lamp that burned and gave light" (John 5:35). John Sung, called the greatest evangelist China has ever known, was termed "a living flame of gospel zeal." Again and again some Christian has been so Spirit-filled and so used of God that discerning Christians have referred to that one as "ablaze for God," "ablaze with God's Spirit," "a flaming servant of God," "a fire-baptized leader," or another similar description. Would the people who know you best, those under your leadership, speak of you in those terms?

Spurgeon spoke of the need for leaders "who live only for Christ, and desire nothing but opportunities for promoting His glory, for spreading His truth, for winning by power those whom Jesus has redeemed by His precious blood .... We need red-hot, white-hot men, who glow with intense heat; whom you cannot approach without feeling that your heart is growing warmer; who burn their way in all positions straight on to the desired work; men like thunderbolts flung from Jehovah's hand, crashing through every opposing thing, till they have reached the target aimed at; men impelled by Omnipotence."

David Brainerd, mighty intercessor-missionary to the American Indians, exclaimed: "Oh, that I might be a flaming fire in the service of the Lord. Here I am, Lord, send me; send me to the ends of the earth ... send me from all that is called earthly comfort; send me even to death itself if it be but in Thy service and to promote Thy kingdom."

God chose fire to be the earliest, most continual major symbol and manifestation of His presence. Throughout Old Testament times His Shekinah glory—a miracle glow and fire—constantly proved His presence, guidance, leadership, involvement, and seal of approval. In the New Testament the Holy Spirit fulfilled and spiritualized the Shekinah. God's Shekinah was lost to Israel when they went into captivity and was not restored until its visible return at Pentecost. It was transformed from being primarily God's presence in a place to His presence in His people. Its visibility was temporary at Pentecost, but its reality is abiding in those who are Spirit-filled.

Jesus wanted all His disciples to be baptized with the

You Can Be Ablaze!

Holy Spirit and fire (Matt. 3:11; Luke 3:16). He desires each of us to be so Spirit-filled that our innermost nature is cleansed as by fire and our life made radiant, filled with Spirit-given power and zeal, and aflame with the Shekinah glory of God.

The Spirit's Shekinah-glory, His holy flame, is for all of us believers in this dispensation of grace. It is to make us beautiful in godly personality, radiant in disposition, and fruitful in life. This is God's New Testament norm for His children. How much more it should be typical for all leaders in Christ's church!

Every Christian leader should be an exemplar, should be a demonstration of Christ's visible standard of Spirit-filled living. You as a leader should maintain your spiritual stature, fervency and consistency, and be so marked by the seal of God's Spirit that those you lead thank God for your leadership. They should be motivated to accept and follow your leadership wholeheartedly, and both consciously and unconsciously be drawn nearer to God under your leadership.

All of us as Christian leaders long to be more used of God, more marked by God's seal upon our lives and ministries. Be of good courage. God will satisfy that longing. You can be more ablaze for God than ever before.

> O Thou who camest from above,
> The pure celestial fire t'impart,
> Kindle a flame of sacred love
> On the mean altar of my heart.
>
> There let it for Thy glory burn
> With inextinguishable blaze,
> And trembling to its source return,
> In humble prayer and fervent praise.
>
> Jesus, confirm my heart's desire
> To work, and speak, and think for Thee;
> Still let me guard the holy fire
> And still stir up Thy gift in me.
>
> Charles Wesley

Chapter 2

The Holy Spirit Will
Set You Ablaze

The Holy Spirit is the wonderful third Person of the Trinity about whom we know so little. He loves so tenderly, cares so personally, and ministers to us so faithfully. How amazing that perhaps the most common symbol of this beautiful Person found in the Bible is flaming fire! Why does Scripture choose fire to illustrate His presence and role? What blessedness does this suggest for us when we are Spirit-filled?

An important symbolical message for us in the fire of the Spirit is undoubtedly His work of purifying. This is the central reality in the experience of being filled with the Spirit (Acts 15:9). However, there are other significant truths taught by the fire-symbol of the Spirit. Let us look at these.

John the Baptist had prophesied of Jesus that "He will baptize you with the Holy Spirit and with fire" (Matt. 3:11;

Luke 3:16). The coming of the Spirit is to have the effect of fire. Christ desired that all the fiery ministry of the Spirit be active in the life of His own. He kindled the holy flame of God in the hearts of His followers as He began His earthly ministry. Only on the day of Pentecost, as visibly symbolized by the descent of the holy flame of the Spirit, did Christ so empower by His fiery baptism that the 120 began to spread God's holy fire across the world.

Jesus had said, "I have come to bring fire on the earth" (Luke 12:49). While not all commentators are agreed as to the meaning of this fire which Christ so longed to have arrive, yet over the centuries a host of noted scholar-leaders of the church have seen it as referring to or including reference to the mighty ministry of the Spirit.[1]

Zeal for accomplishing God the Father's purpose was burning in Jesus like an unquenchable fire. He had a "burning readiness to do all the Father's will, even though it cost Him His blood." Our flaming-hearted Savior should have disciples with hearts similarly aflame.

Bishop William Quayle, speaking of a leader, said he "stands at the center of a circle whose entire rim is fire. Glory envelops him. He is a prisoner of majesty." He says that even the speechless should become ablaze on such themes as the gospel compels us to grapple with. "We must not be insipid. There is not a dull page in all this age-long story of the redeeming of the race."

Quayle pleads with us not to be apathetic but to be vigilant. We "are burdened with a ministry which must be uttered lest we die, and, what is more of consequence, which must be uttered lest this wide world die." Let your heart be kindled with his further words: the minister "has his own heart strangely hot. Love girds him. The Christ applauds him. Eternity becomes his tutor. Heaven owns him as its ambassador. With him is God well pleased. A thousand points of fire leap along the horizon of his loving thought and design."

Benjamin Franklin confessed that he often went to hear George Whitefield because he could watch him burn before his very eyes. We have forgotten the root meaning from which we get our word "enthusiastic." It is from *en theos,* i.e., in God. When God gets His flaming Spirit into our personalities He naturally burns within us with holy dynamic. We become ablaze and we set others ablaze. It is a sin for a Christian leader to be drab and uninspiring.

That prince of English preachers, Dr. Martyn Lloyd-Jones, insists, "Preaching is theology coming through a man who is on fire . . . . I say again that a man who can speak about these things dispassionately has no right whatsoever to be in a pulpit; and should never be allowed to enter one. What is the chief end of preaching? I like to think it is this. It is to give men and women a sense of God and His presence."[2]

A respected educator of New York University, H. H. Horne, said the secret of great teaching is contagion. This is the secret of all great leadership, of whatever kind. Martin Luther did not want to lose the fire from his soul; neither dare we. Fire attracts. Fire motivates. Fire kindles fire; it is the nature of fire to set ablaze.

The Salvation Army and many other evangelicals in the British Isles love to sing this hymn written by William Booth, the Army's founder:

> Thou Christ of burning, cleansing flame,
> > Send the Fire!
> Thy blood-bought gift today we claim,
> > Send the Fire!
> Look down and see this waiting host;
> Give us the promised Holy Ghost.
> We want another Pentecost!
> > Send the Fire!
>
> 'Tis Fire we want, for Fire we plead.
> > Send the Fire!
> The Fire will meet our every need;
> > Send the Fire!
> For strength to ever do the right,
> For grace to conquer in the fight,
> For power to walk the world in white—
> > Send the Fire!

To make our weak hearts strong and brave,
    Send the Fire!
To live a dying world to save,
    Send the Fire!
Oh, see us on Thy altar lay
Our lives, our all, this very day.
To crown the offering now we pray,
    Send the Fire!

God said to Jeremiah, "I will make my words in your mouth a fire" (Jer. 5:14). On that occasion God was referring to fire as a judgment. But God similarly makes our words fiery in order that His people may become aflame with holy love, zeal, and obedience.

When the Holy Spirit sets our heart aflame He will cause our words to be aflame. When our personality is aflame with commitment to Christ and with a burning vision of what He purposes to do for us, our whole leadership comes alive with life and becomes vibrant with power.

We must constantly maintain our consecration, even as the priests maintained the fire on the altar of the temple. God honors when we make repeated occasions to renew our commitment, confess our total dependence upon Him, and appropriate and implore anew His gracious Spirit's ministry within and through us. Let us note more fully this fiery ministry of the Spirit.

He sets you aflame with His fiery baptism. "He will baptize you with the Holy Spirit and with fire," said John the Baptist of Jesus (Matt. 3:11; Luke 3:16). This refers to "the fiery character of the Spirit's operations upon the soul—searching, consuming, refining, sublimating—as nearly all good interpreters understand the words."[3] The inner fire of the Spirit sets the Spirit-filled person ablaze with His divine presence.

He empowers you with His fiery divine energy. The fire of God speaks also of His divine energy constantly ready to empower His own who are totally surrendered to Him. Christ desires that all the fiery ministry of the Spirit be active in your life. "I have come to bring fire on the earth" (Luke 12:49). He

23

kindled the holy flame of God in the hearts of His followers as He began His earthly ministry. But He knew they needed more of the Spirit.

On the day of Pentecost the Holy Spirit visibly descended in holy flame upon the men and women gathered in the Upper Room. Empowered by the Spirit, they began to spread God's holy fire that very day. For decades the Spirit's fire kept burning and spreading. Persecution could not quench their fire, it only served to fan the flames. Pentecost lit a flame that by God's grace will never go out.

He sets you aglow with His fiery radiance and zeal. Romans 12:11 urges, "Never be lacking in zeal, but keep your spiritual fervor." You have spiritual zeal when you are spiritually ablaze. Weymouth translates this, "Have your spirits aglow"; Goodspeed, "on fire with the Spirit"; and the Revised Standard Version states it, "Be aglow with the Spirit."

The Holy Spirit revives your spirit, fills you with abundance of life, love, and zeal, and sets you aglow so that you manifest the vibrant, radiant life of God. He will revive your devotion, accelerate your obedience, and fan into flame your zeal. As a Spirit-filled believer you should be marked by the intense devotion, eager earnestness, and the loyal bond-service which characterizes the heavenly angels. Apollos (Acts 18:25) was thus ablaze. The literal translation can be that he was "burning in spirit," or "glowing with the Spirit."

When the Spirit burns within you in freedom and fullness, your inner life becomes radiant, your zeal intense, and your service dynamic. You, in the words of Ephesians 5:16, are "making the most of every opportunity."

The need for this spiritual glow and zeal is emphasized by the condition of the church in Laodicea which had grown lukewarm (Rev. 3:15–16). The spiritual temperature of a Spirit-filled leader should remain high. The Spirit desires so to fill you with burning, glowing agape love that your life is constantly radiant with His presence. Whether the translation of Romans 12:11 is to be aglow with the Holy Spirit or to be aglow in your own spirit, the Enabler is ever the Spirit

Himself. His active fullness must permeate your personality and service.

He provides you gifts which you are to stir into flame. Spiritual gifts are endowments for service given through the activity of the Holy Spirit. God provides whatever divine enablements we need for the service to which He appoints us. The Holy Spirit Himself is God's great gift to us (Acts 2:38) but He bestows grace-gifts (charismata) providing divine endowment and enablement for serving God and the body of Christ.

"Fan into flame the gift of God which is in you," Paul urged Timothy (2 Tim. 1:6). Notice the gift was "in" him. The Holy Spirit primarily works from within, not upon in some external sense. He does not manipulate us, He enables by His indwelling presence and power.

God never appoints or guides you to do a service without being available to endow and empower you with all you need to do His will. But there is a cooperating role for you to play. You must kindle anew, or fan into full flame the divine endowment. God's gifts are given to be cherished and used. To fail to use them as God desires is to fail God and people. We develop them by use. As we use God's endowment, the Spirit enables us, guides us, and makes us fruitful.

The constant tendency of fire is to go out. The Spirit does not waste divine energy. If we do not obey and use the grace God provides, He ceases to bestow. The Greek tense of the verb emphasizes the continuous rekindling of the flame. The spiritual biography of many a Christian leader is "once ablaze." Was there a time when you were more ablaze for God than you are today?

Praise God, a flickering flame that is almost gone can be fanned into brilliant fire again. That fanning must be a continuous process. Five times in Leviticus 6 God instructed that the fire on the altar of burnt offering was never to go out. He had initially given that fire from heaven (Lev. 9:24; 2 Chron. 7:11). God supplies the fire, but we must keep it burning. We constantly need the Spirit's fire, symbolizing the divine presence within us, and we constantly need the touch

25

of God's grace provided through the atonement upon us. Our consecration to God should never lapse and His presence and power in and upon us should never diminish.

God has created our spirits flammable. We are spiritually combustible. Our nature is created to be set ablaze by the Spirit. We are spiritually most blessed, most victorious, most usable when we are ablaze. We are most Godlike when we glow with holy flame—the flame of the indwelling Spirit.

The fire of God gives an unforgettable attraction to the personality of God's messenger and to the content of his message. It imparts a sacred authority that cannot be counterfeited by human efforts. It so seals with the mark of God that others are unable to ignore it. It gives a holy authenticity and assures of integrity. It impresses with the obvious involvement and partnership of God.

Whatever the cost, we must keep the flame of the Spirit burning on the altar of our hearts. The Greek word in "fan into flame" in 2 Timothy 1:6 refers to the use of a bellows to cause a smoldering fire to flame up. This takes effort. Timothy was to do all in his power to intensify the manifestation of the flame of the Spirit. Our cooperation with the Spirit is essential to consistency of flowing ardor, spiritual radiance, and flaming zeal.

General Booth urged his people, "The tendency of fire is to go out; watch the fire on the altar of your heart." Our constant danger is to cool off spiritually, to lose our fervor, and to slow down in zeal. Personal revival comes through renewed commitment and reaffirmed consecration. Everyone needs such personal revival again and again.

We have the great gift of God, the Holy Spirit, but we need to hunger more for the manifestation of His presence, and open our hearts constantly in faith's expectancy for His working, His empowerings and constant enablings in our life. God gives us capacity and the Spirit wants to imbue our whole being with His reality, making us His channels of expression that His holy fire may be constantly visible in us. We must choose whether we will neglect the Spirit, quench the Spirit, or fan into flame the Spirit's presence.

Chapter 3

Wanted: A Burning Heart!

No alternative to the Holy Spirit is available for the Christian leader. He must have a heart ablaze with love to God and love for people. Dr. George W. Peters said, "God, the church, and the world are looking for men with burning hearts—hearts filled with love of God; filled with compassion for the ills of the church and the world; filled with passion for the glory of God, the gospel of Jesus Christ, and the salvation of the lost."

He adds, "God's answer to a world of indifference, materialism, coldness, and mockery is burning Christian hearts in pulpits, in pews, in Sunday Schools, in Bible Institutes, and in Christian colleges and seminaries."

If you as a leader lack a burning heart, few of your people will be known for their burning hearts, and they will make little impact on the world about them. Our communities are little impressed by our programs and manifold activities. It takes more than a busy church, a friendly church, or even an evangelical church to impact a community for Christ. It must be a church ablaze, led by leaders who are ablaze for God.

Samuel Chadwick, late president of Cliff College in Britain, was called "a burning bush." From the time he was filled with the Spirit "miracles of grace were wrought through the influence of a life that was now on fire for God." Francis W. Dixon tells how "the power of his preaching and the moral influence of his church members were so great that the chief constable of the neighborhood publicly expressed his gratitude for the way in which the whole town had been cleaned up by the influence of men and women who had been set on fire with the love of God."

John Wesley, evangel of the burning heart, was reportedly asked by a fellow minister how to gain an audience. He replied, "If the preacher will burn, others will come to see the fire."

One of Wesley's biographers called him a man "out of breath pursuing souls." On the grave of Adam Clarke, early Methodist scholar and protégé of Wesley, are the words, "In living for others, I am burned away."

A century ago T. DeWitt Talmage wrote, "We want in this age above all wants, fire—God's holy fire, burning in the hearts of men, stirring their brains, impelling their emotions, thrilling in their tongues, glowing in their countenances, vibrating in their actions, expanding their intellectual power and fusing all their knowledge, logic, and rhetoric into a burning stream. Let this baptism descend, and thousands of us who, up to this day, have been but commonplace or weak ministers, such as might easily pass from the memory of mankind, would then become mighty." This is still true.

It is also true in the world about us. Some years ago a soldier in Poland told Dr. Harold John Ockenga: "In Poland, it's a race between Christianity and Communism. Whichever makes its message a flame of fire will win."

A passionless Christianity will not put out the fires of hell. The best way to fight a raging forest fire is with fire. A passionless leader will never set the people ablaze. A passionless youth leader will never set the youth ablaze for Christ. Until we are ablaze we cannot speak to the hearts of our people. Bishop Ralph Spaulding Cushman prayed:

> Set us afire, Lord, stir us, we pray!
> While the world perishes, we go our way
> Purposeless, passionless day after day!
> Set us afire, Lord, stir us, we pray!

There is no greater need in our churches and schools today. It is not enough to be evangelical in faith and heart; we must be utterly possessed by Christ, utterly impassioned by His love and grace, utterly ablaze with His power and glory. Every earthly part of our being, in the words of the great hymn, must glow with God's fire divine. The wood is not enough, the altar is not enough, the sacrifice is not enough— we need the fire! Fire of God, descend upon us anew! Set us ablaze, Lord, set us ablaze!

If we are to be an irresistible force for God where He has placed us, we need the Spirit's baptism of fire. If we are to awaken our sleeping church, we need the holy flame that came upon each waiting believer in the Upper Room to descend upon us today. You need it and I need it.

In a stirring article, "Burn On, Fire of God," T.A. Hegre wrote: "It is fire we need: fire to stir our cold and flat emotions, fire to drive us to do something for those who are going into Christless graves. Untold millions today are dying untold because we as Christians have no fire. We need fire— the fire of the Holy Ghost."

We do not need wildfire; wildfire does not glorify our holy Christ. It is holy fire, the fire with which the Holy Spirit baptizes us. We need the fire and zeal of the early church when almost every Christian was ready, if need be, to be a martyr for Christ.

In a hard-hitting sermon, John R. Rice rebuked our lack of fire. "Listen, it is not sinners that are hard. The trouble is it is the preachers that are hard. It is the Sunday School teachers; it is the Baptist deacons and Methodist stewards and Presbyterian elders that are hard. I find it easier to win a soul and get a drunkard or harlot converted than it is to get a preacher on fire for souls."

George Whitefield was mightily used by God as he and John Wesley turned England upside down for Christ and saved, by God's grace, the British Isles from a duplicate of the French Revolution. It was said of him, "From the time he began, as a lad, to preach to the very hour of his death, he knew no abatement of passion. To the end of his remarkable career his soul was a furnace of burning zeal for the salvation of men."

His soul a burning furnace! Ah! There is the secret. Our tragic problem is that we are trying to lead God's people with hearts that have never been truly set ablaze, or hearts that have lost their flame. Elijah prayed until the fire fell on Mt. Carmel. Then the backslidden people leaped to their feet exclaiming, "The LORD—he is God! The LORD—he is God!" (1 Kings 18:39).

Can the Shekinah fire that set the desert bush ablaze set our hearts aflame until we are burning bushes for God? The Shekinah fire on Mt. Sinai suffused the whole being of Moses till his face radiated the glory of God. Can we draw near enough to God until that Shekinah fire begins to transfigure our vessels of clay and our people see glimpses of the glory of God upon us and in us?

Can the Shekinah fire that Ezekiel saw depart stage by stage from Israel return to us today? It returned on the 120 in the Upper Room. If it took ten days of seeking God's face on our part, it would be more than worth it if we too could be set ablaze for God.

It is not to be earned, worked up, or simulated. Only God can baptize with fire. Only God can send Shekinah. Only God can meet your need and mine. We have labored too long without it. We have come far short of God's glory without it. We have left our people too largely unmoved without it.

We cannot light this fire. In ourselves we cannot produce it. But we can humble ourselves before God in total integrity and honesty, confessing our need. We can seek God's face

Wanted: A Burning Heart!

until His holy searchlight shows us what in our hearts and lives prevent our infilling and empowering.

God's holy fire only descends upon prepared, obedient, hungry hearts. Perhaps the need that underlies all needs is that we are not hungry enough, not thirsty enough, not whole-souled enough in our desire. "If you then, though you are evil, know how to give good gifts to your children, how much more will your Father in heaven give the Holy Spirit to those who ask him" (Luke 11:13).

Come! Oh Come! We Plead!

Blessed Holy Spirit, come again today;
Come, indwell us fully in a mighty way.
We are longing, waiting for Your grace and pow'r;
Blessed Holy Spirit, come on us this hour.

Chorus:
Come upon us now! come upon us now!
Hungry, thirsty, longing we before You bow.
Work in all Your fullness in and through us all;
Hungry and obeying, Lord, in faith we call.

Blessed Holy Spirit, let Shekinah fall;
May Your holy glory come upon us all!
May Your fire and glory now on us descend;
Put Your seal upon us; then in service send.

Blessed Holy Spirit, work so all can see;
Exercise Your Lordship—all Your ministry.
Work in pow'r more fully than we've seen or heard;
'Tis Your blessed promise, 'tis Your holy Word!

Blessed Holy Spirit, Oh! do not delay!
Come in might and glory; come on us today!
'Tis for You we hunger; it is You we need.
Blessed Holy Spirit, come, oh come! we plead!

Wesley L. Duewel

YOUR POWER

Chapter 4

Do You Long for Power?

It is natural for you as a Christian leader to long for God's power to rest upon you and be evident in your ministry. You have often longed for more power in prayer, in your speaking, and in your touch upon the lives of those to whom you minister. This is a God-given longing. It was placed in your heart by the Holy Spirit because He wants you to ask and trust God for more of His powerful ministry through you.

God is a God of power. He demonstrated this in creation. Throughout the Old Testament God demonstrated His power in leaders of Israel, in the deliverance of Israel from Egypt, and in godly kings and prophets. He still bestows that power upon His people. "The LORD gives strength to his people" (Ps. 29:11). He himself is the strength, the power of His people (Ps. 28:7). God's power and strength is a major theme of the praise of God's people: "Ascribe to the LORD glory and strength" (Ps. 29:1; 96:7).

God is a God of love and power; He gladly and graciously manifests both. The Christian leader is to demonstrate God's love and God's power through the enabling of the Holy Spirit. To lack either love or power is to have an incomplete seal of the Spirit upon your ministry.

During Old Testament times perhaps a greater emphasis was placed upon God's manifesting His power on behalf of His people than manifesting it within and through His people, although that was also very definitely present. We who live in New Testament times live in the dispensation of the Holy Spirit. God is still as much for us as He was for His people in Old Testament days (Rom. 8:31). This is our constant experience and strength. But in a special new sense God now desires to manifest His power within us and through us.

THE "UPON-NESS" OF THE SPIRIT

This emphasis of the Spirit of the Lord coming upon God's chosen leaders is frequently mentioned in Bible history. "The Spirit of the LORD came upon" Othniel, and he became Israel's judge, went to war, and a forty-year peace resulted. Why could he overpower the enemy even though he had no trained army? Because of God's power upon him.

Today we have not only the spiritual powers of darkness arrayed against us (Eph. 6:12; Col. 1:13), but in addition often we face forces within our secular culture, vested interests, and the unrighteous media. How dare we conclude that we can defeat and rout the forces opposing God's will without His repeated special empowering of our efforts? We must not just take it for granted. We must request it of God, if we would receive it. Just because this is the dispensation of the Spirit does not assure that the Spirit will always automatically undergird, empower, and manifest God's triumph to the maximum.

We are in constant danger of relying too exclusively upon

our human efforts and wisdom. The secret of the manifestation of the Spirit is our asking for it (Luke 11:13; James 4:2).
These promises were recorded long after the outpouring of
the Spirit at Pentecost. This is the Spirit's dispensation, but
His working is often dependent upon our special asking.

The Spirit of the Lord came upon Gideon and he blew a
trumpet and rallied the tribes (Judg. 6:34). Perhaps we at
times have inadequate success in rallying God's people to
worship, witness, give, and pray because the Spirit of the
Lord has not come upon us in power. We try too often to do
God's work without earnestly seeking God's powerful enabling.

The Spirit came upon Jephthah (Judg. 11:29), and he
advanced against strong enemy forces. The secret of advance
for God is the same today. The Spirit must come upon us
again and again. Slow advance may be caused by our failure
to ask and appropriate adequately the Spirit's power.

The Spirit came upon Samson with such power that he
confronted a young lion (Judg. 14:6). The Hebrew literally
says that the Spirit "came rushing" upon him. This same
Hebrew word is also used two other times when Samson
faced emergencies (Judg. 14:19; 15:14). Does this suggest the
instant availability of God's power? God can come rushing
upon us. The requirement of time is usually for our sake or
the sake of others involved. To be endued with God's power
need not be only a long, gradual process. God is able to meet
our need instantly and abundantly.

The Spirit came upon Samson again in power and he
defeated the Ashkelonites (Judg. 14:19). Again the Spirit
came upon him in power and he struck down a thousand
Philistine oppressors. If Samson had continued fighting the
Lord's battles without compromising with sin, the Spirit
would have come on him in power again and again—whenever God saw that there was need.

We are too easily satisfied and glory in occasional past
moments when God touched us by His power. God is
delighted to empower us as often as we need Him, and we
need Him more often than we realize. We have become too

complacent and too easily satisfied with minimum manifestations of His power.

Samuel promised Saul, "The Spirit of the LORD will come upon you in power ... and you will be changed into a different person" (1 Sam. 10:6). When the power had come upon him he was to do whatever his hand found to do. Before the day was over the Spirit "came upon him in power" (v. 10) as he obeyed the Lord. Soon after, as Saul got word of a great national need, again "the Spirit of God came upon him in power" (1 Sam. 11:6). But Saul quickly began to assert his own will and ceased to obey the Lord. We do not read that he again asked God's help. He lost the power and fought his later battles largely on his own.

How tragic when a Christian leader, like Samson, has once known special times of the Lord's enabling when the Spirit came upon him "in power" and then begins to rely on his own "know-how," his busy endeavors, and his administrative skills more than on the Lord. Paul realized that it was when he was aware of his weakness and cast himself upon the Lord that he was most strong (2 Cor. 12:10). Jesus said to him, "My power is made perfect in weakness" (v. 9).

The Holy Spirit empowered David for his role. "From that day on the Spirit of the LORD came upon David in power" (1 Sam. 16:13). The empowering of the Spirit became a continuing experience of David. Repeatedly the hand of God was upon him for accomplishing God's will. A Christian leader has every spiritual right to ask for and receive repeated enduements and enabling touches from God.

Has God touched you with His power? It is His sample of what He delights to do for you whenever you need it. While you cannot dictate how God should manifest His assistance, you have every right to ask and, by faith, appropriate special divine enablings in your ministry and in urgent times of need.

Of Gideon (Judg. 6:34), Amasai (1 Chron. 12:18), and Zechariah (2 Chron. 24:20) it is said that the Spirit of God came upon them and "clothed" them. This suggests a powerful envelopment with the Holy Spirit, a complete enfolding with the presence and power of God. It suggests not just a momentary touch of power, but an abiding envelopment in the Spirit, at least until the particular ministry or God-given assignment is complete.

As Christian leaders chosen by God, we have every right to experience the enveloping Spirit of God. Whether our role is to meet a particular and special need, guide God's people, teach them, encourage them, or rebuke them—God's clothing of our human best by the holy enduement of His Spirit and His power is our privilege. It can be ours through prayer and faith.

Micah testified, "As for me, I am filled with power, with the Spirit of the LORD, and with justice and might [courage, heroism], to declare . . . to Israel his sin" (Mic. 3:8). Even before the coming of the Spirit at Pentecost to fill God's people, Micah knew the infilling of the Spirit's power. Is our lack of true prophetic courage, faithfulness, and forthrightness in proclaiming God's truth, whether in the pulpit or in private counseling, because of our not being filled with the Spirit as God expects us to be?

Our assignments for the Lord are of a different kind today, but the same power is available to us according to our need. God's power is as available for our generation as for any that has ever lived. This is still God's day of grace. It is still the dispensation of the Spirit and His power. God has not changed. We are the ones who fail to appropriate. Ask God today to clothe you with His power!

Chapter 5

The Hand of the Lord
Upon You

"The hand of the Lord" is a term frequently used in the Old Testament to express God's Spirit resting upon a person whether in grace or in power. When God gave Ezra the vision and burden for Jerusalem he went to Artaxerxes with his requests. He reports that the emperor "granted him everything he asked, for the hand of the LORD his God was on him" (Ezra 7:6).

Ezra was conscious of God's gracious hand in his life. In two chapters he refers to it five times. He told Artaxerxes, "The gracious hand of our God is on everyone who looks to him" (Ezra 8:22). He then called his people to prayer and fasting for a safe journey. The dangerous and long trip from Mesopotamia to Jerusalem as the caravan carried the enormous store of gold and silver without armed protection was safely completed. "The hand of our God was on us, and he protected us" (Ezra 8:31).

We too can be unusually conscious of God's gracious hand upon our leadership and our people. This should be our experience repeatedly in this New Testament dispensation. God is longing to be gracious to us (Isa. 30:18). "How gracious he will be when you cry for help!" Isaiah added (v. 19). Normally we do not need to have protracted dry periods in our ministry, prolonged times of only minimal evidence of God's presence with us and His using us for His glory.

We can and should frequently experience God-given empowering, refreshing, and fruitfulness. Many times, like Jacob, we may discover the full realization after the event. "Surely the LORD is in this place, and I was not aware of it" (Gen. 28:16).

We should not require supernatural manifestations to know that we are in the will of God. Nevertheless, God has repeatedly revealed Himself as the God of the supernatural. It often glorifies God when He gives special and visible indications of His favor and blessing. In non-Christian lands that is often needed to confirm the reality of Christ as the living God, and of His gospel as "the power of God unto salvation." Perhaps it is also becoming increasingly important in our own all too skeptical and secular society.

Nehemiah had a similar testimony. "I also told them about the gracious hand of my God upon me and what the king had said to me" (Neh. 2:18). This immediately motivated all the others to join in the task to which God had called them (v. 18). Perhaps there is nothing more effective in uniting a group in faith and love around a leader. Spiritually discerning people quickly notice the evidence of blessing or lack thereof. Because of God's mighty and gracious hand upon you, the people whose prayer backing and cooperation are most essential to the spiritual aspects of your leadership are most confirmed in their loyalty to you. They are zealous to follow your leadership. God's people need to see God in you and God using you.

41

When the hand of the Lord came upon Elijah, he was given superhuman augmentation of his strength (1 Kings 18:46). In the service of the Lord one can receive a divine touch which renews and refreshes spiritually, mentally, and physically. God's touch benefits our whole being (Isa. 40:31).

Ezekiel is the prophet who speaks most of God's hand upon him. The first instance was at the beginning of his recorded ministry. The word of the Lord came to him, the hand of the Lord was upon him, and he saw a vision of the cherubim. The account of his overwhelming call occupies Ezekiel 1:1–3:15.

Eight times Ezekiel reports that the hand of the Lord was upon him. Seven times he tells how the Spirit lifted him up or raised him to his feet. Twenty-four times he tells how the Spirit "led" him, "took" him, or "brought" him. Many of these experiences were part of a vision. The important point is that Ezekiel was conscious that God was touching him, speaking to him, leading him, and using him. He knew the hand of God in his ministry; his ministry would not have been the same without it.

Is it possible for us to be so overwhelmingly aware of God's hand upon us? Does God intend that His conscious touch should be a part of our leadership experience? Perhaps today we do not often use this vivid form of speech. But is the reality behind it available today? Should you be clearly conscious from time to time of God's hand upon you while you lead and minister?

Luke tells us that the hand of the Lord was so evident with John the Baptist even in his childhood (Luke 1:66) that people noted it. As a result of the presence of God with the early Christians "a great number of people believed and turned to the Lord" (Acts 11:21). Is our lack of observable spiritual results at least partly due to our lack of God's hand upon our life and ministry?

How much should we expect to experience something like what Scripture describes in this Hebrew phrase, "the hand of the Lord"? It is another of God's attempts to impress upon us the availability of His power to us and our leadership.

It is a totally biblical emphasis. There is little danger that we will take this to fanatical extremes. Our far greater danger is that we will remain content to work and minister on an almost totally human level. Have you noticed the difference between a Scripture lesson read with or without the hand of the Lord on the reader? The difference between a solo beautifully sung with merely human skill and quality of performance and a solo sung with the hand of the Lord upon the singer?

Why do some messages seem so lifeless? so deadening? so much like a mere secular lecture? Undoubtedly one reason can be that the speaker has not received his message from the Lord. Another reason can be that the messenger does not really believe the message. But have you noticed the difference between a sermon delivered with a tone of faith and enthusiasm and a similar one given when the hand of the Lord is also upon the speaker?

God wants us to receive anew the experience of God's hand upon us, adding His divine dimension to our human best. God wants us to learn a new dependency upon His added enabling, His presence, and His power. We may prefer to describe it in more modern terms. But there is a divine dimension of spiritual reality which God has available and which He longs to add to our leadership.

Our whole culture and the spirit of our age tends to make us self-dependent rather than God-dependent. We do much of our Christian work with very little God-awareness. If we would be ablaze for God we need to cultivate new God-dependency, God-consciousness, and God-imbued living. The leader as a man or woman of God must have a new dimension of God-involvement in his or her leadership. We must become alive to God and to all of His holy influences and enablings. God must become all-essential to us.

Chapter 6

The All-Essential Power

"You are witnesses . . . but stay in the city until you have been clothed with power from on high" (Luke 24:48–49). This was said to a large group of the disciples by Jesus. The command is clear. We are not ready for Christian witness, service, or leadership until we are clothed with the promised power of the Spirit. There was a tremendous difference in the ministry of the disciples before and after the power enveloped and clothed them. Jesus had told them that the Spirit was already with them as His disciples (John 14:17). If any person does not have the Holy Spirit he does not belong to Christ (Rom. 8:9).

But there is always a tremendous difference between being a disciple of Christ indwelt by the Spirit, and being clothed with the Spirit, filled with the Spirit, and empowered by the Spirit. The Spirit must penetrate and possess all of our being. He must control us in all of His lordship. He must pervade our personality. He must add a dimension of supernatural power. It is not enough for us to say that since Pentecost every Christian has the power of the Spirit. The question is, "Are you and I fully appropriating the power available to us?"

James Hervey, one of John Wesley's ministerial associates, describes in these words the difference the Spirit made in Wesley's ministry: "While his preaching was once like the firing of an arrow, all the speed and force depending on the strength of his arm in bending the bow, now it was like the firing of a rifle ball, the whole force depending on the power needing only a finger touch to let it off."

You dare not serve merely with a love for Christ. You must serve in the authority of Christ, with a personality consecrated to Christ. You must be infused with power from on high, suffused with the supernatural, imbued through and through with the holy, dynamic power of God (1 Thess. 5:23).

This is not a power that spectacularly sparks, crackles, and arcs as you reach out and touch needs. It is not a divine shortcut to instant miracles. It is not a superseding of the authority of the Spirit so that you can choose to perform a miracle, heal the sick, or manifest any other gift or demonstration of the Spirit. It is not a power under your control. You do not use the Spirit's power; the Spirit uses you as He works in power. I am not putting a premium on the sensational. Power always makes a dynamic difference, but it is not necessarily spectacular.

But the one clothed with the power from on high, though still a dependent child of God, is enabled to live and serve in a new level of Spirit-given effectiveness. It is not the effectiveness of the person, but of God working through the person. It is the divine clothing, pervading and empowering the human as long as the person serves in total dependence upon the divine Person, in total obedience to the divine guidance, and in total appropriation of the divine provision.

The sacred mystery of divine empowering is that it is all of God in and through you, but it is always dependent on the obedient cooperation of your surrendered being. God does not force Himself upon you. He does not violate your will. He does not manipulate you. Satan manipulates, the occult manipulates. God works in and through you.

God does not automatically manifest His presence in us and His power through us just because we accept Christ as our Savior. He indwells us from the moment we are born of the Spirit. But indwelling and manifestation are two different things. God chooses when to manifest Himself. We must prepare the way of the Lord by remaining cleansed, obedient, consciously dependent upon Him, and hungering for His manifested presence and power. Is this true of you?

Paul was conscious of his total dependence upon the power of God. He knew that God's power must saturate his message so that the faith of the converts would rest upon that power. "My message and my preaching were not with wise and persuasive words, but with a demonstration of the Spirit's power, so that your faith might not rest on men's wisdom, but on God's power" (1 Cor. 2:4–5).

Are you more concerned to choose wise and persuasive words for your messages, your teaching, or your words of counsel than you are to secure "the demonstration of the Spirit's power"? What do you understand by this Bible phrase? To what extent has this "demonstration of the Spirit's power" been your primary concern and experience in your ministry this past year? What steps have you taken to experience this divine enabling?

Dr. Martyn Lloyd-Jones insists, "If there is no power, it is not preaching. True preaching, after all, is God acting. It is not just a man uttering words; it is God using him. He is under the influence of the Holy Spirit; it is what Paul calls in 1 Corinthians 2, 'preaching in demonstration of the Spirit of power'; or as he puts it in 1 Thessalonians 1:5, 'our gospel came not unto you in words only, but also in power, and in the Holy Ghost, and in much assurance.'"[1]

Paul testified that his ministry was based on two things— God's grace and God's power. "I became a servant of this gospel by the gift of God's grace given me through the working of his power" (Eph. 3:7). Both his call to the ministry and his continuing daily ministry was through God's energy and enduement "which so powerfully works in me" (Col. 1:29).

Paul was always conscious of God's mighty power working in and through him. To him it would have been unthinkable to labor for God without that power. God's working in and through him was far more important than his working for God. He labored tirelessly because God worked in him so powerfully. To Paul, the outworking was dependent on God's inworking. He could do for God only as God did in and through him. There is no other way to effective ministry. We are foolish to think that training, skill, and experience constitute an alternative to God's power. There is no alternative.

God's power does not make us passive. Far from it! God's mighty power was the reason that Paul could labor day and night with an intensity which he referred to as a struggle. "I labor, struggling with all his energy, which so powerfully works in me" (Col. 1:29). The Greek word is *agonizomai*. It is the word used for those contending in the Olympic-type contests in Greece. It can be translated "to fight, to engage in fierce conflict, to wrestle, to strain every nerve to attain an object." It involves toil, perseverance, and maximum effort.

So God's power does not work while Paul remains passive. Paul works to win everyone possible to Christ and to "present everyone perfect in Christ" (v. 28). It is "to this end" that he labors, agonizes, wrestles, exerts his maximum effort "with all [Christ's] energy which so powerfully works in [him]." He immediately adds, "I want you to know how much I am struggling for you," how great an agony he has on their behalf. This is the only way to secure New Testament results. We must do our best. God deserves our best. But we must be clothed, filled, and saturated with the power from on high. We must be overwhelmed by the divine energy coming upon us and working through us.

Oh, my Christian co-leaders! We need a new drenching, a new outpouring of the Spirit upon us. We need again and again to have God's power descend upon us, enter into us, fill us, and permeate us until we can truly say of our lives, "Not I, but Christ," and of our ministry, "Not I, but God's Spirit."

We are not ashamed to confess His role. Humble testimony, selfless acknowledgment of the working of God is glorifying to God. But the moment we boast, touch God's glory with our own unworthy hands, or become self-confident and take God's power for granted—that moment God will withdraw His hand and let us labor on entirely on our own.

In fact, after a period of God's mighty working, He in His sovereign wisdom may be pleased to let us labor for a time without such overwhelming consciousness of His presence. We never reach the place where we cease to live and labor by faith.

Sometimes God works with great might without our being aware of it. God is often working silently in the hearts and lives of people as His prevenient grace prepares them for His great day of salvation, revival, and victory. We must persevere in prayer, total obedience, and total dependence on God through those waiting times. God has not forgotten us or His divinely chosen goals. He is marshaling His resources. He is building up His all-essential preparations for His great day of power and triumph toward which He is leading.

Don't demand a constant sense of God's power at work, but expect repeated gracious occasions when God makes you blessedly aware of His holy presence and the silent or open working of His power. God's power is all-essential. Your awareness of it is not essential. But if you rarely, if ever, are made aware of His power at work, it is time to search your heart.

If you perceive that God's powerful Spirit is strongly burdening you for prayer, guiding you in prayer, and adding His might and authority to your praying, you know His power is clothing you, even if you do not see the mighty outworking of His answers to your prayer.

At times Satan seems able to cast a shadow of darkness over you as you pray and try to minister for God. He seems able to block all awareness on your part for a time of God's presence and power. Is that your experience today? Don't be alarmed by these faith moments. Hold steady and pray; labor on in total dependence on God's power even when you cannot see or feel it at work.

As certainly as you have sensed God's presence and power in the past, just so certainly you will sense it again. You are in the midst of a conflict with the power of darkness. Your experience is not unique. God's choicest saints have at times had days, weeks, and even months of such darkness. But God's answer always comes again. Don't try to get off the train while you are going through the tunnel. You are still en route to God's great victory. Hold on, and God's power will be revealed again.

Chapter 7

It Takes Power
to Extend the Kingdom

The kingdom of God, of heaven, of Messiah is a great Bible theme that was proclaimed by Old Testament prophets and repeatedly mentioned by Christ in the Gospels. God is our Sovereign King. His reign in our hearts today and in the world until the return of Jesus is His saving kingdom. It is built through human hands but not by human hands. It is built by the power of God working through the cooperating joint ministry of the Holy Spirit and the Spirit-filled.

"The kingdom of God never means an action undertaken by men or a realm which they set up . . . the kingdom is a divine act, not a human accomplishment, not even the accomplishment of dedicated Christians."[1] The power of the kingdom is operative in and through God's representatives. But the power is not their power; it is the power of God. Christ gives to His own the keys of the kingdom to use in

50

binding and loosing through prayer and obedience (Matt. 16:19; 18:18–20). But the power of the keys remains God's power and is usable only by the Spirit's guidance and enabling.

Kingdom power was present in the ministry of Jesus, and it was present in the ministry of His followers. Indeed, it can be present in your ministry today. But it is not your power. It continues to be given and manifested through you only as God makes it operative and evident.

Our best efforts of themselves do not build or advance the kingdom. Christian efforts are not sufficient. Even the best endeavor of the Spirit-filled is totally inadequate. Nothing less than the Holy Spirit guiding, empowering, and using the efforts of the Spirit-filled can extend Christ's reign in any heart or in any group. The extent to which God can use the influence, witness, and service of a holy people is governed by the extent to which He sovereignly empowers and works through them.

Purity and power are closely associated, but they are not identical. We need both. God wills both for us. They are essential in our living. They are even more essential in our service. Purity can be beautiful and positive, or it can be largely negative. Purity can be retained; power must be renewed. Purity in the form of positive goodness and righteousness is the result of power to be what God wants us to be. God wants to give us the Spirit's power both to be and to do what He has called us to be and do. Purity pertains to living, power specially to service.

The spiritual measure of Christian leaders is the fullness of the Spirit and His enduement of power. Oratory, effectiveness of delivery, and speech are good, but they are not enough. Content, orthodoxy, and solid biblical truth are essential, but they are not enough. Personality, graciousness of speech and action are important, but they are not enough. The power of the Lord must be upon them. All these qualities can exist on the human level. The kingdom must be built, advanced, and manifest on the level of the divine empowering of the human. It must be God working through us.

When some in Corinth began to criticize Paul and his ministry judgmentally, it did not concern Paul greatly. The apostle regarded the Lord as his judge (1 Cor. 4:4). Only God knows the measure of His power working within us. Paul makes it very clear: "The kingdom of God is not a matter of talk but of power" (v. 20). Paul said he would come to Corinth and check both the words and the power of those who were creating confusion. Truth is essential, but in Christ's service it must be truth on fire. Truth without power does not accomplish the will or work of God. It may only deaden or offend.

By the presence or absence of God's power in their lives and ministry, Paul wanted the Corinthians to evaluate the credentials of Christian leaders who came among them. How would you have passed Paul's scrutiny and inspection? In 2 Corinthians 6 Paul gave a list of many ways in which he commended himself as a servant of God. Important among them was ministry "in the Spirit" and "in the power of God" (vv. 6–7).

Paul reminded the Thessalonian church, "Our gospel came to you not simply with words, but also with power, with the Holy Spirit and with deep conviction. You know how we lived among you for your sake" (1 Thess. 1:5). Paul was deeply conscious that the power of God was at work. The Christian leader is usually aware when God's power is specially present. Are you frequently aware of this in your ministry? It was normal to Paul.

Leon Morris spoke the truth when he said, "Whenever the gospel is faithfully proclaimed, there is power. Not simply exhortation, but power."[2] Paul knew that a faith built on words alone, i.e., the message alone, might be tempted to waver. This is why he reminded the Corinthians that both his message and his manner of preaching the message were with a "demonstration" of the Spirit's power (1 Cor. 2:5) and so their faith could be based on that demonstration of power that added to the content of his words. The Greek word translated "demonstration" suggests evidence or proof. "It was a technical term for a compelling conclusion drawn from the premises."[3] God's power was so evident in Paul's message that the Corinthians were compelled to conclude that his message and he as the messenger were from God. Power confirms truth. We dare not depend on truth alone; we must minister truth aflame with God's power.

To Paul this power was so all-essential, so characteristic of his ministry, that he was willing to pay any price so that Christ's power could rest on him. It was as if Paul kept crying to God, "Oh, for more of Your power upon me; oh, for more of Your power manifest through me!" Paul had already known so much of the power of the Spirit that to him this is the mark of his being in the will of God. It is not visions and revelations which are important to him. With reluctance he had just testified to such precious and secret dealings of God with him (2 Cor. 12).

No, what Paul wants is more of the abiding power of Christ communicated through the Spirit. What he desires is not an occasional mountaintop experience. He longs for the continuing experience of God's power every day of his life and ministry. He hungers for, yearns for, and is willing to pay any price if only that power can abide upon him day after day.

"So that Christ's power may rest on me" (2 Cor. 12:9) is his heart cry. Christ had promised power when the Holy Spirit came upon His disciples (Acts 1:8). Paul had over and over experienced that power. It had become characteristic of his ministry. He testified to it repeatedly. He wanted that power to "rest" on him. The Greek word means "to tabernacle." Just as Christ came and tabernacled among us during His incarnation (John 1:14, where the same Greek word is used), so Paul counts his highest ambition in ministry to have Christ's power tabernacle over him. He wants to live day by day within that atmosphere of power.

Most commentators recognize in this heart cry a reference to the Shekinah glory of God which was over the tent in the wilderness, which entered the tent and covered the ark of the covenant in the tent. Later it entered the temple and "tabernacled" over the ark in the Holy of Holies in the temple. As the Shekinah covered the ark, Paul wanted

Christ's power to cover him, overshadow him, and continually rest upon him.

Jesus had told him that such power "is made perfect in weakness" (2 Cor. 12:9). Weakness does not create power. But weakness drives us all the more to God, the source of all divine power. When we recognize how weak and insufficient we are, we call on God, cling to God, and make this the constant cry of our hearts.

When through revelation Paul recognized that his thorn in the flesh (v. 7), all the other opposition, dangers, and sufferings during the years of all-out service for Christ (2 Cor. 11:23–30) served to drive him closer to God and to constant dependence upon God, the apostle responded, "That is why for Christ's sake, I delight in weaknesses, in insults, in hardships, in persecutions, in difficulties. For when I am weak, then I am strong " (2 Cor. 12:10).

For Christ's sake, for the continuing experience of His power, His Shekinah glory tabernacling over me, resting upon me, I will accept any suffering, says Paul. I am completely satisfied, in fact, I rejoice in anything which increases Christ's power on me. This is not the cry of a fanatic volunteering to be a martyr. This is the cry of the foremost apostle of the church who has experienced so much of the power of God that he counts all else as nothing if he can only experience constantly more of that power.

How important is it to you to have the power of Christ, yes, more and more of the power tabernacling, resting, remaining upon you? What have you experienced of this holy power? Not visions, not miracles, not gifts or manifestations— but the silent, all-pervading, all-crowning power of Christ upon you? Filled with that power, energized by that power, clothed with that power, endued for your ministry by that power! That power is the Spirit; that power is Christ himself (1 Cor. 1:24) manifest through the Spirit (1 Peter 1:11). Is that power available today?

Chapter 8

God's Power in the Ministry of John Wesley

John Wesley (1703–91), the evangelist with the burning heart, is one whose ministry was repeatedly characterized by the power of the Holy Spirit. His conversion story is well known. His godly home environment during his childhood, his intention throughout youth methodically to discipline himself for a holy life, his promotion of the Holy Club at Oxford, his two-year missionary experience in North America, and his deep piety yet lack of the assurance of salvation— these are often cited.

Then came his life-transforming new birth on May 24, 1738, when this deeply committed clergyman found Christ while a passage from Martin Luther was being read. Wesley reported that his heart was "strangely warmed," and from that day on he became the proclaimer of the glorious witness of the Spirit to salvation.

What was the secret of his prodigious ministry from that day forward? Respected secular historians have said that through the ministry of John Wesley and his helpers and converts and the great awakening across England that resulted, the nation was saved from the bloodbath that characterized the French Revolution which began two years before Wesley's death. Robert Southey added that Wesley was "the most influential mind" of his century, whose life would influence civilization for "centuries or perhaps millenniums" if the human race lasted that long!

A British nobleman passing through a village in Cornwall, England, and after searching in vain for a place to purchase alcoholic beverages, asked a villager, "How is it that I cannot get a glass of liquor in this wretched village of yours?" The old man, recognizing the rank of the stranger, respectfully took off his cap and bowed and then said, "My lord, something over a hundred years ago a man named John Wesley came to these parts." The peasant then turned and walked away.

For fifty-three years of a tireless ministry Wesley called himself "a man of one book"—the Bible. Yet he wrote over 200 books, edited a magazine, compiled dictionaries in four languages—all in his own handwriting. He crisscrossed England on horseback for a total of some 250,000 miles. For years he averaged twenty miles a day and often rode fifty to sixty and even more miles in a day, stopping to preach along the way. He preached 40,000 sermons—rarely less than two a day and often seven, eight, or even more.

When he was eighty-three he complained that he could no longer read or write more than fifteen hours a day without his eyes hurting. He regretted that he could no longer preach more than twice a day, and confessed his increasing tendency to lie in bed until 5:30 A.M. At eighty-six he was still rising at that hour each morning for prayer.

What was the secret of his tremendous energy, or, even more, the secret of God's tremendous continuous seal upon his ministry? His journal entries for October 3 and 15, 1738, point to his longing for a deeper experience. Historians point to an occasion six months after his new birth. Listen to his own words from the journal: "Monday, January 1, 1739. Mr. Hall, Kinchin, Ingham, Whitefield, Hutchins, and my brother Charles were present at our love-feast in Fetter-lane, with about sixty of our brethren. About three in the morning, as we were continuing instant in prayer, the power of God came mightily upon us, insomuch that many cried out for exceeding joy, and many fell to the ground. As soon as we were recovered a little from that awe and amazement at the presence of His majesty, we broke out with one voice, 'We praise thee, O God, we acknowledge thee to be the Lord.'"

The account reminds one, in some ways, of the experience of the apostles in Acts 4:23–31. This outpouring of the Spirit upon this union meeting of the several Methodist societies seems to have been a profound turning point in Wesley's ministry. From then on he preached with unusual anointing and power, and that preaching resulted in powerful conviction of sin in the hearts of multitudes of people.

Wesley's printed sermons do not contain illustrations, which often are used by God today to touch people's heartstrings. Nothing else in his messages would seem to arouse emotions. When you read them today you may wonder why they were so effective. Yet God used them to lead thousands to the Lord. It was not the word; it was God's power on the word.

From that time on Wesley preached with such new authority and power that thousands came to the Lord. His journals, which he kept faithfully over the years, tell of people seized suddenly with tremendously deep Holy Spirit-given conviction for sin. The accounts remind one of Paul's experience when God's power struck him down on the road to Damascus. Under Wesley's preaching people often suddenly cried out aloud in great soul anguish, many falling on the ground from the hand of God upon them as they repented. Within minutes they would be rejoicing with a wonderful assurance of sins forgiven and a deep awareness of the peace of Christ. People saw their sins as they appear in the sight of our holy God and cried out for deliverance. Some were seized with trembling before God's awesome presence.

Others were gripped by tremendous conviction of sin as much as three weeks afterward. They would suddenly cry out as if in the agonies of death, repent, and soon rejoice in the forgiveness of sins. On April 21, 1739, at Weaver's Hall, Bristol, "a young man was suddenly seized with a violent trembling all over, and in a few minutes, the sorrows of his heart being enlarged, sunk down to the ground." Soon he found peace.

On April 25, while Wesley was preaching "immediately one, and another, and another sunk to the earth; they dropped on every side, as if thunderstruck." It seemed to be almost repetition of Paul's experience on the road to Damascus. Always people were gripped with an awesome revelation of God and of the sinfulness of their sin. Critics standing by would suddenly be gripped by similar conviction and be converted on the spot. One strong opponent was suddenly knocked off his chair and fell calling on God.

Wesley tells of another place as God's power was on his preaching: "One and another and another was struck to the earth; exceedingly trembling at the presence of his power. Others cried with a loud and bitter cry, 'What must we do to be saved?'"

The evangelist was repeatedly and heatedly opposed, often mobbed, and in danger of his life. But of his preaching Wesley wrote, "The power of God came upon his word; so that none scoffed, or interrupted, or opened his mouth." At Wapping twenty-six people were gripped with such conviction of sin that "some sunk down and there remained no strength in them, others exceedingly trembled and quaked." Wesley prayed that no observer would be offended by these happenings. He neither encouraged them nor tried to stop them, recognizing that it was the hand of the Lord.

With great liberty and power he often preached to vast audiences in the open air. Even in rain or biting cold he preached to the crowds, at times his sermon being two and three hours in length. On December 23, 1744, another mighty

58

anointing came upon him as he preached at Snow Fields. He wrote, "I found such light and strength as I never remember to have had before."

Again and again when exhausted from his constant ministry he found new physical and spiritual strength as he prayed. One such occasion was March 17, 1740. Wesley tells of a trip on horseback when great weariness was upon him. "I then thought, 'Cannot God heal either man or beast by any means, or without any?' Immediately my weariness and my headache ceased, and my horse's lameness in the same instant."

I have cited only a few of the many instances of God's power on Wesley. There is no human explanation except his life of prayer and repeated sense of God's power. It was nothing worked up. He did not seek emotion or outward demonstration. God simply clothed his constant ministry with power.

Chapter 9

God's Power in the Ministry of Charles G. Finney

As a young law student Finney became interested in the Bible and purchased a copy. He was greatly hindered as he listened to prayers in church which never seemed to be answered. As he became more and more concerned about his soul, Christians offered to pray for him, but he told them he did not see how it would do any good, for they were continually asking and not receiving from God.

In October 1821, after several days of increasingly deep Spirit-given conviction of sin, Finney came to a clear experience of Christ in the morning and was filled with the Spirit in the evening.

I was powerfully converted on the morning of the 10th of October, 1821. In the evening of the same day I received overwhelming baptisms of the Holy Ghost, that went through me, as it seemed to me, body and soul. I immediately found myself endued with such power from on high that a few words dropped here and there to individuals were the means of their immediate conversion. My words seemed to fasten like barbed arrows in the souls of men. They cut like a sword. They broke the heart like a hammer. Multitudes can attest to this . . .

This power is a great marvel. I have many times seen people unable to endure the Word. The most simple and ordinary statements would cut men off their seats like a sword, would take away their strength, and render them almost helpless as dead men. Several times it has been true in my experience that I could not raise my voice, or say anything in prayer or exhortation, except in the mildest manner, without overcoming them.

This power seems sometimes to pervade the atmosphere of the one who is highly charged with it. Many times great numbers of persons in a community will be clothed with this power when the very atmosphere of the whole place seems to be charged with the life of God. Strangers coming into it and passing through the place will be instantly smitten with conviction of sin and in many instances converted to Christ.

When Christians humble themselves and consecrate their all afresh to Christ, and ask for his power, they will often receive such a baptism that they will be instrumental in converting more souls in one day than in all their lifetime before. While Christians remain humble enough to retain this power, the work of conversion will go on, till whole communities and regions of country are converted to Christ.[1]

The morning after Finney's enduement with power, or baptism of the Spirit as he himself often called it, God began to use him mightily. Almost every person Finney talked to that day was seized with conviction for sin and then or later found the Lord. He left his law office to talk to people about their salvation. He won a Universalist and a liquor distiller that day. The word spread around the village and although no meeting was announced, most of the people gathered in the church that night. No one spoke, so finally Finney got up and testified. Many were immediately convicted of sin. From then on a meeting was held each night for some time, and all but one of Finney's former companions and many others from there and from surrounding communities found the Lord.

Shortly afterward Finney began to fast and pray and meetings continued. One day as he approached the church building, God's "light perfectly ineffable" so shone in his soul that it almost prostrated him. It seemed brighter than the noon-day sun, and reminded him of Paul's conversion on the way to Damascus. Many were saved, some were healed in body, and Finney learned what it meant to travail in prayer for the unsaved. Isaiah 66:8 was repeatedly impressed on his heart by God: "No sooner is Zion in labor than she gives birth to her children."

After his ordination in 1824 his first regular meetings were at Evans Mills, New York. For several weeks he preached without results. In one service he demanded that the congregation decide for or against Christ, which angered them. Finney spent the next day in fasting and prayer. That night an unusual sense of anointing and power came upon him and a wave of conviction swept over the people. Throughout the entire night people sent for him to pray with them. Even hardened atheists repented and were saved.

From then on, with increasing power and results he preached the gospel across America and later in Britain. Sometimes the power of God so came upon a service that almost the entire audience fell on their knees and prayed, while some were prostrate on the floor. At times the power of God would be so mightily upon him that he felt himself almost lifted from his feet. At other times it seemed that "a cloud of glory" descended upon him as he ministered.

Often in towns and cities where he ministered a divine solemnity, a hallowed calm came over the area until even the unsaved remarked about it. Sometimes unsaved people felt deeply convicted of their sins as soon as they entered the city.

In one New York town as Finney preached against sin and unbelief, within fifteen minutes an awesome solemnity from God "seemed to settle upon them. The congregation began to fall from their seats in every direction, and cry for mercy. If I had had a sword in each hand, I could not have cut down as fast as they fell. Nearly all were either on their knees or prostrate."

In 1826 in Auburn, New York, some of the professors in the theological seminary became hostile to his ministry. They wrote to ministers in areas where Finney had not preached, with the result that many opposed his revival ministry. Spies were sent to try to find something that could be reported to damage his influence.

God's Power in the Ministry of Charles G. Finney

One day while Finney was praying at length, as he regularly did, Jesus appeared to him in a vision. "He drew so near to me while I was engaged in prayer that my flesh literally trembled. I shook from head to foot under a sense of the presence of God." Finney described the experience as like standing atop Sinai with its thunderings.

But instead of wanting to flee, he felt drawn nearer and nearer to God. As His presence filled him Finney felt "unutterable awe and trembling" like Daniel (Dan. 10:8–11). God gave him special promises of assurance that no opposition would prevail against him, and he had nothing but love and kind feelings to the ministers opposing him. He was so sanctified in soul that he never felt one unkind feeling toward his opposers.

At times God gave Finney detailed instructions on what to say and how to approach seemingly impossible individuals and then the Spirit came on them in conviction and salvation. He seemed constantly led or restrained regarding places of ministry.

The power of God that came upon people under Finney's ministry was not something due to his presence, but to the presence of the Spirit. People gripped by God during a service often continued under the awesome hand of the Spirit after they returned home. Until they completed their repentance, restitution, and confession they found it practically impossible to go about their normal duties.

A well-known businessman in Auburn strongly opposed his wife's Christian experience and did not let her attend the meetings for some days. One night before the service she prayed at length, and when her husband arrived he announced that he would take her to the meeting. He intended to find things to ridicule and oppose.

Finney knew nothing of this, but early in the service God gave him a text, "Let us alone!" from Mark 1:24, and anointed him with special power as he preached. Suddenly the businessman screamed and fell from his seat. Finney stopped preaching and went to him. The man had recovered some strength, had his head in his wife's lap, crying like a child and confessing his sins. People began to weep across the church. Finney dismissed the service.

The man had to be helped to his home. Immediately he sent for his former sinful companions and confessed his sins to them and warned them to "flee the wrath to come" (Matt. 3:7). For several days he remained so overcome by the power of God that he could not walk around, but kept sending for people, making confessions and asking forgiveness, and exhorting people to be saved. He became, in time, a useful elder in the Presbyterian church.

On the other hand, at times God used the physical presence of Finney to bring people to Christ. The power of Christ was so on him and such a holy influence for God seemed to emanate from him that people were led quickly to Christ. It seemed as though Finney's arrival was so accompanied by the presence of the Lord that unsaved people were gripped by the Spirit of God. Until the very end of his life not only did revivals break out almost anywhere he began to labor, but often salvation came to the homes of the people where Finney visited.

One evening they arrived in Bolton, England. Their host had invited a few people in for conversation and prayer. Mrs. Finney noticed a woman deeply moved upon, so she took her by the hand and motioned for Finney to come. Within minutes she was rejoicing in Christ, and the woman's face glowed with her new experience in Christ.

During his ministry at New York Mills, he visited a cotton factory. When he got within eight or ten feet of a young woman trying to mend a broken thread, she sank down and burst into tears. Others in the room noticed and began to weep, and in a few minutes nearly everyone in the large room was in tears.

The conviction of the Lord spread from room to room. The owner of the factory told the superintendent to close down. All the workers were gathered in a larger room and Finney spoke to them. Revival went through the building with such power that in a few days nearly everyone in the mill had been converted.

Finney was persuaded to preach in Rome, New York, one Sunday. The next day many convicted people gathered in a home, so deeply moved that after a few remarks by Finney he suggested they dismiss the service. He prayed "in a low, unimpassioned voice." People began to sob and sigh. Finney tried to restrain the emotion by asking each to go home in silence without speaking a word to anyone. But they went weeping and sighing down the street.

Early the next morning, calls came from all over town for him to visit various homes to pray for the deeply convicted. He and the pastor would enter a home and neighbors would rush in. All morning was spent moving from home to home.

In the afternoon, people literally ran from every direction to a large room for a service. Many were converted and the meeting lasted till night. So mightily did God work that for twenty days a prayer meeting was held each morning, a meeting for inquirers each afternoon, and a preaching service each evening.

Three men ridiculed the work, and spent a day drinking till one of them fell dead. The other two were speechless. Nearly all of the lawyers, merchants, physicians, and other leading people were converted; in fact, it seemed that almost the entire adult population of Rome came to Christ. In twenty days at least 500 were converted. A pastor said, "So far as my congregation is concerned the millennium is come already."

HOW THE POWER WAS MANIFESTED

1. *Power was manifested in Holy Spirit-given conviction.* Through Finney's ministry the power of the Lord was manifested in overwhelming conviction of sin and spiritual need. While one normally thinks of such conviction leading to the convicted person's loss of appetite or desire to sleep, in Finney's ministry people were even more powerfully seized by the Spirit. This was not brought about by conscious use of psychology or any form of manipulation of emotions. Rather, it seemed the direct effect of the Spirit upon people, usually after hearing Finney speak or pray.

Often people lost strength to sit, stand, or even to speak aloud for a time. Sometimes they collapsed on the floor; at other times they were suddenly smitten off their chairs. At times strong men became so weak they had to be helped home by friends.

Often the Spirit's conviction pierced the people with intense inner pain and remorse for their sins and resistance to

God. Finney described it frequently in words like this: "The work was with such power that even a few words of conversation would make the stoutest men writhe in their seats, as if a sword had been thrust into their hearts . . . the pain that it produced when searchingly presented in a few words of conversation would create a distress that seemed unendurable."

While Finney preached for some months in Philadelphia in 1829 God began to work among lumbermen who brought their logs down the Delaware River to sell. Many found God and then went back up the river to their places and began praying for the salvation of others. Many instances were reported of two or three lumbermen living alone in little shanties who had attended no meeting and knew almost nothing of God. They would be suddenly convicted in their shanties, go out and ask other lumbermen what to do, and then be wonderfully saved. More than 5,000 people over an eighty-mile range were converted in this way.

2. *Power was manifested in tremendous prayer burdens.* Finney was converted while praying in the woods. That evening as he sat by a fire the Spirit baptized him in a mighty way and wave after wave of love swept over his soul.

Shortly, Finney began the habit of rising long before daylight to pray. At times others joined him in those prayer seasons. Often converts were gripped with a tremendous zeal for prayer. In his later ministry two ministers at times set aside almost all activity and gave themselves to prayer for months for Finney's ministry.

As a young Christian, Finney often had such precious seasons of communion with God that, he said, could not be described in words. He had frequent days of fasting, a practice which characterized his ministry throughout his life. At times God's power burdened him so deeply for others that he literally groaned deeply and loudly. Throughout his life-long ministry he often mentioned giving himself to intense prayer and fasting.

Often tremendous prayer burdens came upon the new converts. Sometimes they prayed whole nights until they were physically exhausted with the burden for the salvation of the unsaved. Prayer meetings multiplied. At times several converts would agree in prevailing prayer for the salvation of one unsaved person after another, and would see many brought to the Lord.

Finney himself felt at times a tremendous spirit of importunity and daring faith. It seemed to him that he was enabled to pray without ceasing. He testified that God's power gripped him with both prayer agony and faith. He spoke of being able to "put on the harness for a mighty conflict with the powers of darkness" for an outpouring of the Spirit. Repeatedly he felt the power of the Spirit coming on him for intercession.

WIDESPREAD EFFECT OF FINNEY'S MINISTRY

About 1830, according to the estimate of Dr. Henry Ward Beecher, at least 100,000 were converted and joined the churches in one year through the Finney-related revivals and their spreading influence. Probably this was the greatest harvest since Pentecost.

In 1849 God began to use Finney in revival in London. At times 1,500 to 2,000 would respond to an invitation to receive Christ. Ten years later he was told that nearly all of the converts of those years were still standing true.

The great revival that swept America in 1858-59 was sometimes called the revival of the united prayer meetings. Dr. Lyman Beecher called it "the greatest revival the world has ever seen" with at least 600,000 conversions. It was considered a direct result of Finney's ministry over the previous years, although he was not usually present.

Bishop W. A. Candler asserted that at least one million were converted in this revival. Dr. J. Edwin Orr, historian of Christian revivals, agrees with the bishop.[2]

The permanence of the results of Finney's ministry was outstanding. After the revival in Gouverneur, New York, it is said that no dance or theatrical play could be held for six years. Careful research showed that eighty-five percent of those converted in Finney's meetings remained true to the Lord. Even the ministry of evangelists like Moody showed a permanence of only thirty percent. There is no substitute for the power of the Lord as was so manifested in Finney's life and ministry.

Chapter 10

God's Power in the Ministry of Duncan Campbell

My dear friend, the Rev. Duncan Campbell, minister of the United Free Church of Scotland, was mightily used in the Hebrides revival which began in December 1949 and continued in several waves in succeeding years. Perhaps no minister of this century experienced so many remarkable manifestations of the power of the Lord. He was not a part of the charismatic movement, and there was no emphasis upon gift manifestations. To the day of his death in 1972 he remained the humble prophet of the Lord.

In April 1918, bleeding profusely from almost fatal wounds in one of the last cavalry charges of World War I, Duncan Campbell was flung across a horse for evacuation and treatment. He prayed McCheyne's famous prayer, "Lord, make me as holy as a saved sinner can be." Instantly he felt the mighty power of God like a purging fire sweep through his whole being. God's presence and power were so real that he thought he was going to heaven.

As he lay on a stretcher among the wounded in the Casualty Clearing Station, he quoted, in the Gaelic speech of the Scottish highlands, the metrical version of Psalm 103, so beloved by Scots. Within minutes the mighty conviction of the Holy Spirit fell upon the other wounded, and seven Canadians were born again in the same instant. Then one by one they began to testify. Duncan had discovered the secret of the supernatural power of the Holy Spirit. From then on until his death he had a consuming thirst for God, revival, and the manifestation of God's power.

When the war was over and his recuperation completed, he started out in the country districts of Argyllshire, visiting from home to home, reading Scripture, testifying, and praying with the people. He soon joined the Faith Mission Training Home in Edinburgh for a concentrated nine-month course. In his practical assignments he began to win people to Christ. One day before class began, Duncan rose to his feet and testified that Jesus was his dearest Friend. God's power descended on the class, the students fell to their knees, studies were forgotten, and they prayed on for hours. This was the first hint of God's plans to use Campbell mightily in real revival.

After graduation Duncan, with a Faith Mission team, began to preach in country school buildings and churches. God poured out His Spirit in power. A schoolteacher was so gripped by God as she rode her bicycle that she had to kneel by the roadside as she received salvation. Up to 200 people began to attend services. Old and young were deeply convicted of sin and turned to Christ.

Much opposition faced him when he began ministry on the Isle of Skye. Duncan walked the roads at night praying for God's help. Three young women were given a great prayer burden and prayed all night in their home while Duncan did the same in a barn. The next evening God's power fell on the meetings. People were so seized with the conviction of the Holy Spirit that they groaned for mercy. Attendance increased and God's power was felt throughout the community. Whole families were converted.

Duncan went from village to village, preaching wherever he could and praying with people by the roadside, on the hillsides, in homes, or wherever he found them. New converts began to pray for unsaved relatives and many were converted. One, returning from Australia, became convicted by the Spirit on shipboard and was converted before he reached Scotland.

Sometimes people were drawn from their homes by the mighty power of the Spirit and came to places where some of the congregation were gathered—even outside a police station. God was so present that people fell on their knees and began to pray. At times people in the services were bowed before the awesome presence of God by the Spirit's power. Christians groaned and sinners cried out for mercy.

During the awakening at Barvas, God's power so worked throughout the community that most secular work was abandoned and people sought God throughout the day in their homes, barns, sheds, by the roadside, and in the fields. It was Duncan's custom to extend his ministry in a place as long as people continued to come to the Lord, and then he would move on to another community.

During the revival on Lewis, the northernmost island of the Hebrides, it seemed as if the whole island were saturated with God. Visitors were gripped by the Spirit before their feet touched the island. A man said to a local minister that he had not attended a service, but he could not get away from the Holy Spirit. A young bus driver stopped his bus and pleaded with the passengers to repent.

At times God's convicting power fell upon the people until they wept so much that Campbell had to stop preaching. No one could hear him. People began to weep as they walked alone. Some were prostrated by the power of God while they were alone in their fields or at their weaving looms. Some walked the roads at night, unable to sleep because of such deep conviction of sin.

A group of Christians gathered one night to pray for the

70

people still unsaved and apparently unmoved by God. About midnight Duncan turned to the local blacksmith and asked him to pray. Suddenly the whole house shook as if by an earthquake. Dishes rattled, and "wave after wave of Divine power swept through the building."[1] Rev. Campbell pronounced the benediction at once. As they left the building the whole community seemed to have come alive with an awesome awareness of God's presence. Night after night people found God in their homes.

In one service, "with the force of a hurricane the Spirit of God swept into the building." (An almost identical event happened in the ministry of Andrew Murray in South Africa.) Instantly many were prostrated before God, while others wept or sighed. The effect spread throughout the island, and people hitherto indifferent were conquered by the Holy Spirit.[2]

While Duncan Campbell was in the middle of a convention service in Northern Ireland, the Holy Spirit suddenly impressed upon him the name of the little island of Berneray off the coast of Harris. This was repeated three times in the next minutes. Duncan told me that he had never been to the island, never corresponded with anyone nor ever known anyone on the island. Immediately he left the service (to the consternation of the convention coordinator), gathered his things from his hotel, and left at once for the airport.

When he reached Berneray, he found that a local elder had prayed all night for revival and that God had told him He would send Duncan Campbell and work through him. The elder had been so sure of God's work that he had already sent word around the island, and had announced a service for a few hours after Duncan stepped on the shore.

On the third or fourth evening as the people were leaving the church, the Holy Spirit suddenly fell upon them as they reached the gate. No one could move—so mightily were they arrested by the Spirit's power and a tremendous sense of the presence of God. Duncan called them back into the building, and a mighty movement of God began. All over the island lives were shaken and transformed. Twenty years later

71

Campbell was told that those converted in the revival were still walking with the Lord.

In his later years, like Finney, Duncan gave himself to leadership in a Bible college. At times students trembled as he opened the Word of God to them. "There was something sacred about the way he used God's name, and often the atmosphere of heaven filled the room when, with reverence and tenderness, he simply said, 'Jesus.' We felt we were standing on holy ground."[3]

In March 1960 in a college prayer session, God suddenly came in power and "did in seconds what others had been trying to do for months."[4] God's power was so present that many wept silently. One young woman reported, "It seemed that if I lifted my head I would look upon God." Wave after wave of God's power passed through the room. Suddenly all in the room heard heavenly music coming from the skies.

On at least two other occasions that we know of, people present with Duncan suddenly heard similar singing by heavenly choirs. Once at about two o'clock in the morning, the congregation in one church left and walked together across the fields to another church where the Spirit had brought others and suddenly fallen upon them. As they walked in the night, they suddenly heard the choirs singing in the skies, and all 200 fell on their knees. The experience was overwhelmingly sacred.

While Duncan appreciated all manifestations of God and heaven, he was not a charismatically inclined person. He remained a Scottish Presbyterian churchman. He did not encourage people to seek spectacular manifestations. He did not want people to get their attention focused on emotion and off the awesome majesty of God. He had received a mighty infilling of the Holy Spirit and lived in the fullness of the Spirit. But he believed that the most important thing about anyone was the silent influence of his personality filled with the fullness of God.

One day in Lisburn, Northern Ireland, the chairman of the convention where Duncan was speaking was alone in the dining room when he suddenly sensed "the brightness of the presence of the Lord" transforming the whole atmosphere. He felt so unworthy of being in such an awesome manifestation of God's presence that he stepped out into the garden, where he stood weeping silently. Then Duncan appeared—his face glowing as he told of a promise the Lord had just given him of outpoured blessing.

All day long God's presence hovered near. In the evening service, after the final message and benediction, the organist was so overcome by the presence of God that her fingers were powerless to touch the keyboard and play the postlude. The entire congregation was so held by the power of God that they sat in holy stillness and for half an hour no one moved. Then some began to pray and weep. Four people later testified to hearing indescribable sounds from heaven.

To sit by Duncan Campbell and hear him humbly recount some of his experiences of God's supernatural working—even pointing to the spot where we sat as he told what God had done at that very place—or to hear him recount to a group of ministers, by my request, some of these tremendous scenes of God's presence and power, was to have one's heart revived and to glimpse anew that we have learned only the ABC's of all God longs to do for us.

Chapter 11

You Need Repeated Empowerings

The more you experience God's power working in your life and through your ministry, the more you will sense your repeated need of the Spirit's new touch. The Holy Spirit is leading you into this deep awareness of your need and your joy in the Spirit's availability to you.

When He fills us, that is, takes complete lordship in our lives, He cleanses and gives us power to be victorious in our Christian living. As the gospel song states, "His power can make you what you ought to be." But in the service of God, indeed, in dynamic Christian living of the Spirit-filled life, you need new infillings, new empowerings, new anointings, new outpourings of the Spirit from time to time.

In the book of Acts the 120 born again disciples who gathered in the Upper Room were all filled with the Holy Spirit at Pentecost (Acts 2:4). Later God used Peter and John to heal a man crippled from birth who had begged each day at the temple gate. Such a crowd gathered that Peter preached to them and another 2,000 new believers were added to their number. The Sanhedrin threatened Peter and John and commanded them not to speak again in the name of Jesus.

The Christian leadership group went to prayer. The Holy Spirit came upon them. The place where they met was shaken as by a mighty earthquake, and we read, "they were all filled with the Holy Spirit" (Acts 4:31). Many of these, if not all, had been present at Pentecost and had all been filled then. Thank God, once one has totally surrendered to the lordship of Christ through the Spirit, one can be refilled again and again as often as one needs it.

The Spirit mightily anointed Stephen as he spoke to the Sanhedrin (Acts 6:10), and filled him as he was being stoned to death (Acts 7:55). While Peter preached to Cornelius and his family, the Spirit came upon them (Acts 11:15).

When Ananias placed his hands on Paul's head and prayed, the Holy Spirit filled Paul (Acts 9:17). The Holy Spirit filled him when he confronted the sorcerer Elymas (Acts 13:9). When he prayed for the Ephesian disciples, the Holy Spirit came on them (Acts 19:6). At Antioch after Paul's ministry, the report was that "the disciples were filled with joy and with the Holy Spirit" (Acts 13:52).

It is spiritually natural for the Holy Spirit to come upon God's children again and again, once they have been initially filled with His presence and power. Whenever new special times of need arise, the Spirit is available to empower and fill again. God is delighted to anoint us, empower us, and cause His Spirit to flow through us out to others with their needs. As we walk close to God in obedience to His will and as we seek His face for new enduements, we receive by faith His new outpourings.

Says Dr. Martyn Lloyd-Jones, "This 'accession of power,' or if you prefer it, this 'effusion of power' upon Christian preachers is not something 'once for all,' it can be repeated, and repeated, and repeated many, many times."[1]

Often these new outpourings, new anointings, are not

accompanied by any visible evidence, or even strong emotions. The Holy Spirit is a holy *Person,* not a holy emotion. Yet as this holy Person works within us He imparts His holy power, His divine adequacy, to us in such a way that we feel new inner strength, new enablement above our own resources, a sense of special spiritual authority and faith, and we recognize a new effectiveness which we must credit entirely to the Spirit, not to ourselves.

On the other hand, this awareness of God's hand upon us in new empowering and enabling gives us deeper inner joy, a pervading sense of resting on God's faithfulness, an abiding peace that may be beyond words to describe. In this sense it very profoundly moves our emotions. It may bring tears of humility and joy as we recognize our own unworthiness. It may instill a deep holy excitement at what God can do and what we increasingly expect Him to do. It may fill our lips with praise and our heart with song.

Yes, the holy Person, the third Person of the Trinity, as He indwells us profoundly affects our inner life. He is not superficial emotion, worked up by singing choruses over and over or by waving of hands or shouting of praises. Holy hands may be raised in faith and prayer to God, holy praises may be spoken and sung. But these occur not in human zeal but as the outflow of a heart glorying in God's presence, goodness, and grace.

The deepest emotions are often the most overwhelmingly private and quiet. Sometimes God's presence is so sweet or so awesome that we almost hesitate to move or speak. Yet at other times God's famous leaders as well as hidden saints have broken out in song, praise to God, or loud exclamations of "Glory to God," "Praise to the Father, Son, and Spirit," "Thank you, Jesus," or other spontaneous exultations.

Power is not an emotion; power from God is inner strength and enabling. Power is God's bestowal of inner holy dynamic (indeed, *dunamis* is the Greek word from which we derive such words as dynamic, dynamite, and dynamo).

Praise God, it is often recognizable when He has added His special power to our unworthy efforts.

This holy awareness was a frequent experience in the life of Wesley, many of the early Methodist leaders, and Charles G. Finney during his years of ministry. It has been a frequent experience of many a comparatively unknown servant of God. I trust that you know from experience what I am writing about and that your own heart testifies that though you may feel most unworthy, yet God is truly present in your leadership and ministry. It is an experience we must never boast about and may seldom mention, but we need it repeatedly in our service for Him.

Sometimes this special empowering of the Lord comes upon a group of people at the same time, as recorded in the book of Acts. Almost simultaneously many sense God's unusual nearness, or the enveloping presence of God that descends upon a gathering of God's people. Sometimes there comes an awesome and profound sense of the majesty and holiness of God that results in a holy hush. This has been a frequent experience over the centuries among God's children of various denominational backgrounds, especially among the Friends.

Perhaps most of the time this empowering has come as a personal and private experience. Just as Paul was reluctant to mention often his deepest experiences of God, yet constantly mentioned the power of God, so you too will want to strike the balance of not drawing attention to yourself, nor priding yourself in God's hand upon you, yet not neglecting to point constantly to God's presence and power so that God will receive all the glory.

Chapter 12

Do You Lack Spiritual Power?

Over many a Christian leader's record could be stamped these words: LACKS POWER. Why do so many ministers and lay leaders have a vague restless awareness that something is lacking in their leadership? They have had adequate training; they make all the needed preparation; they work faithfully and hard. But it all remains largely on the human level.

If you rely on training, you accomplish what training can do. If you rely on skills and hard work, you obtain the results that skills and hard, faithful work can do. When you rely on committees, you get what committees can do. But when you rely on God, you get what God can do.

God's work deserves our best, but God's work demands more than our human best. God's work always needs His supernatural touch added to our human best. God's work is a cooperative work in which He has called us to be His coworkers. Our part is to supply the human personality and human effort at its best. God's part is to supply the Holy Spirit in all His efficacy and power.

But we are in danger of being better trained and equipped on the human level than we are empowered by the Spirit, of being more skilled and more experienced than Spirit-anointed. We can be trained to be adept in our leadership, skills, and administration. But we cannot be trained to be anointed and empowered. These are divine additives.

Perhaps the greatest lack in most Christian leadership and ministry is this divine bestowal, the Spirit's empowerment. We are attempting to do God's work depending only nominally upon God, but in fact depending primarily upon ourselves—our training, our personalities, our past experience, our knowledge, and our sincere efforts.

Perhaps the greatest and most revolutionary change that could happen to your leadership would be for you to receive and continually experience the divine dimension. Once you receive it and experience the difference it makes, you will not want to minister without it. There must be the initial reception, the initial clothing of the Spirit (Luke 24:49), but you must also learn to receive His renewal day by day.

Let it not be said of you, as Paul asked the Galatians, "Are you so foolish? After beginning with the Spirit, are you now trying to attain your goal by human effort?" (Gal. 3:3). Human effort is God's will for you; but it is His will that you be empowered by the Spirit for that effort.

God has made every provision for you to have as much of the Holy Spirit's presence and power as you need to live and serve effectively for Him. He never expected you to have to rely exclusively on your own efforts and resources. He did not expect the apostles and first disciples to do so.

Why did Jesus tell His appointed leaders not to begin their witness and ministry immediately after His ascension? They had been with Him for three or more years. He had trained them carefully. And had He not given them authority to represent Him and proclaim His message? Had He not given them authority to use His name and cast out demons? Did He not rejoice over the way God was using them (Luke 10:17–21)?

But it was all-important that they be endowed with the Spirit's power in a specially equipping way for the work which would now become their lifetime commission. "Don't leave Jerusalem and begin your work," commanded Jesus. "Don't rush into busy activity for Me yet! Wait for the Spirit's empowering. Put the Spirit first in your ministry."

This is a lesson we all have to learn over and over again. Pray and beseech God till He gives you His message, His word for the people. Then pray and earnestly seek God's presence in the service. Also pray, hunger, and trust for God's special anointing on you as you lead or minister in any way.

Don't plan and then ask God to bless your plan. Get your plans from God. Don't prepare and ask God to bless your preparation. First ask God to prepare you. First ask God to guide you—not in a ten-second prayer, but take time to seek God's face. Then ask God to anoint and empower you as you minister in His name.

Those who receive fresh blessing upon their own hearts before they lead, speak, or sing in the service of God on any particular occasion will see the Spirit descend in blessing upon those present as they minister. Those who lead in their own self-sufficiency, without fresh anointing from on High, may give a beautiful message, song, or other ministry, but spiritually it will be largely barren. Barrenness is a continuing tragedy in too much Christian service. It may be intellectually stimulating, emotionally moving, and may receive plaudits from people, but the long-term spiritual results will be minimal. Our church services and all forms of Christian activity will seldom rise above the level of our spiritual preparation.

Those who minister in any way, after careful heart preparation and with the consciousness of the fresh touch of God upon them, will perform no less acceptably. But they will have the added divine dimension upon their ministry or leadership. Those who listen will sense the added touch of

God upon the remarks, the music, the message, or whatever the form of leadership activity. Recognizing the touch of God, they will be more alert, more receptive, more moved by the Spirit, and will experience more lasting spiritual benefit.

The fact that the special touch of God is upon you as you counsel today is no guarantee that the same touch will be upon you tomorrow. Even though you may have been strongly anointed in one service, you may not necessarily experience the same anointing the next time. You are not such a favorite with God that He will bless you whatever you do regardless of how constantly you hunger for and seek His help. Don't take God's empowering for granted.

The Christian life is a life of faith, and Christian ministry is an activity for which we constantly appropriate by prayer and faith the ministry of the Holy Spirit. A spiritually presumptuous person leads without daily, and at times hourly, appropriation of divine enabling and empowering.

We experience little of God's touch upon us because our asking for it is so casual and superficial. We recognize that it would be nice if God would bless our efforts and plans. But if not, we are content to carry on in our own strength as we have done so often. We tend to be more concerned to perform our part creditably than we are about God's mighty involvement in our efforts. We tend to be more hungry for success than we are for God's empowering.

Indeed, some of us have so rarely experienced the added dimension which the Holy Spirit can give, that we hardly understand what God longs to do in our ministry. We fear it might tend to fanaticism. Far from it! When God came upon Jonathan Edwards in power till members of the congregation gripped the seats and pillars of the church for fear they would fall into hell, was Edwards pacing back and forth across the platform haranguing the people? Not at all. He was reading his message, holding the paper barely ten inches from his eyes because of his shortsightedness, and speaking in a conversational voice. Human emotion or loudness of voice is not the equivalent of the power of the Spirit.

The quietest, most non-emotive word empowered by the

Spirit may accomplish far more spiritual results than a highly oratorical display. You can work up emotion by psychology; you cannot manipulate the Spirit of God. Only when we ourselves are arrested by the message of God and feel the deep inner working of the Holy Spirit within—whether in total quietness or with deep-felt emotion—only then will those present be gripped by the Spirit when we speak, sing, or lead.

Out of our innermost being, said Jesus, are to flow streams of living water (John 7:38). By this, John added, Jesus meant the Spirit. But there is only outflow of such life-giving streams when there is copious inflow of the Spirit into our own being. No inflow; no outflow. It is as simple as that.

Christian leaders with a desert condition in their souls will experience no outflow of living water. Living in a minimum experience of the Holy Spirit will not result in overflowing spiritual blessing to others. Spiritual blessing comes only from the Spirit flowing into and through your personality. Do such streams of blessing flow from your life? You can bless others no more than you are blessed yourself.

If you feel the lack of the power of the Spirit in your life and ministry, why not determine to look to God for His answer? There is no lack of power with God. When God placed the Holy Spirit on the seventy Israelite elders just as He had on Moses, Moses said, "I wish that all the LORD's people were prophets and that the LORD would put his Spirit on them!" (Num. 11:29)

God longs to give His Spirit abundantly to all His children, and especially to all in Christian leadership. Do you hunger and thirst as deeply for the Spirit's presence and power as God hungers to grant this to you?

Chapter 13

Depleted Spiritual Power
Can Be Renewed

When the Holy Spirit fills us He imparts purity and power. The person who dedicates his all as a living sacrifice in absolute surrender (the term Andrew Murray loved to use) and asks for and trusts for the Spirit's infilling is given a new dimension of spiritual life. The Holy Spirit cleanses and makes one pure in the inner person to a degree he never knew before, and in the same moment fills with a divinely greater power.

After one is filled with the Spirit, as one walks in the light of the Word as guided by the Spirit, he seeks constantly to please the Lord. Moment by moment he depends on the Spirit who indwells, and the Spirit enables him to be victorious over temptation. Through the Spirit's help purity can be preserved. In some sense we can keep ourselves pure (1 Tim. 5:22) by careful obedience to the Spirit (1 John 3:3), by testing everything, holding to the good and avoiding the evil (1 Thess. 5:21–22). We thus help to keep ourselves from being soiled and spotted by sin (2 Peter 3:14).

But spiritual power is different. Spiritual power cannot be preserved indefinitely. The power of the Spirit is His energy flowing into and through our spirits. Energy gets used up. Power must be renewed. This spiritual secret is beautifully symbolized in Zechariah 4.

God gave an important vision to Zechariah to strengthen and encourage the two God-anointed leaders who were rebuilding the temple after the captivity—Joshua, the high priest, and Zerubbabel, the governor. Great opposition had delayed the work for twenty years.

God used symbolism to illustrate and confirm His pithy dictum: "This is the word of the LORD. . . 'Not by might, nor by power, but by my Spirit,' says the LORD Almighty" (Zech. 4:6). God showed Zechariah a vision of a gold lampstand furnishing light through a bowl that channeled olive oil to seven lamps (symbolizing fullness of light). The oil supply to the bowl came from two golden pipes that received oil from a living olive tree. The lamps burned and gave light as long as oil flowed.

The Spirit's power is the great essential for doing God's work, but it is expended by use. We cannot minister today in yesterday's power. We cannot accomplish God's full purpose on memories of past blessing and empowering. God does not want us to live in the past, but in a moment-by-moment present appropriation of His power.

There may be rare occasions when God uses us in spite of ourselves. That was probably the way He used Samson, Balaam, and King Saul on occasion. But the rule of God is that we can give only what we receive. God wants us to be daily empowered so that we are daily usable for His glory. God forgive us if the only time He uses us mightily is when He is compelled to work in spite of our spiritual condition.

HOW SPIRITUAL POWER IS DEPLETED OR LOST

Jesus Christ did not begin His ministry until He received a special bestowal of Holy Spirit power. Hear His words: "The Spirit of the Lord is upon me, because he has anointed me to preach" (Luke 4:18). Peter summarized Christ's ministry by saying, "God anointed Jesus of Nazareth with the Holy Spirit and power" (Acts 10:38). Jesus used the same power in His earthly ministry that we must use today—the power of the Spirit. He chose primarily not to minister through His inherent deity, but through the anointing of the Spirit.

Luke 6:19 explains, "The people all tried to touch him, because power was coming from him and healing them all." This was the power of the Spirit. When the woman who had been suffering for twelve years touched the edge of Jesus' cloak, He said, "Someone touched me; I know that power has gone out from me" (Luke 8:46).

What was true of Jesus is true of you. As you minister to people, you expend spiritual power. If you want to be used of God, if you want to heal the wounds of humankind, God's power must be upon you continually and flow through you.

1. *Spiritual power is expended naturally by your ministry.* The more you minister, the more you need your power renewed. The busier you become, the more you need your power renewed, the more you need spiritual refreshment and replenishing. It is not just mental weariness or physical exhaustion that you experience. Without spiritual renewal you will become a spiritual has-been.

Once when Luther was asked about his plans for the next day he replied, "Work, work, from early until late. In fact, I have so much to do that I shall spend the first three hours in prayer." Busy ministry without adequate prayer and spiritual renewal leads to loss of spiritual power. The input is not keeping up with the outflow. Have you been giving to others so constantly that you yourself are spiritually depleted? Have you once known more of the power of God upon you and more of His anointing than you know these days?

2. *Spiritual power is expended by involvement in non-*

spiritual affairs. We are living in a basically secular world. We are not an island, but live with all kinds of human associations. God does not want us to be recluses, to isolate ourselves from the contaminating influences of life. We are to be light and salt in our world. But the source of light is expended by burning, and salt is expended by use.

There is no conflict between work and spirituality. Hard workers make the best Christian workers and the best prayer warriors. Many people are too lazy to be blessed greatly. They do not know how to pay the price of self-discipline to find time for God's Word and prayer. They let almost anything take priority over spiritual replenishment. They have not learned the lesson of Zechariah 4. They try to succeed by their own power rather than by God's Spirit.

In many forms of work there are wonderful opportunities for moments of brief prayer, praise, spiritual communion, and expressions of love for the Lord. But too often we live as if the Lord were not by our side. We ignore Him. We fill our minds with fantasies, self-pity, and self-made plans. We can invest moments with God while washing, grooming, walking, driving, or a thousand other activities, if we only will.

But there are activities or environments where this is more difficult. The atmosphere in some places is not conducive to spiritual activity and may even be anti-spiritual. You cannot breathe the atmosphere of noise, levity, suggestiveness, sinful jokes, materialism, or blaspheming of God's name without its effect upon you—unless you resort constantly to the Lord. You will begin to sense gradual loss of spiritual power. Like Lot (2 Peter 2:7), you will feel constantly distressed and almost tormented.

You need quiet of soul for spiritual communion and renewal. Some people are so accustomed to being entertained by radio or television that they hardly know how to use quiet time for spiritual refreshment and renewal of soul. In Bible times the priest washed before ministry in the tent or temple. We too need to take spiritual baths, or at least to freshen the face, as it were, with frequent moments with the Lord.

3. *Lack of unity with other Christians depletes our*

spiritual power. David says that unity, like the dew from heaven, brings spiritual refreshment and blessing (Ps. 133:3). Disunity does the opposite. It dries the soul, withers spiritual life, and evaporates spiritual refreshment and keenness. Power is dissipated by critical attitudes, thoughts of resentment, or any unforgiveness or bitterness of heart.

Nothing will drain away God's blessing, power, and anointing from your life more rapidly than unkind thoughts of others. Unloving words, gossip, laughter at the expense of others, and negative talking cuts your power and the sweetness of God's presence. Anything contrary to the tender love of the Holy Spirit is devastating to spiritual power.

Are you sensitive enough to recognize quickly what grieves the Holy Spirit? Whoever touches God's people touches the apple of God's eye (Zech. 2:8). With one critical remark, you can destroy the blessing you received from hours of prayer. The Holy Spirit is the gentle Spirit of perfect love. One of His roles is to pour in abundance the love of God into our hearts and out through our lives (Rom. 5:5). We cannot afford to grieve His loving nature.

Paul speaks sharply and abruptly to this subject. "You, then, why do you judge your brother? Or why do you look down on your brother?" (Rom. 14:10). "Who are you to judge someone else's servant?" (Rom. 14:4). Judgmental thoughts always grieve the Spirit.

"Do not grieve the Holy Spirit of God . . . . Get rid of all bitterness, rage and anger, brawling and slander . . . . Be kind and compassionate to one another, forgiving each other, just as in Christ God forgave you. Be imitators of God, therefore, as dearly loved children and live a life of love, just as Christ loved us" (Eph. 4:30–5:2).

4. *Lack of obedience depletes spiritual power.* Failure to continue to walk in God's light, or failure to accept and use God-given opportunities can bring loss of the power of the Spirit. God constantly gives us opportunities to do little extra things for Jesus. They are not demanded of us; it depends upon how intensely we love Jesus, how eager we are to please Him with little gestures of love.

Just as active expression of your love to Him increases His nearness and blessing upon your life, so neglect of these gestures of love can lead to loss of the sweet awareness of His presence.

Failure to be alert to express your love in thought, word, or deed can lead to spiritual carelessness and to a gradual decrease in the Spirit's presence and power upon you. Are you as sensitive to what pleases the Lord as you are to what pleases your dearest companion?

Delayed obedience, ignoring the Spirit's suggestions, any controversy between your heart and the Lord, resisting His highest will for you—these can short circuit the flow of God's power into your life. Spiritual power is governed by God's spiritual laws just as certainly as electrical power or nuclear power are governed by God's laws of nature.

5. *Self-indulgence, a self-centered, luxurious lifestyle can deplete your spiritual power.* Dr. R.A. Torrey, the Bible teacher and co-worker of D.L. Moody, was deeply convinced of this. He wrote,

> Power is lost through self-indulgence. The one who would have God's power must lead a life of self-denial . . . . I do not believe that any man can lead a luxurious life, over-indulge his natural appetites, indulge extensively in dainties, and enjoy the fullness of God's power. The gratification of the flesh and the fullness of the Spirit do not go hand in hand . . .
>
> If we would know the continuance of the Spirit's power we need to be on guard to lead lives of simplicity, free from indulgence and surfeiting, be ready to "endure hardness as a good soldier of Jesus Christ" (2 Tim. 2:3). I frankly confess I am afraid of luxury; not as afraid of it as I am of sin, but it comes next as an object of dread. It is a very subtle, but a very potent enemy of power. There are devils today that "go not out but by prayer and fasting."[1]

The Holy Spirit always reaches out to others, is always sensitive to the welfare of the entire church and of the world. Self-centeredness is the opposite of Christ-centeredness and kingdom-centeredness. In numerous ways Christians may spend their time or indulge themselves, ways that are contrary to the sacrificial spirit of holiness, the recognition of the needs of a hurting world, and the extension of Christ's kingdom. His "inasmuch as you did not" will be said to evangelical Christians of our generation as truly as it was said to some of His generation. How can the Spirit bless us with outpourings of His power when we are so little concerned about what concerns Him?

6. *Self-sufficiency and pride will deplete spiritual power.* Power can be almost instantly lost through pride. God will not share His glory with any other. God condescends to work through Spirit-filled people, but if anyone reaches out his proud hand and takes to himself the glory of which only God is worthy, He will withdraw His power, often instantly. That is one reason Satan tempts you so constantly to pride.

Billy Graham has repeatedly made such statements as, "If God should take His hand from my life, these lips will turn to lips of clay." We are only earthen vessels, "jars of clay to show that this all-surpassing power is from God and not from us" (2 Cor. 4:7).

God could reveal Himself so fully to Moses in a more face-to-face relationship than with any other human being (Deut. 34:10), and could work more mighty miracles through Moses than through any other person (Deut. 34:12) because Moses was the most humble person on the face of God's earth (Num. 12:3).

Uzziah was greatly helped by God until he became strong and grew proud (2 Chron. 26:15–16). Many a Christian leader's history could be written in the same words. God worked mightily on behalf of Hezekiah until almost unbelievably his heart became proud over the answer to his prayer (2 Chron. 32:25). Nebuchadnezzar was honored and used by God until he became proud (Dan. 5:20).

Satan's own downfall was through his pride (perhaps Ezek. 28:2, 5, 17; 1 Tim. 3:6). Pride makes us more like Satan than like Christ. Pride will cause God to turn His face away from us. God opposes the proud, but gives grace to the humble (James 4:6; 1 Peter 5:5).

Any step of self-sufficiency is the first step to pride. Any

89

acceptance of praise for oneself is probably denying God the praise due Him. Self-confidence can be humble if based on God's usual help and if we remain in complete dependence on Him. But self-confidence can be carnal, can become a carnal form of self-reliance, and can rob us of God's sweet presence and His mighty power.

Any power manifested in the ministry of one who is not marked by deep humility is counterfeit power. It is not God's power. It may be psychological power. It could even be the power of Satan who delights to pose as an angel of light (2 Cor. 11:14).

7. *Excessive levity can deplete spiritual power.* Humor is a gift of God to us, but it must be used only in appropriate ways and to a modest extent. God is obviously a God who Himself enjoys wholesome humor. That is why He created us to enjoy humor and to be able to laugh. But there is a time, a place, and a limit on the humor God will bless. Even too much wholesome humor can dissipate God's power. I have noticed that just before a special spiritual responsibility, even when I was not aware that it was just ahead, Satan has at times tried to get me and others so amused that we lost the spiritual preparation we had made. Satan delights to rob us of God's anointing and power just before a spiritual crisis or time when we will greatly need His power. The presence and power of the Spirit available to a person through several hours of prayer can be lost by five minutes of improper humor, or humor at the improper time.

8. *Sin always depletes and destroys the power of the Spirit.* Conscious disobedience, sin against light, sin against another, and all forms of failure to walk in God's light will stop the awareness of the presence and smile of God's favor. Sin stops the Spirit's power from filling you and using you. Sin robs prayer of its effectiveness. "If I had cherished sin in my heart, the Lord would not have listened" (Ps. 66:18). This refers, of course, to sin according to the Bible definition of 1 John 3:4, a willful breaking of God's law in spite of clear light.

When Israel disobeyed God and broke the covenant with

God, God paid no attention to their tears and prayer (Deut. 1:45). Just as Samson was shorn both of his locks of hair and of God's power upon him because he trifled with disobedience and sin, so there have been Christian workers who have just as completely lost the power of God upon their lives.

Sometimes we may be unaware that we have disobeyed the Lord, but feel in our hearts that we have grieved the Spirit in some way. This may be merely the accusation of Satan as he tries to depress and discourage. On the other hand, this may be the restraint of the Spirit. He is so loving and faithful that if we grieve Him without fully realizing it, He speaks to us or touches us. If we have developed a listening ear for God's guidance, God will find it easy to get our attention and will be faithful to speak to us.

Thank God, there is forgiveness and cleansing available. There is always a way back to God's favor, presence, and power (1 John 2:1–2). Contrition, humbling ourselves before the Lord, repentance where necessary, and forgiveness can open the gate to God's full favor and the flood tide of His power upon us again.

YOUR LOVE

Chapter 14

Love—The Secret of Your Leadership

Christian leadership is a leadership of love. You can lead without loving, but it is not genuine Christian leadership unless you are marked by a Christlike love. As a Christian leader you lead in the name of Christ, on behalf of Christ, in the spirit of Christ, and for the glory of Christ. This can be done only as you lead with a Christly love.

Love is the hallmark of every Christian. He who does not love is no Christian (1 John 3:10, 14; 4:8). The more nearly pure and perfect your love for others, the more Christlike you prove yourself to be. Every Christian is to love with a love like Christ's. His love is infinite, ours is finite; His is perfect, ours is all too imperfect. Yet our love, like His, must be personal, practical, holy, self-giving, and sacrificial.

Love is God's seal upon every Christian; it is the all-important seal upon you as a Christian leader. Though you possess all other leadership abilities and leadership skills, you are not qualified to be a Christian leader until you love those you lead with a Christlike love. First Corinthians 13 is essential for all Christians; it is the all-essential standard for you.

YOU MUST LOVE WITH A CHRISTLIKE LOVE BECAUSE:

1. *You were created to love.* You were created in the image of the God of love. You were created so Godlike that you have the capacity to respond to and understand the love of God. Your whole being, when touched by the Holy Spirit, can receive and, to a blessed degree, transmit God's love to others.

God rejoices to receive your love, and He rejoices to see you share His love with those He also loves so dearly and infinitely. He finds holy satisfaction in your love to Him and your love to others. One important way you love Him is to love others, especially those you lead. The more you transmit and express His love to others, the more He can flood you with love and the more fully you will be able to share the love He expresses to you.

2. *He first loved you* (1 John 4:9). You do not originate love; it originates in the heart of God. You do not manufacture love, imitate His love, or fake His love. You receive and pass on His love. The only *agape* love you have is what you receive from Jesus. We first saw God's love in Him. "This is love: not that we loved God, but that he loved us and sent his Son as an atoning sacrifice for our sins" (1 John 4:10).

Love is incarnate in Jesus—visible, constantly active, and self-sacrificing unto death. You love because you have seen this *agape* love of God in Christ and because that love has so transformed you that it expresses itself through you.

3. *The Holy Spirit pours this agape love of God into your nature.* Paul describes it beautifully: "God has poured out his love into our hearts by the Holy Spirit, whom he has given us" (Rom. 5:5). He fills you with his Spirit so that He can pour

His own holy nature of love through you as a constant, abundant, gushing river. This is the chief stream of living water that Jesus promised you (John 7:38).

You love because the Holy Spirit pours His own loving nature into you as fully as you are open to receive. The more you pour out God's love on others, especially those you lead and those in need, the more God the Spirit is able to pour into you His holy self—which is holy love, for God is love.

The more you pour out, the more He pours in—ever fresh, ever new, ever cleansing, ever transforming, ever filling, ever Christlike, ever reaching out to and blessing others. Oh, what a life and leadership of love as He pours in as fast as you pour out!

To be filled with the Spirit is to be filled with the love He is pouring from the innermost nature of the Trinity into and through us. To be filled with all the fullness of love, for God is love! There is nothing higher, deeper, more holy, more blessed, more wonderful in all of human experience. This fullness of love, this gushing river of love, this indescribable bliss of love is God's plan for every Christian.

If this is true, and it is, then you as a Christian leader are to demonstrate its truth and reality more than anyone else. You are to be a model of love. You can model this love of God in Christ in only one way and that is by being filled with this river of love and then letting it pour out of you into the church and into the world for which He died.

If this fullness of divine, supernatural love is not constantly streaming out from you as a Christian leader, you are not a true representative of Jesus. You are a misrepresentation. God is love; Christ is love. Christ can be represented only by love. The only true ambassador of Christ (2 Cor. 5:20) is an ambassador of love. He who does not pour out love slanders the God of love he claims to represent.

Love is the essential ingredient for all Christian service. Love is the key for all Christian success. Love is the fragrance, the glory, and the power for all Christian living. Love makes a leader a shepherd. Love makes a witness an ambassador for Christ. Love makes work for God a ministry.

Love is the secret of holiness, saintliness, and fruit-fulness. Love is the summation and fulfillment of the law. Love is the transforming power of Pentecost. Love is the secret of Christlikeness. Love is the basic fruit of the Spirit. The measure of the fullness of Christ is love (Eph. 4:13).

On the last great day of the feast Jesus stood and called in a loud voice, " 'If anyone is thirsty, let him come to me and drink. Whoever believes in me, as the Scripture has said, streams of living water will flow from within him.' By this he meant the Spirit" (John 7:37–39). So anyone who does not have this river of love is not thirsting, not believing, not obeying, for the Holy Spirit is given to those who ask (Luke 11:13), believe (John 7:38), and obey (Acts 5:32).

Since love is to be the most constant, most evident, and most attractive aspect of the Christlikeness of each believer, it is to be even more your daily nature, your visible glory, and your mighty power as a Christian leader. You dare not rest content with only a nominal, minimal experience of this love.

How can we describe the love that must characterize you as an effective pastor and leader? It must be based on the adoring, ardent, fervent love for Christ. It must be poured out in love for the church. And it must be constantly yearning, hungering, and thirsting for and seeking the unsaved.

Chapter 15

Ablaze With a Passion for Christ

Passion for Christ is the highest passion for any Christian and for you as a Christian leader. This was the overwhelming passion of the apostle Paul, the greatest leader the church has ever known. Paul exultingly proclaimed, " . . . to me, to live is Christ" (Phil. 1:21). "I no longer live, but Christ lives in me" (Gal. 2:20).

Hear Paul's ringing testimony: "Whatever was to my profit I now consider loss for the sake of Christ. What is more, I consider everything a loss compared to the surpassing greatness of knowing Christ Jesus my Lord, for whose sake I have lost all things. I consider them rubbish, that I may gain Christ . . . . I want to know Christ" (Phil. 3:7–10).

As leaders called by Christ this must be our ruling passion also. Such a passion for Christ sets a leader apart from all others. Alas, so few are really possessed by, absorbed in, and committed to this one passion. How few can say, "My passion is He, only He, supremely He!"

Our deepest commitment must be to Christ, our unswerving devotion, our supreme love, our life's absorbing passion must be Christ. To know Him more and more must be our most desired knowledge, to please Him more and more our greatest hunger, and to glorify Him more and more our highest ambition.

For Him, like Paul, we live or die, to Him we turn for His wisdom, guidance, and power. In Him we glory, in Him we stand, and unto the whole measure of His fullness, His image, and His likeness we aspire. Our passion for Christ as a Person must be above and beyond our passion for His cause or our commitment to His service. This is the passion underlying all other Christian passions.

He, He is our goal and our exemplar; He is our whole desire and our eternal reward. He is our Alpha and Omega, our Beginning and our End. And because He is all this He must become our intensely personal Beloved One. The passion for Christ transmutes into a thrillingly deep and personal love for Christ.

ABLAZE WITH LOVE FOR CHRIST

Your deepened passion for Jesus must begin with your passion of love, your deeper dimension of love for Him, your more intensely personal devotion to Him, your more constant delighting in His love and more frequent resting in His love. It is not a mere commitment of orthodoxy or of duty, but rather the whole-souled self-giving of yourself in joyous personal abandonment. The name *Jesus* must be far more than the official, God-given name of our wonderful Savior. It must be the delightfully sweet and soul-thrilling name of your Beloved.

The goal of Scripture is intensely personal love for Jesus possessing your whole being. The goal of redemption is your love-relationship, your love-life with Jesus. Christian living is living in love with Jesus. Prayer communion is looking lovingly into Jesus' eyes, thrilling to Jesus' voice, resting in Jesus' arms.

Christ's passionate lovers have bejeweled the history and heritage of the church. No Christian leader is greater than his love. Few today realize the intense devotion to Christ in the early church and in our sainted martyrs. The Holy Spirit can develop in us just as ardent devotion as He did in those days.

Do not consider abnormal the passionate love for Christ in such flaming-hearted souls as Thomas à Kempis, Madame Guyon, John Fletcher of Madeley, Gerhard Tersteegen, Samuel Rutherford, David Brainerd, Robert Murray McCheyne, John (Praying) Hyde, Fanny Crosby, and Amy Carmichael. They were perfectly normal when compared with the church of the first century. The twofold hallmark of the early church was ardent flaming love for Jesus and overflowing practical love for one another.

The most crucial danger to a leader is to be so busy as to neglect to love Jesus, to fail to live a life of ardent devotion and "in-loveness" to Jesus. Love's expression takes time. Love must be frequently expressed, unhurriedly expressed. The Holy Spirit is eager to lead you into ever-more-thrilling love to Jesus, to supply you with all the love you are willing to lavish on Jesus.

Love's commitment and expression is a volitional thing. It is far deeper than emotion. You must choose to be whole-souledly His. But whole-souled, passionate commitment to Jesus becomes a deeply emotional reality—too deep for words.

Love for Jesus is not a religious feeling we work up, an occasional passing affection. Deep, deep love for Jesus becomes inexpressibly emotional because it is the living reality of our whole being. We rejoice in Him, rest in Him, commune throughout the day with Him, lift up our eyes and smile in His face—but we may be moved to tears as we catch the love-light in His beautiful eyes as He beams back His Calvary-love smile to us.

A.W. Tozer once said, "The great of the kingdom have been those who loved God more than others did." Those who

101

have really looked into the face of Jesus cannot but be captivated by His love. Too often our love for Jesus is sadly impersonal. We believe in His Person, we worship His Person, but we relate to Him far too impersonally. There is too much distance, a tragic remoteness in our fellowship.

True, He is our infinitely holy God and we are but sin-deformed creatures before Him. He is our Sovereign King, and we bow before His majesty. But He is also our Savior who loved us with such everlasting love that He forsook heaven's throne to become the incarnate Son of Man, to die for us, to redeem us for Himself and make us the special and eternal object of His love. Indeed, He came to make us collectively His bride and personally His beloved.

The words of Jesus to the church at Ephesus are searching to us as Christian leaders. Ephesus was a model church. When Paul wrote to the Ephesian church he mentioned love twenty times. Now, perhaps some thirty years later, Christ speaks through John, accusing them of having "forsaken their first love" (Rev. 2:4–5).

In spite of the fact that they worked strenuously, faithfully persevered, were orthodox and separated (v. 2), and were unwavering and unwearied in suffering, they were a disappointment to Jesus. They needed to remember the height of love from which they had fallen and repent (v. 5).

It is much easier for us leaders to maintain doctrinal orthodoxy and faithful work patterns than it is to maintain the sweet intensity of deeply personal love. The resurrected Jesus who examined Peter about his love (John 21:15) may, in effect, be asking you and me the same basic question, "Do you truly love me more than these?" Whether we interpret this to mean more than others do or more than we are committed to our work, the essential question remains: How much do we truly love Jesus?

Let's humble ourselves before Him. Let's confess how cool and casual we too often have been in our expression of love to Him. Let's ask the Holy Spirit to give us a new baptism of love for Jesus. We need the Spirit's help to love Jesus as we should. Perhaps we have had too little of the

Spirit's fullness to enable us to love with the personal ardor Jesus desires. Paul tells us that it is the Holy Spirit who pours such love into our hearts (Rom. 5:5). Let's pray with William Cowper:

> Lord, it is my chief complaint
> That my love is weak and faint;
> Yet I love Thee, and adore;
> Oh, for grace to love Thee more!

Jesus' response to us is: "He who loves me will be loved by my Father, and I too will love him and show myself to him" (John 14:21).

LOVING JESUS WILL TRANSFORM YOUR LIFE

Loving Jesus makes you a happy Christian, an expectant Christian full of hope and faith. Loving Jesus will transform your prayer life, both your communion and your intercession. It will make putting priority on prayer much easier. Loving Jesus will make you a radiant witness of all He means to you and does for you. Loving Jesus makes you God-conscious and surrounds you with His presence. A passion for Jesus will bring new life and power to your public speaking and preaching. It will add a new reality, joy, and often a poignancy to your personal conversations about Jesus.

All other passions build upon or flow from your passion for Jesus. A passion for souls grows out of a passion for Christ. A passion for missions builds upon a passion for Christ. When Hudson Taylor was once asked what was the greatest incentive to missionary work, he instantly replied, "Love of Christ." William Booth's passion for helping the underprivileged, the derelicts of society, and for world evangelization was built upon his passion for Christ.

The most crucial danger to a Christian leader, whatever his role, is to lack a passion for Christ. The most direct route to personal renewal and new effectiveness in leadership is a new all-consuming passion for Jesus. Lord, give us this passion, whatever the cost!

Chapter 16

Ablaze With a Passion
for Souls

What a beautiful phrase! Yet how many of us have almost forgotten the expression "A Passion for Souls." For years it was a tremendous motivating force for God's children. Today with the emphasis upon such terms as church growth, counseling, Christian education, and youth ministries we have almost forgotten the emphasis upon constantly winning people to Christ.

Every Christian leader, whatever his official title or role, should be characterized by a passion to lead others to Christ. We all give nominal adherence to winning people. We seem to feel a little embarrassed to speak about "souls" since we hear the constant emphasis upon treating people as "whole persons"—body as well as soul. But every human being has a spiritual aspect of his nature which will live forever and ever. When the body dies, the spirit will live on. It will be eternally saved, at home with Christ, or eternally lost to Christ and heaven, lost in a Christless eternity in hell.

The word "soul" is still in the Bible. Throughout Scripture the concept is emphasized that we are more than body. We dare not let psychology rob us of the emphasis upon the soul. If you prefer, use "spirit" for the individual spiritual nature, but it seems more common to use "soul" for the whole being of humankind but with particular emphasis upon the spiritual nature. Salvation affects the whole being, lifestyle, and inner nature. We will use "soul" for the purpose of this discussion. Jesus asked, "What good will it be for a man if he gains the whole world, yet forfeits his soul? Or what can a man give in exchange for his soul?" (Matt. 16:26).

Our danger is that although in our busy schedules and ministry we recognize that soul-winning is part of our responsibility, yet it becomes almost incidental in our work plan and time plan. It remains our goal in theory, but in practice it is often not a priority in our public or private ministry.

WE NEED A PASSION FOR SOULS

No Christian leader is the person of God that our Lord wants him to be unless day after day the consuming desire of his heart is that people come to Christ. For this we must live, must long, must seek opportunities, must pray, and must believe. You have not drunk deeply of the spirit of Christ if you do not share His tears over the unsaved who are blindly hastening to an eternity forever separated from the love of God, the presence of Christ, and with all hope of change forever gone.

We need to feel the love for people that drew Christ from heaven to earth, that fills His heart on heaven's throne today. We need to imbibe the infinite longings of His heart as He looks out on a world filled with people lost in their sins, their sorrows, and their spiritual helplessness. The passion for souls must come from the heart of Christ. From Him we must seek it until we find it.

Why was Jesus a Man of Sorrows (Isa. 53)? Surely it was because He took our sins upon Himself, because He totally identified with us in our sorrows, and because today His infinite loving heart still longs so ceaselessly for the lost of earth. We as Christian leaders do not deserve His grace and we sin against His love if we do not live close enough to His yearning heart to receive and share His longing for the sheep still outside the fold.

D.L. Moody once said, "When I see young men by the thousands going in the way of death, I feel like falling at the feet of Jesus with prayer and tears to come and save them." Paul S. Rees wrote in *World Vision*, "In heaven's name and for earth's sake, let's never allow to cool that 'insatiable desire that men and women should be won to Christ.'"

Eloquent Bishop Joseph Berry, in describing our Lord's parable of the great banquet (Luke 14:16–24), applying it to our gospel feast today at Jesus' table, pleaded, "Have you no concern, O happy guests, for the starving ones in the streets? Out, out of the light and warmth! Out into the chilling storm! Out into the dismal streets! Invite them to come. That is not enough. Persuade them to come. That is not enough. Compel them to come!"

The good bishop added, "The man who sits down to the banquet and selfishly enjoys its light and warmth, with never a thought of the hungry multitude outside, is a caricature of a Christian. He has caught no true vision of his Lord; nor have the fires of Christian evangelism been kindled in his heart. He may be a church member, but he is not a Christian . . . . Is anyone a real disciple of Christ who is not swayed by this consuming passion?"

LET THE PASSION FOR SOULS KINDLE YOU

Many of the greatly used people of God, giant leaders of God's people who moved the church and their world for Christ, were marked by this passion for souls. Read the following words not with a spiritual nonchalance nor a hurried casualness. These words poured forth from hearts of

106

Christlike yearning, from their own Gethsemane of longing. They are the essence of their whole being. They cost them all in a Calvary commitment regardless of the price.

John Knox constantly carried the burden for his land. Night after night he prayed on the wooden floor of his hideout refuge from Queen Mary. When his wife pleaded with him to get some sleep, he answered, "How can I sleep when my land is not saved?" Payne reports that often he would pray all night in agonizing tones, "Lord, give me Scotland or I die!" God shook Scotland; God gave him Scotland. God respects such a passion for souls.

John Wesley, as he exhorted his pastors upon whom the future of their revival movement depended, urged, "Let us all be of one business. We live only for this, to save our own souls and the souls of those who hear us." Again, Wesley cried, "Give me one hundred preachers who fear nothing but sin and desire nothing but God, and I care not a straw whether they be clergymen or laymen, such alone will shake the gates of hell and set up the kingdom of heaven on earth."

David Brainerd, missionary to American Indians, shared his heart cry in his diary: "I set apart this day for fasting and prayer to prepare me for the ministry . . . . In the forenoon, I felt a power of intercession for immortal souls . . . . In the afternoon . . . God enabled me so to agonize in prayer that I was quite wet with sweat, though in the shade and the cool wind. My soul was drawn out very much for the world: I gasped for multitudes of souls. I think I had more enlargement for sinners than for the children of God, though I felt as if I could spend my life in cries for both" (April 19, 1742).

Again, "I cared not where or how I lived, or what hardships I went through so that I could but gain souls to Christ. I continued in this frame all evening and night. While I was asleep, I dreamed of these things, and when I waked, the first thing I thought of was this great work of pleading for God against Satan" (July 21, 1744).

Philip Doddridge wrote, "I long for the conversion of souls more sensibly than for anything else. Methinks I could not only labor, but die for it."

James Caughey said it similarly: "Oh, to burn out for God! All, all for Him! Jesus only! Souls! Souls! Souls! I am determined to be a winner of souls. God help me."

John Smith (English soul-winner) said, "I am a broken-hearted man; not for myself but on account of others. God has given me such a sight of the value of precious souls that I cannot live if souls are not saved. Give me souls or else I die."

Of George Whitefield, great evangelist and friend of Wesley, William Cowper wrote,

> He followed Paul—his zeal a kindred flame,
> His apostolic charity the same.

Prayed Whitefield, "O Lord, give me souls or take my soul." It is said his face shone like the face of Moses when he sobbed that prayer.

When William Booth, founder of the Salvation Army, was asked by the king of England what the ruling force of his life was, he replied, "Sir, some men's passion is for gold, other men's passion is for fame, but my passion is for souls."

Charles Cowman, founder of OMS International (formerly The Oriental Missionary Society), as he wrote of the millions of Japan, resolved, "By the help of God they shall hear if it costs every drop of my life's blood. Here I am, Lord, send me! Send me!" It was said of him, "The winning of a soul was to him what the winning of a battle is to a soldier; what the winning of a bride is to a lover; what the winning of a race is to an athlete. Charles Cowman lived for just one thing—to win souls for Christ. This was his soul passion, and in a very extraordinary manner God set His seal upon it."[1]

It was further said in tribute to Cowman, "Whenever the evangelization of the Orient was mentioned, his soul took fire and you felt he would die a martyr through his own ferventness before he reached the sunset of life, and it was even so. He belonged to the class of early martyrs whose passionate souls made an early holocaust of the physical man."[2]

John Hyde ("Praying Hyde"), so mightily used in salvation and revival in India as the Apostle of Intercession, often cried out, "Father, give me these souls or I die!" He alternated in agony of intercession and joyous praise, receiving tremendous answers to prayer and by the end of his missionary service was averaging more than four souls a day, largely won through prayer.

President Walters of the British Methodist Conference recalled a Monday morning when he went into the study of Hugh Price Hughes who had launched the Wesleyan Forward Movement which founded churches and central halls. Walters was there to report on his Sunday work. "That morning Hughes looked like a broken man, his eyes were wet with tears—broken, and he was but fifty years of age! 'Are you ill, sir?' I asked. 'No,' he answered, and then continued, 'Walters, we have had three Sunday nights at St. James Hall without anyone in the inquiry rooms—no conversions—and I can't stand it. It will break my heart . . . When God sent me to West London, it was that, whenever I preached, I should win a verdict for Christ.' "

HOW TO RECEIVE THIS PASSION

Do you long to be a person of God with such a passion for souls that God begins to add a new dimension of fruitfulness to your leadership? Dare you believe that God will give it to you if you ask? Not everyone is called to be a Whitefield, a Billy Graham, or a Praying Hyde. But everyone of us is called to bear fruit—both the fruit of the Spirit and the fruit of souls.

Your leadership assignment may involve you primarily in administration, teaching, or other non-evangelistic duties, but you can still be fruitful. Aletta Jacobsz of South Africa, a teacher and counselor, visited the OMS work in China in 1938 and '39. Before long God through her brought revival to OMS and many Presbyterian centers. She was not a public speaker, but her radiant love for Jesus so attracted people and moved them toward Christ that people came constantly to her room or asked her to share with small groups. Hundreds found a new experience in Christ during her visit.

R. Stanley Tam, Lima, Ohio, businessman and president of U.S. Plastics, tirelessly leads his successful business, but is also in constant demand to speak to church and business groups across the country. He has deeded his business to God, receives a modest salary, and all profits go to missionary evangelism. He has the joy of constantly leading people to Christ during his travels, over the phone, through gospel booklets in all his shipments, through the film and books on his life, and through his public witness. People have even come across the country to find Christ in his office. In 1987, he led 1,644 to Christ—more than four per day.*

There is no greater joy than to lead a person to a transforming experience of Christ. The more you taste this joy, the more you will want God to make you a soul-winner. How can you increasingly find this joy in your own experience?

1. *Become more passionately committed to Jesus Christ than ever before.* This is the foundation of soul-winning motivation and this is the secret of radiant Christian attractiveness. The more personal your daily fellowship with Jesus, the more thrilling your personal prayer communion, the more naturally and eagerly you speak about Jesus as you share with others, the more God will be able to use you. It is not professional motivation to witness that brings results. You need personal love for Jesus so real and so preciously rewarding that you overflow with love for Jesus. Then you will not be able to keep silent.

2. *Specifically ask God to give you a passion for souls.* Make it part of your daily prayer to ask God to help you lead people to Christ. Make it one of your daily priority requests.

3. *Ask God to give you a sensitivity to others.* Ask Him to give you eyes to see and ears to hear those about you. Ask Him to help you discern the hurts, heart cries, and needs of those you meet.

---

*Dr. Tam's tract, "Witnessing Everywhere," has blessed thousands. For a copy write: United States Plastics Corporation, 1390 Neubrecht Road, Lima, Ohio 45801.

4. *Ask God to make you spiritually radiant.* Each day ask Him to make you Christlike, overflowing with joy in the Lord, and anointed by the Spirit in all your contacts. Ask Him to put something of His presence and glory so evident in your face and in your actions so that others will be attracted to Him.

5. *Ask God for winsome boldness in witnessing.* Ask Him for a loving, caring spirit of initiative to make you recognize open doors and help you buy up your opportunities. Ask Him to make you alert to seize strategic moments for the Lord.

6. *Ask God to make you confident and positive.* He will gladly deliver you from fear. The more you speak to others about Christ and about their personal spiritual life, the more confident you will become and the easier it will become for God to use you.

7. *Put constant priority on prayer.* Put priority on both communing prayer and interceding prayer. Prayer is the key to your personal spiritual radiance. Prayer is the key to guidance in your contacts and witness. Prayer is the key to the anointing of the Spirit on your life and efforts. Prayer is the key to God's power clothing you so that there is a divine dimension in your soul-winning efforts. Prayer is the key to a passion for souls and to all your spiritual life. Put priority on prayer.

A century ago God greatly used Dr. A. T. Pierson, a Presbyterian minister, as a pastor both in America and at Spurgeon's Tabernacle in London, and as editor and leader of the Student Volunteer Movement. Here he tells how to receive this fiery passion for souls:

> There is a secret fellowship with God where we get this heavenly fire kindled within, and it makes personal work for souls easy, natural, a relief, and a rest. To linger in God's presence until we see souls, as through His eyes, makes us long over them with a tireless longing.
>
> This passion for souls is probably the highest product of spiritual communion with God. It absorbs us, and even our own salvation is forgotten in that passionate yearning which made Moses ready to have his name blotted out of God's book for

111

Israel's sake, or Paul willing to be anathema for the sake of his brethren.

It seems to me that such passion is the highest form of unselfish love, and the nearest approximation to the divine motive that impelled the Lord Jesus Christ to empty himself of his original glory and majesty, and assume "the form of a servant," enduring even the cross.

No man can kindle in himself that celestial fire; it must come from the live coal from the altar above.

Chapter 17

Your Love for the Unsaved

God so loved the world that He gave Jesus for the salvation of the world of sinners. All we are and all we have we owe to God's great love for us while we were rebels by our sinful acts. Jesus died for us, not because we were so wonderful or good, but out of pure love. There is no more important way to repay God the Father and our loving Savior than to love the world which they still love with the same longing, redemptive love.

GOD GIVES AGAPE LOVE

God depends on you and me to pass on His love. Every Christian has a debt to discharge that he can repay in no other way. God's love was "agape love" (the Greek word repeatedly used for God's love in the New Testament)—love for the

113

unworthy, for the undeserving, love for sinners who by their actions and attitudes were His enemies (Rom. 5:10; Col. 1:21).

The Holy Spirit pours that same divine agape love into our hearts so that we love others with the same love for the unworthy, the undeserving, the sinners. We must love people because God loves them and calls us to represent and manifest His love to them.

It is comparatively easy to love God the Father, Jesus our Savior, and the Holy Spirit our Counselor and Helper. We respond to their great love which they lavish on us. It is usually not too difficult to love our fellow Christians, for the church is to be a family of love. Love becomes most costly, often most difficult, and most God-given when we love the sinful, the hateful whose lives are filled with evil. But this is the love God calls Christians to manifest. This is the agape love He gives us and gladly multiplies within us to pass on to our needy world.

LOVE FOR SOULS IS YEARNING LOVE

The love of Christ creates in us a yearning for the salvation of the unsaved. This should be the characteristic emotion of a Christian worker's heart. There must be a constant, ever-present tender desire for the salvation of all. There are moments when you may not be conscious of this longing, but it springs up again instantly into consciousness as you mingle with people who do not know Christ.

When you see beautiful children or youth, you long for them to grow up and live for Christ. When you see them already showing evidences of the hardening process of sin, you grieve and covet them for God. When you see the unsaved enslaved by evil habits, you long to see Christ set them free. When you hear them blaspheme the name of Jesus, your heart bleeds and you long to bring them to our loving Christ. When you see those who evidence the presence of demonic power or control, you instantly yearn for Christ to set them free.

114

Your Love for the Unsaved

Love for souls is always a yearning love. The person who loves souls with Christ's agape love goes through life constantly yearning and praying brief prayers of holy longing for those about him.

There are also those sudden temporary, intense prayer burdens of yearning love which the Holy Spirit specially entrusts to those who live a life of hunger for souls. Often this is because a particular person for whom God gives you a burden is facing a special temptation, despondency in his life, or is grievously defeated and in bondage to Satan. The Holy Spirit so desires the salvation of this one that He pours His agape love into your heart at the very time of need and you sense an instant, heavy prayer burden.

You are blessed indeed if the Holy Spirit entrusts to you such a special prayer burden. Go instantly to prayer if at all possible. It may well be that after an hour or two of prevailing prayer or perhaps even a longer time of prayer and fasting God will break the bonds of sin and Satan and set the captive free. What wonderful testimonies have been given around the world of spiritual victories when God's children have been faithful to such Spirit-given prayer burden. God can send it to you whenever He needs your special intercession if you are living a daily life of yearning love for souls. Does God give you such intense prayer burdens? If not, perhaps you have not really yearned for souls.

At other times the Spirit over a period of days or weeks deepens a prayer concern or special hunger in your heart for the salvation of particular persons until you literally hunger and thirst for their salvation. This also is a special privilege— to be entrusted with such holy thirst and prayer concern.

At times God gives a long-term assignment and a continuing yearning love for a particular place or people. God can give such a holy burden to any pastor for the people of the community where God has placed him. Often God puts such a hunger on the hearts of other people also. My mother for years carried a hunger for the people of China and India. For many years practically every day as she prayed during family prayer for these two nations she would break down and weep

115

before she finished praying. Her love was deep and constant, and she will be rewarded eternally for her years of love-burden for those lands. This is the love of Jesus reaching out and mediated through Christians by the Holy Spirit.

Great soul-winners have always been those who longed for and prayed for souls. T. DeWitt Talmage said, "If God does not give me my prayer, I cannot endure it. I offer myself. I offer my life to this work. May a great multitude of souls be born of God." Matthew Henry, the great commentator, wrote, "I think it a greater happiness to gain one soul to Christ than mountains of silver or gold to myself."

Rutherford said to his people, "My witness is above, that your heaven would be two heavens to me, and the salvation of all of you as two salvations to me." In other words, his joy in heaven would be double if only his people be saved. David Stoner on his deathbed cried, "O Lord, save sinners by the score, hundreds, thousands."

David Matheson, Scots evangelist, said of his ministry, "Never for many minutes was the thought of the conversion of souls out of my view. I have served the Lord for two and twenty years. I have sought to win souls. It has been my passion."

Dr. Oswald J. Smith of Toronto shared his love for souls in these excerpts from his diary: "Never will I be satisfied until God works in convicting power and men and women weep their way to the cross." "Oh that He would break me down and cause me to weep for the salvation of souls." "Oh, to burn out for God! All, all for Him. Jesus only! Souls! Souls! Souls! I am determined to be a winner of souls. God help me." "About two this afternoon I was praying, when suddenly, I stopped and began to praise God. Tears flowed copiously. All I could do was sob out, 'They're lost! They're lost! They're lost!' and so I wept and prayed for the people."[1]

Thomas Collins said, "I went to my lonely retreat among the rocks, I wept much as I besought the Lord to give me souls." "I have pleaded with God this day for hours, in the wood, for souls. He will give them. I know His sign. I shall have souls tonight."

When a praying president of a college was told that he would die within a half-hour, he said, "Then take me out of bed and put me on my knees, and let me spend it calling on God for the salvation of the world." And he died upon his knees.

David Brainerd had holy hunger for the salvation of North American Indians. They resisted the gospel and feared and distrusted the white colonists. But David Brainerd went into the forests where they lived and wept and wrestled in prayer month after month. He constantly hungered and thirsted for their souls. He prayed hour after hour with such intensity until he became totally exhausted.

Brainerd was literally consumed with holy love and holy longing for the salvation of the Indians. He poured out his life physically and spiritually for those he loved so deeply. He wrote in his diary on July 21, 1744, "I exceedingly longed that God would get to Himself a name among the heathen."

For nearly three years Brainerd's intense concern continued. Over and over his diary records times of "wrestling" in prayer. All the time he kept pouring out his love and his life for them. Then suddenly the Spirit of God came upon them. Those who a few days before were living in drunkenness and heathen feasting, participating in "wild hooting war dances and carousals" were suddenly gripped by deep Holy Spirit-given conviction of their sins. From all directions Indians crowded in and around his house, standing speechless as he preached to them.

Many fell to the ground in great distress of soul as they now prayed to the Jesus Brainerd had been telling them about. While he did personal evangelism with some of them, God's Spirit came suddenly like a mighty rushing wind reminiscent of the day of Pentecost. People of all ages prayed and cried to God for mercy. All through the house and around the outside Indians repented and prayed for salvation. Many were so seized by God that they could not walk or stand, and collapsed on their knees before Him. Whole tribes began to hunger and thirst for salvation.

What was the secret? Overwhelming love for souls, all-

117

consuming love for souls that literally compelled Brainerd to pray on, weep on, and love on for these unresponsive pagan Indians. He poured out his soul and his strength month after month, often frail in body and weak from tuberculosis. But he held on until suddenly the Holy Spirit came in tides of salvation power.

Oh, the irresistible power of Holy Spirit love and Holy Spirit-empowered prevailing intercession! This is our all-important need today. Each movement of the Spirit has different characteristics. God has infinite love and infinite originality. The details will vary each time and place when God works in power and revival. But the basic principles are the same. Holy Spirit love and Holy Spirit-energized prayer are the secret and mighty preparation for Holy Spirit power and Holy Spirit harvest.

LOVE FOR SOULS IS A SEEKING LOVE

When the Holy Spirit fills your heart with inexpressible hunger for souls He will guide you, wherever possible, in ways to express that love in seeking the lost. Jesus taught us that love seeks. The father of the prodigal son saw his wayward, wretched son long before he reached the father's home. The loving, longing, hungry heart of the father drove him to run to meet and welcome back his long-lost son.

The loving heart of a good shepherd cannot rest content with ninety-nine sheep in the safety of the sheepfold as long as one is lost in the night. Seeking love drives him out alone across the hills and valleys seeking, seeking for the lost sheep until he finds it. And when he does, he joyfully puts the sheep on his shoulders and takes the sheep home. He calls to his friends and neighbors to rejoice with him (Luke 15:3–7).

THE GREAT JOY WHEN THE LOST IS FOUND

Tremendous joy comes when the lost is found. Heaven and earth rejoice. The person newly saved finds a thrilling new joy in his heart—the joy of the Lord. Often the new believer's family rejoices at the change Jesus has made.

The church of a soul-winning pastor is a happy church. Think of the constant joy of new brothers and sisters in the family of God, the joy of personal testimonies of God's transforming grace, the joy as church members catch the vision of soul-winning and then themselves experience the thrill of leading people to Christ. No leader's joy compares with the soul-winner's joy, the joy of seeing the answers to prayers for the lost.

Jesus spoke of joy in heaven over each repentant sinner. He did not say who rejoices, but I am sure all heaven rejoices. Certainly the angels rejoice over the triumphs of the gospel. How they thrill to watch our gospel ministry when the Holy Spirit is working mightily (1 Peter 1:12). But Jesus does not specifically say the angels rejoice. He says there is joy in heaven (Luke 15:7) and joy "in the presence of the angels of God over one sinner who repents" (v. 10). To whom is He referring? Relatives or friends of the new believer who are already in heaven? Probably they are informed, but we cannot be sure. If they are, they will greatly rejoice.

But who rejoices most of all? Who invested most and the costliest effort to make the salvation of this one possible? Certainly the Triune God—Father, Son, and Holy Spirit. All have been involved in providing and applying redemption. Their infinite hearts must rejoice inexpressibly more than the hearts of any other creatures in heaven or earth. If you want to bring joy to heaven and if you want rich eternal reward, bring souls to Christ.

"Those who are wise will shine like the brightness of the heavens, and those who lead many to righteousness, like the stars for ever and ever" (Dan. 12:3). What greater wisdom can you show than winning souls, when the salvation of each soul is so important to the entire Trinity? What greater fool could you prove yourself to be than to fail to pray and do everything possible for the salvation of as many as possible? Are you personally winning souls?

Chapter 18

You Have No Alternative but to Seek the Lost

Love for Jesus will drive you to seek the lost. Respect for God, for the price Jesus paid for your salvation at Calvary, will compel you. What kind of love for God do we have if it does not cause us to hunger for and seek the salvation of those for whom Jesus yearns so constantly? Even love for humanity ought to drive us to seek the lost. When we know it is salvation or hell, mere respect for fellow human beings should move us to do all in our power to bring people to Christ, for He is their only hope of heaven.

There is no alternative. Whatever is necessary to find them, persuade them, win them—agape love drives us to do it. Whatever steps prepare the way for the salvation of others, the Spirit wants to guide us to take them.

God has ordained that the Holy Spirit work through us. You can hinder the Spirit's working. You can be the missing link in God's plan of redemption. Oh! the tragedy of non-soul-winning churches! What an account their pastors will have to give to Christ at the judgment! How long has it been since you won new people to Christ? What a tragedy when ministers have never learned the joy of constant soul-winning! What makes us so blind? What makes us so unmoved by heaven and hell? Do we believe what we preach? George Whitefield said, "I am persuaded that the generality of preachers talk of an unknown and unfelt Christ. Many congregations are dead because dead men are preaching to them."

A notorious British murderer was sentenced to die. On the morning of his execution the prison chaplain walked beside him to the gallows and routinely read some Bible verses. The prisoner was shocked that the chaplain was so perfunctory, unmoved, and uncompassionate in the shadow of the scaffold. He said to the preacher, "Sir, if I believed what you and the church say you believe, even if England was covered with broken glass from coast to coast, from shore to shore, I would walk over it—if need be on my hands and knees—and think it worthwhile, just to save one soul from an eternal hell like that."

Moses threw himself into the gap between God and sinning Israel again and again as he fell on his face before God. Many times it is mentioned that he asked God to forgive them and not to destroy them (Exod. 32:11–13, 31–32; Num. 11:2; 12:13; 14:5–20; 16:4, 22, 45; 20:6; 21:7). He sent Aaron to run with the censor and stop the plague, standing between the living and the dead (Num. 16:46–48). Will Moses at the judgment seat of Christ or in heaven ask you why you did not intercede more for your people and seek more faithfully and assiduously to rescue hell-bound sinners?

When Nehemiah heard of the plight of Jerusalem he was so overcome by grief of heart that he could not keep standing. He sat down and wept. For some days he mourned and fasted and prayed (Neh. 1:4–11). He gave up his influential and honored position of cupbearer and confidant of the greatest emperor of his day to pay any price, risk his life, and go and seek the welfare of the Jews. Will Nehemiah one day ask you why you did so little to seek the lost of your city and area?

When Jehoshaphat was king in Jerusalem he became so burdened at the sin of his people that he sent his officials to take that portion of the Old Testament which was then available and go to every town in the nation to teach the people the will and Word of God. Apparently King Jehoshaphat himself went from city to city to teach and evangelize (2 Chron. 17:9).

A second time he went out among the people from one end of the land to the other to bring the people back to God. He exhorted his officials to consider carefully what they were doing, for they were God's representatives. He said, "Warn them not to sin against the LORD; otherwise his wrath will come on you and your brothers" (2 Chron. 19:10). If Jehoshaphat, although king, felt he would sin if he did not go to seek the lost, what will he say to you and me? We are Christ's servants, we have the clear gospel message today, we are set apart to reach the lost. How can we justify doing so little to seek and save the unsaved all around us?

What will the saints of God in heaven say to you, asking you why you did not do more to seek to save their sons and daughters, their loved ones and friends? What excuse will you and I give to them that we did not seek more continually, even desperately, to keep their loved ones from going to hell?

If the rich man in Hades pleaded with Abraham to send Lazarus to warn his five brothers so they would not come to the fire and torment of Hades (Luke 16:27–28), what will you say at the judgment seat of Christ if damned neighbors and friends of yours point their fingers at you and protest your going to heaven when you knew about hell and yet did so little to warn them and save them from its torment? What will you say when they ask you why you did not do everything humanly possible to keep their loved ones from hell?

No, there is no alternative. If we love God the Father we must seek the lost. If we love Christ who died for the unsaved, we must seek to lead them to Jesus. If we have any human love, we must seek the lost and try to keep them from the eternal flames of hell. One day when we stand before the judgment seat of Christ we will wish we had done, oh, so much more to seek to save the lost.

Is there significance that twice we are told in the book of Revelation that after the resurrection our tears will be wiped away? God will wipe them away after the great multitude of believers, including those from the Great Tribulation, are safe in heaven. They are the multitude that no one can count from all the nations of the earth, and they rejoice before the throne (Rev. 7:17). But we are again told, after the final judgment when every sinner has been judged and sent to the lake of fire, that God will wipe every tear from our eyes (Rev. 21:4). Will you and I weep at the judgment over the lost we failed to win? Is that why we are again told at that point that God will wipe our tears away?

HOW TO SEEK THE LOST
MOST LOVINGLY AND EFFECTIVELY

Recognize how essential to both God and the race that you seek the lost. Recognize how crucial it is that the unsaved be reached as quickly as possible since anyone's last opportunity to be saved may come at any moment.

Recognize that the Holy Spirit is the great Seeker. He alone knows the full need, the circumstances and inner attitudes and thoughts of each person. You need Him to coordinate and help your evangelism. Your own best efforts can so easily fail. You must realize that although the Holy Spirit longs to use you, there is no alternative to your being totally dependent on Him in all your seeking love.

1. *Ask the Spirit to give you eyes to see* when a person's heart is ready, when he faces a crisis where you can help, when the Spirit has brought him across your path for a purpose. Ask the Spirit to give you eyes to see people as He sees them and to see them with the love with which He sees them.

2. *Ask the Spirit to guide you* so that you are in the right place at the right time to speak to or bless and love the right

person. Only He knows which person He is assigning you to help at any moment. Only He knows all the circumstances. Only He knows all the changing thoughts and desires of the person. God's guidance is perfect and God's timing is perfect.

3. *Ask the Spirit to give you His anointed touch.* Only He knows the deepest heart cry and emotions of each person. There are certain standard approaches which are helpful in evangelism. But God may plan for you to have a different approach. And He may plan for you to have several initial contacts preparing the way before His strategic moment comes. Only He knows the way to contact, the time to smile, offer help, express friendship or goodwill, or the time to press the point. Only He knows the best way to empathize, to express understanding and appreciation. He may even, on the other hand, use you to awaken a person to his need by correction, verbal restraint, or suggestion.

No person knows enough to have the right touch on each occasion. It is the role of the Holy Spirit to guide you, anoint you, give you understanding and love, and make your touch exactly what is needed. Ask Him to take complete control of you and to use you.

4. *Ask the Spirit to give you the right words.* The right word at the right time can attract the attention of a person and interest him. On the other hand, the wrong word can cause him to turn away in disgust or aversion. The wrong word can prejudice a person whom the Spirit is drawing toward Christ. But who is able to know constantly the right word to use? Only the Holy Spirit.

One Sunday morning at a guest house in Bombay where I was staying for several days while transacting business in the city, a chance word of mine in answer to a question caught the ear of another guest. He had been introduced as a journalist. After the meal he asked why I used that word and what I knew about that word. The minutes stretched to hours and by noon I had led a backslidden minister to Christ as he wept his tears of repentance.

This appointment chosen by the Spirit had tremendous implications. He had arrived in India to launch a cult with the aid of one of India's political leaders. It could have had serious implications for Christians in India. God used me to block Satan's plan. The man destroyed all the literature which was already prepared, and Christ's cause was protected. God had used a "chance" word in my conversation which, unknown to me at the time, the Spirit had guided me to use.

On another occasion while traveling by train across India, God used one word I spoke in answering a question to interest another traveler. Before it was over I had a three-hour opportunity to answer questions about Christ and Christianity before a group of some twenty government leaders. One word, at God's time, when the Spirit had prepared the way was the key. Ask God to guide your words, even in your casual non-evangelism conversations. You can begin seeking souls any moment when the Spirit is in control.

LOVE FOR SOULS IS A SACRIFICING LOVE

Love does not hesitate to pay any price. Seeking love can be costly. There is always a price in loving people to Christ. For the sake of the gospel we must be willing to deny self whatever the cost. Jesus spoke clearly, "Anyone who loves his father or mother more than me is not worthy of me; anyone who loves his son or daughter more than me is not worthy of me; and anyone who does not take his cross and follow me is not worthy of me" (Matt. 10:37–38). What does it mean to follow Jesus? Not only does it include forsaking our sin and receiving Christ as Savior, it also includes making Christ our Lord and following Him in costly discipleship. Jesus searched for the lost, often having no place to lay His head (Matt. 8:20). Jesus searched even at the cost of precious family ties (Matt. 12:48–49). Following Jesus in evangelism often involves such supreme devotion to Christ that it costs us precious times of family fellowship (Luke 14:26–27). It involves a cross.

Sacrificially following Jesus with agape love as we seek the lost involves a price for us today. John Henry Jowett in his book *The Passion for Souls* pleads, "My brethren, are we in this succession? Does the cry of the world's need pierce the heart, and ring even through the fabric of our dreams? Do we 'fill up' our Lord's sufferings with our own sufferings, or are we the unsympathetic ministers of a mighty passion?"

Jowett also said, "To be . . . in the sacrificial succession, our sympathy must be a passion, our intercession must be a groaning, our beneficence must be a sacrifice, and our service must be a martyrdom."

Christlike identification with persons in need takes upon itself their heartbreak and their woes. We feel the chains of sin which bind them. We feel the pangs of broken vows, the bitter heart cries of both those sinning and those sinned against. We cringe at the hatred spawned from hell. We struggle against the evil tyrants that bind these poor lives. We wrestle with satanic powers of darkness that enslave them. We seek to snatch them from the fire kindling upon them (Jude 23).

Soul-winning involves spiritual battles. Battles with Satan are often not quickly won and are not easily won. Love gets wounded, love suffers scars, but seeking, sacrificing love does not give up because the seeking Spirit of God does not give up. Even though the cost involves laying down one's life as a living sacrifice, love seeks on. Even though it shortens life or involves a martyr's death, love seeks on.

Love, as Paul admits, often not only spends what it has but expends itself as well (2 Cor. 12:15). Love always carries the cross in its heart. Seeking love has the character of Calvary. Paul was not ashamed to bear on his body the marks of Jesus (Gal. 6:17). Heaven is filled with battle-scarred veterans of God's holy war of love. Jesus will glory in showing us His nail-scarred hands in heaven, even as He did on resurrection Sunday (John 20:20).

Amy Carmichael, one of India's living missionary martyrs of some years ago, wrote a searching poem called "No Scar?" in which she asked you and me if we bear a scar from wounds suffered in sacrificially serving Christ. Her closing words to us are

You Have No Alternative but to Seek the Lost

Can he have followed far
Who has nor wound nor scar?

The secret of soul-winning ministry is love. Love that yearns, love that seeks, love that gladly suffers. Love that is willing to earn a scar.

Chapter 19

Your Love for the Church

It is part of Christ's eternal plan that He have a beloved body of people called out of the world, redeemed by His blood, and specially committed in love to Him. Jesus said, "I will build my church" (Matt. 16:18). He is "head over everything for the church" (Eph. 1:22). "He is the head of the body, the church" (Col. 1:18). He wants God's wisdom to be proved to the angel world by the church (Eph. 3:10).

"Christ loved the church and gave himself up for her to make her holy, cleansing her by the washing with water through the word, and to present her to himself as a radiant church, without stain or wrinkle or any other blemish, but holy and blameless" (Eph. 5:25–27).

Christ loved the church and chose the church to be His eternal bride (Rev. 21:1–3). Christ wants the church to be spiritually well-fed, spiritually secure, spiritually radiant, and spiritually adorned as His beloved, beautiful, lovely bride.

YOU ARE CALLED TO LOVE THE CHURCH

Christ has chosen you to care for His church or a group within it on His behalf. He wants you to love the church with His love. As a Christian leader you are responsible to care for it for Him. He wants to fill you with His ardent love for it.

There is only one way you adequately can be a shepherd-leader of the church or a group of God's people, caring lovingly for them until Christ comes Himself to get her for His very own. You must love the church with Christ's own special love provided by the Holy Spirit.

It is not enough for you to love the believers as fellow-human beings, as your friends, or even to love them as fellow-believers. You must love them with Christ's own love given by the Spirit. Christ calls you to love for Him, to be His love-gift to the church. He has sent the Holy Spirit to give you the love you need. You are appointed to be His channel of love. Paul is probably the greatest example of Christ loving the church through us. His letters reveal the intensity, commitment, and sacrificial fullness of his love.

HOW TO LOVE THE CHURCH

1. *Thank God for the church.* It is Christ's great treasure, His precious, beloved bride. It is His constant joy. He eagerly waits for the time when His bride will be complete and He can come to receive her to Himself (Eph. 5:25–26). As Christ thanks God for the church, so should we. Here, again, Paul is an outstanding example.

"I always thank God for you" (1 Cor. 1:4). "Ever since I heard . . . I have not stopped giving thanks for you, remembering you in my prayers" (Eph. 1:15–16). "I thank my God every time I remember you. In all my prayers for all of you, I always pray with joy" (Phil. 1:3–4). "We always thank God, the Father of our Lord Jesus Christ, when we pray for you"

(Col. 1:3). "We always thank God for all of you, mentioning you in our prayers. We continually remember before our God and Father ..." (1 Thess. 1:2–3). Are you constantly thanking God for your church? Thanking God over and over increases your love.

Only love, Pauline love, Christlike love, can sustain you and enable you to be the leader of your people God wants you to be. Again and again you will need to pray God to baptize you anew with His love. Time and again you will need to call to the Holy Spirit to pour His love in new rivers of fullness through your soul. It is a costly ministry—costly in love, in tears, in pleadings, in agonizing intercession, in time, and in soul energy. But love you must—more, and more, and more.

2. *Make the church your special joy.* When you love people intensely they become your constant source of joy, especially as they respond to your love. Just as a parent receives joy observing the child's play, growth, interesting sayings, and constant development, so your heart of love for your people will rejoice constantly as you see the Spirit of God at work in them.

Paul calls the Philippians his joy and crown (Phil. 4:1). To the Thessalonians he writes, "Now we really live, since you are standing firm in the Lord. How can we thank God enough for you in return for all the joy we have in the presence of our God because of you?" (1 Thess. 3:8–9).

Paul not only rejoiced constantly over the church, it was his pride and glory. He delighted with deep spiritual satisfaction. He wrote to the Corinthians, "I glory over you in Christ Jesus our Lord" (1 Cor. 15:31). "I have great confidence in you; I take great pride in you" (2 Cor. 7:4).

3. *Keep the church in your heart.* Paul testified, "I have you in my heart" (Phil. 1:7). They were written on his heart (2 Cor. 3:2). They had such a place in his heart that Paul could hardly find words to describe it. "You have such a place in our hearts that we would live or die with you" (2 Cor. 7:3). David Brainerd, in describing his love for the American Indians, wrote, "When I was asleep I dreamed of these things, and when I waked, the first thing I thought of was this

great work." He kept the people on his heart. Are the people to whom you minister constantly in your heart?

4. *Open your heart in love to the church.* Paul wrote to the Corinthians, "We have . . . opened wide our hearts to you" (2 Cor. 6:11). He referred to the depth of his love for them which caused him to weep for them when he saw their struggles and needs (2 Cor. 2:4). Paul testified that he commended himself by kindness and sincere love (2 Cor. 6:6). He proved himself a true fellow-worker of God (v. 1) by his love. He sent his love to them in writing (1 Cor. 16:24). He told the Thessalonians that his love for them increased and overflowed (1 Thess. 3:12). The longer you are with your people, the more the Spirit wants you to love them, and the more the flood tide of your love is to gush out to them.

Paul called God as his witness that he deeply and truly loved his people (2 Cor. 11:11). Though he was absent from them in the body, in love and prayer he was with them in spirit, observing them and delighting in them (Col. 2:5). You never dare react to the disappointing attitudes or actions of some of your people and begin to shut your heart against them. Christian leaders must consciously endeavor always to keep their hearts open through love to their people.

5. *Have constant holy longings for the church.* Paul wrote to the Philippians, "God can testify how I long for all of you with the affection of Christ Jesus" (Phil. 1:8). His longing was so great because Jesus had shared with him such deep affection for the church. Can you testify that God has given you a special love for the ones to whom you minister? What did Paul do because of such God-given love? He tells us in the next verses. Since he could not be with them he prayed constantly for them.

Again Paul said of them in Philippians 4:1, "You whom I love and long for, my joy and crown." Paul longed to see the Thessalonians (1 Thess. 3:6). He testified that his longings for them moved him so deeply it was almost unbearable. "Brothers, when we were torn away from you for a short time (in person, not in thought), out of our intense longing we made every effort to see you. For we wanted to come to you—

certainly I, Paul, did, again and again . . . So when we could stand it no longer . . . when I could stand it no longer" (1 Thess. 2:17–18; 3:1, 5). When Paul was away from his beloved people he longed for them so intensely it was painful. Such longing kept him constantly praying for them. Do you have such deep longings for your people that it constantly drives you to prayer?

6. *Love by constant intercession for the church.* While your prayer for your people is never fully obvious to them, yet the love invested in prayer for your people becomes apparent in many ways. The leader who invests much prayer in his people does not need to announce it to them. They will sense his loving concern and it will bind their hearts to him. Certainly prayer is often the most powerful way to love people. It is not the only way; it cannot take the place of concrete demonstrations of love, but it is basic to all else and upon it depends the effectiveness of all else.

Christ lives to intercede for the church and the world. It is He who directs the Spirit to place upon the heart of a godly leader prayer burdens for the church. Every prayer concern for your people comes direct from the heart of God to you. It is a trust from God to you. You dare not fail Christ by failing to spend extended time each week interceding for your people. Nothing is more important.

If the apostles were led by the Spirit to assign many administrative tasks to others in order to devote themselves more exclusively to prayer and the ministry of the Word, we can do no less. No pastor is faithful to his pastoral role unless he spends a number of hours each week in intercession. This must include prayer for the church as a whole, for each family and individual in some orderly way so that none is missed, for the various sub-groups in the church (youth, children, mothers, fathers, etc.), and for each of the ministries of the church—the missionaries supported by the church, the choir, and other forms of outreach. The pastor will also spend much time in prayer for God's anointing on his ministry, for the Spirit's revival touches, and for world harvest.

7. *Have a parental love for the church.* To bring a church

into existence is often as costly and as painful as bringing a baby to birth. Paul used the same expression that is used for childbirth. Even after a church has been planted, crises will come during which the God-given leader again goes through the labor and pains of spiritual childbirth. Paul speaks of his "dear children, for whom [he is] again in the pains of childbirth until Christ is formed in you" (Gal. 4:19). Paul had to go through this suffering more than once for the same churches.

Satan may tempt you to give up on your church or group or on some of the people. You may have to ask God to give you a new and deeper love and faith than you have ever had before. The Holy Spirit is always ready to pour more of the love of Christ into your heart.

Paul testified, "We were gentle among you, like a mother caring for her little children" (1 Thess. 2:7). The leader often has to nurse sick Christians as if they were spiritual babies again. All Christians do not attain spiritual maturity at the same rate. Carnal Christians at times seem to regress in maturity. If you carry a Pauline burden for them, you will often go through prayer travail like spiritual birth pains. You will often have to be a nurse to weak believers.

Paul not only testified to a motherly role, but also to a fatherly role. "You know that we dealt with each of you as a father deals with his own children, encouraging, comforting and urging you to live lives worthy of God" (1 Thess. 2:11–12). Every parent knows that each child has a different personality. Even so, each believer must be given personal fatherly spiritual help to grow in grace and to become spiritually mature. This requires constant wisdom, the guidance of the Spirit, and the special touch of the Spirit in counseling, strengthening, correcting, and helping.

Only by the constant enabling of the Spirit can the leader bring every believer to the spiritual maturity and perfection of Christ. "We proclaim him, admonishing and teaching everyone with all wisdom, so that we may present everyone perfect in Christ. To this end I labor, struggling with all his energy, which so powerfully works in me. I want you to know how much I am struggling for you" (Col. 1:28–2:1).

The Greek words Paul uses here illustrate the intensity of the agony and soul travail involved in this process. *Labor* means "toil unto weariness." *Struggling* comes from a Greek word which means "to contest, fight, agonize, straining every nerve and making every effort" like a wrestler in an agony of sweat and pain.

This is what it takes to defeat Satan and bring souls to birth and maturity. It often is more costly in intense prayer and personal parenting to bring Christians to maturity than it was to bring them to Christ in the first place. This is not a physical struggle, except in the physical toll the prayer-wrestling with Satan and the powers of darkness entails. But the agonizing is a spiritual struggle in prayer, an inner price that is paid. This is why Paul compares it with birth pains. Many leaders can never be said to wrestle in prayer. Can you?

As the spiritual parent, you will probably wake to spend undisturbed night hours watching and praying for your people, just as a parent sits all night by the bed of a child seriously ill. You become so identified with the ones you love that, like Paul, you carry a constant concern for all in the church (2 Cor. 8:16). "Besides everything else, I face daily the pressure of my concern for all the churches. Who is weak, and I do not feel weak? Who is led into sin, and I do not inwardly burn?" (2 Cor. 11:28–29). He so identified with them that he burned with shame when they did, and burned with indignation against Satan who misled them.

Leadership is costly, time-consuming, energy-consuming work that makes its demands upon you day and night.

8. *Love the church enough to spend yourself and be willing to suffer.* You are called to give yourself for the church. Christ was willing to give Himself even to death for it. You may not be called upon to make that extreme a sacrifice, but Paul was willing to suffer whatever it took, even unto death. Listen to his testimony: "Now I rejoice in what was suffered for you, and I fill up in my flesh what is still

lacking in regard to Christ's afflictions, for the sake of his body, which is the church" (Col. 1:24). "I will very gladly spend for you everything I have and expend myself as well" (2 Cor. 12:15). "We loved you so much that we were delighted to share with you not only the gospel of God but our own lives as well, because you had become so dear to us" (1 Thess. 2:8).

There is still a price to be paid for the church. This commitment of time, love, effort, and life-blood will make you, like Paul, a servant of the church. Paul called himself a servant of Jesus Christ (Rom. 1:1) and a servant of the gospel (Col. 1:23). This may not seem so difficult to you. But Paul went on to rejoice in being a servant of the church (v. 25). This can be difficult. Are you tempted at times to say of some people, or of the governing body of your church, "Who do they think I am? Am I their servant?" Yes, Paul says, for Jesus' sake we become in many respects servants of the church.

Then how do we maintain our dignity? Not by trying to assert our dignity. Not by saying that certain tasks are beneath our role. The leader's respect, honor, and dignity are maintained only by the presence and power of God upon his life and ministry. Humble servanthood can actually exalt you in the estimation of your people.

You are not called to run errands for everyone, but you are called to be their friend and helper. You may have regretfully to decline to help in some situations because of spiritual priorities. This will be understood if you are recognized as a person of God, of prayer, and one mightily used by the Holy Spirit. Live so full of God's Spirit that young and old respect you as God's person, and want you to give yourself primarily to spiritual ministry.

Chapter 20

The Shepherd Heart

Do you have a shepherd's heart? Nothing is more essential to Christian leadership. There are several Bible descriptions of Christian leaders. They are to be watchmen. God told Ezekiel He had made him a watchman for Israel, with two duties: to hear the word from God, and to give the people God's message (Ezek. 3:17). Thirty chapters later God repeated the same basic message. He then went on to say that the leader was responsible to let everyone know adequately God's warning and message. If he failed to give God's message, God would hold him accountable for the blood of the people (Ezek. 33:1–9). In Isaiah 62:6 God added to the role of the watchman the responsibility of intercession.

There were really no pastors in the Old Testament period, although both prophets and kings chosen by God at times exercised some of the roles of the watchman. Shepherd was another term used in Old Testament times for the spiritual responsibility of leaders.

God wants you as a Christian worker to have the heart of a shepherd. Every leader is responsible to shepherd all the people under his influence and care. Each elder and deacon in a local church shares some of the shepherding responsibility. Every Sunday school teacher or leader of a church group has a like responsibility. A bishop of a denomination or superintendent of a Christian organization is responsible to shepherd the pastors or Christian workers under his supervision. Shepherding is one of the most important and needed roles among the people of God. To some extent every Christian is responsible to help shepherd those younger in faith and also those young in age.

JESUS, THE MODEL SHEPHERD

God has a shepherd heart. Moses in his song called God the Shepherd of His people (Gen. 49:24). David said of God, "The LORD is my shepherd" (Ps. 23:1). His shepherd psalm outlines just how God is our Shepherd and the assurance we have because of this glorious truth. The writer of Psalm 80 prayed to God the Shepherd who leads His people like a flock (Ps. 80:1).

Isaiah rejoices that God the Sovereign Lord has a Shepherd heart. "He tends his flock like a shepherd: He gathers the lambs in his arms and carries them close to his heart; he gently leads those that have young" (Isa. 40:11). Jeremiah prophesied that God would "watch over his flock like a shepherd" (Jer. 31:10). Repeatedly in the Old Testament when their human shepherds failed them God took His sovereign authority and promised to intervene (Jer. 23:4; Ezek. 34:11–16, 23; Zech. 10:3).

Then in John 10 Jesus announces that He is the Good Shepherd that God had promised. He will fulfill all the Old Testament promises and the role outlined in His own parable of the faithful shepherd (John 10:2–5).

1. *The sheep listen to His voice.* They recognize His voice but not those of false shepherds.

2. *He knows all His sheep individually and calls each by his own name.* This expresses His detailed care of us, His intimate knowledge of us, and His love for us. In this He is the pattern Shepherd for all His leaders today. Ideally, every pastor, Sunday school teacher, and church leader should know each of those under him by name in a detailed and personal way. Do you?

3. *He leads them to where their needs are supplied.* He is responsible for their every need and especially their constant need of guidance. Are you providing or arranging for the provision of all the spiritual needs of your people?

4. *He goes on ahead of them and they follow Him.* He is the example of all He teaches, the example for every leader and pastor. You as shepherd must be the example of all that you teach for all whom you teach. You must personally model all the truth you present.

5. *He came that His sheep might have full, abundant life.* He is concerned about all of life for His own. Spiritual life is His primary concern, but Christ as Lord of all of life is interested in all of life. Prayer is to cover all of life. Guidance is for all of life. Every so-called "secular" aspect of life can be lived in a way compatible with spirituality.

Even so, you as a shepherd-leader of God's people must follow Christ's priorities. The spiritual must always take precedence, but nothing else need be neglected. As a shepherd you need to be well acquainted with all the joys, sorrows, successes, failure, wounds, hurts, and needs of your people.

Either the local church must be of a size where this can be done, or else the church must make full provision for under-shepherds who meet with smaller shepherd groups each week, and who know the intimate details of all in his group. They, in turn, must channel all urgent prayer needs to the senior shepherd or to the whole shepherd group. Each believer must have a responsible shepherd who knows him by name, prays for him by name, and gladly shares in as many details of his life as is appropriate. This fullness of prayer and guidance should be available for all of the life of each member.

In Korea I found that many of the larger churches of the Korea Evangelical Church, established by OMS International, with which I have served nearly fifty years, have extensive statistics each week in their church bulletins. The local church is divided into shepherd groups of ten to twenty people. Each has its appointed shepherd, who conducts the weekly group prayer meeting and who gathers the statistics for each person in his group: services attended, offering given that week in the group meeting, number of chapters of the Bible read that week, number of souls won to Christ that week. The church bulletin insert each week gives this information for each group and the total for the church as a whole. Each shepherd must inform the pastor of anyone ill and any urgent prayer request from his group.

I asked one pastor what one special statistic reported. He replied, "You know how it is with a pregnant woman. These are the unsaved people that the particular group are now carrying on their hearts like a pregnant woman carries her baby until it is born." Each group, as it were, was pregnant with one or more souls!

6. *He is the Good Shepherd.* Jesus repeated this important claim. Each time He added a significant statement which must be true in the case of any good shepherd. Every Christian shepherd should be a good shepherd.

a. *Christ is the Good Shepherd because He lays down His life for the sheep* (John 10:10, 15). He did this in two ways. He spent Himself fully and always in His ministry for His own. He thus laid down His life every day of His life. The entire incarnation was a laying down of His life. He also laid down His life to the ultimate degree. He did not hesitate to die for His sheep.

You as a Christian shepherd must be willing to lay down your life daily for your people. You must daily deny yourself for their sake. You must rejoice with those who rejoice and weep with those who weep (Rom. 12:15). You must grieve and inwardly burn over those who sin (2 Cor. 11:29). You must feel weak with everyone who is weak (v. 29). But you must also be willing to defend your people even with your life if this proves necessary in time of persecution.

b. *Christ is also the Good Shepherd because He knows His sheep and His sheep know Him* (John 10:14–15, 27). How fully does He know them? As fully as He knows the Father and as fully as the Father knows Him. Again Jesus is the Model, the Example for all His under-shepherds. You are not fully shepherd to a person whom you do not know. And your sheep need to feel they know you. Only then can you meet their needs and only then can they fully trust you. They need to know your very heartbeat. They cannot receive your full shepherd ministry to them except as they know you.

The key to leadership or any form of shepherd ministry is knowledge of your people. Only then can your care for them be effective. Only then can your love for them be personal and fully an identifying love. There must be an intensely personal dimension and identification in the heart of a shepherd.

Twice in this chapter Jesus says that He knows His sheep (vv. 14, 27). This, He says, is all-important in the shepherd role. The only way you can know a person is to be with him, available to him, and to go where he is when he needs you. May God help you to know adequately your people.

YOUR
ACCOUNTABILITY

Chapter 21

The Shepherd's Role

No better picture of the role of a shepherd can be found than that provided by David, the shepherd-king, in Psalm 23. From his boyhood he knew the life of a shepherd. He lived out in the fields with his sheep so he came to know his sheep well. Even in the beginning of his service for Saul he still went back and forth to his flock.

David had the heart of a shepherd both for his sheep and later for his people as their shepherd-king. He risked his life when he faced a lion and later a bear to defend the flock (1 Sam. 17:34–36). He repeatedly risked his life fighting for his people.

So ideal was David the shepherd-king that in the prophecies of Christ's future reign as King, He is called David, i.e., a Shepherd-King like David (Jer. 30:9; Ezek. 34:23–24; Hos. 3:5). It is David the ideal shepherd who

Ablaze for God

describes God as our Divine Shepherd in Psalm 23. He outlines for us the shepherd-role which we should emulate.

THE SHEPHERD PROVIDES ABUNDANT SPIRITUAL NOURISHMENT

"He makes me lie down in green pastures" (Ps. 23:2). Adequate spiritual food is a primary reason for needing a shepherd. Lying down suggests eating to satiety and then resting in satisfaction and blessing. The sheep that lies down in good pasture has all he desires.

Nothing creates more satisfied sheep, more happy loyalty, than adequate spiritual nourishment. This assures constant spiritual growth—growth in the knowledge of God, His Word, and growth in personal Christlikeness, in the fruit of the Spirit.

Hungry sheep do not lie down; they go searching for more pasture. A church or group losing members is probably a church not being adequately fed. The spiritual diet may be true to the Bible, but something is lacking in quality of deep exposition and in variety of doctrinal teaching. Or the seal of the Holy Spirit may not be strongly on the ministry. Anointed ministry constantly brings out things new and old (Matt. 13:52); it is full of the deep things of God (1 Cor. 2:10). It provides rich, abundant food.

The leader or pastor who during his daily prayer and meditation constantly experiences the Holy Spirit revealing to him those things which "no eye has seen, no ear has heard, no mind has conceived," but which "God has prepared for those who love him" (1 Cor. 2:9) is himself feasting on the deep things of God as found in God's Word. He is so thrilled and excited by the Spirit's illumination of the Word that he is anointed to preach or teach "by the Holy Spirit sent from heaven" (1 Peter 1:12).

When his people sense the holy thrill of God in his voice and the excited joy of the Spirit in his face as he unfolds God's great truths which the Spirit is making so real to him, they feast with him on the spiritual grapes of Eshcol and the milk and honey of Canaan. People who are richly blessed week after week by the sense of God's feeding them through their shepherd become the best advertisement to invite other hungry people to come and be fed. A surprising number of true Christians are unsatisfied with the ministry they receive and feel hungry and semi-starved on the spiritual diet they are given in their church. Are your people left still hungry after they hear you?

God has created us so that a spiritually alive Christian longs for rich spiritual food. Woe to the shepherd who does not know how to get deep and spiritually thrilling messages from God and His Word. God always has a message for His people, and a real person of God who is diligent in prayer, Bible reading, and Bible study will be given God's message for the people week after week. If your people are spiritually starved, they will be restless. They know something is lacking. Are your people restless?

THE SHEPHERD LEADS CONSTANTLY TO SPIRITUAL REFRESHMENT

Every Christian needs special times of spiritual refreshment. "He leads me beside quiet waters" (Ps. 23:2) speaks of God's provision of constant opportunities for spiritual thirst to be quenched. It is normal for a Christian to long for more and more of God. Christians without spiritual thirst are spiritually ill.

Water speaks of the ministry of the Holy Spirit. God created us to be filled with the Spirit, to recognize the presence of the Spirit, and to long for evidences of the Spirit's working. I am not speaking primarily about spiritual gifts. The primary evidences to which I refer are God's anointing, guidance, assistance in prayer, and answers to prayer through the Spirit. I am also speaking of the pervading sense of God's presence in a service and evident in the ministry of God's servant-leaders.

Truth without this special blessing of the Spirit is not sufficient to satisfy. The most wonderful truth may be presented in a deadening way (2 Cor. 3:6). In some services the human so clearly predominates that little of the Spirit's working is evident. The leader cannot control the working and manifestation of the Spirit. But the leader can do much to prepare the way for the Spirit's refreshing presence to be manifested.

1. *Your personal prayer life will decide to a large extent how fully the Spirit anoints and refreshes through your ministry.* Every spiritual person knows it when the speaker is anointed. Even unsaved people can at times sense God's presence in a service and upon the ministry of God's Word, the prayer, and the songs.

2. *Your instruction to the choir or special singers prepares for God to refresh.* Your urging them to prepare their hearts by prayer, to select their musical numbers in prayer, to put emphasis upon the words being fully understood and not just the display of the voice, to seek to make their song God's message, and your emphasis that their musical numbers must become part of the Spirit's ministry— all this can help them to be used by the Spirit. Your prayer time with them before the service can do much to help them sense their dependence on the Spirit.

3. *Your preparing your own heart for public prayer prepares for the Spirit's refreshing ministry.* You must commit your pastoral prayer in advance to God for His blessing just as much as your message. Lead the entire congregation into the very presence of God. All this is of great significance in preparing the way for the Spirit's refreshing your people.

4. *Your preparation of your own heart to read the Holy Word of God prepares the Spirit's way.* Let God guide you in the choice of Scripture selections, in your emphases on specific words as you read, and let Him give you anointed freshness. This too prepares the way for the Spirit. Paul Rees tells how he found as a young minister that just to hear G. Campbell Morgan read the Scripture lesson before he preached was an experience of worship. Do your people hear God speaking when you read the Scripture?

146

5. *Your preparation of your congregation to cover each service with prayer prepares for the Spirit's refreshing ministry.* You may arrange for a selected number of your people, chosen by rotation, to spend a half-hour in prayer on Saturday and again on Sunday morning (or at least 15 minutes both times). They must intercede for God's refreshing presence throughout the service. Or you may arrange for a volunteer group to gather forty minutes before the service and to pray until ten minutes before the service begins. Spurgeon had a large group praying during the service, but he had a larger membership from which to draw, so it did not reduce too largely the attendance.

Your goal must be such a sense of God's presence in your service that all—saved and unsaved are gripped by the Spirit of God, are aware of the presence of God, and bow before God in new obedience to His will. Paul indicated that this is possible when the Spirit uses the service to search the hearts of those present, revealing inner needs, forgotten sins and failures, and God's great provision for every need. Paul said the unsaved can be so convinced of God in their midst that they "fall down and worship God, exclaiming, 'God is really among [us]!'" (1 Cor. 14:25).

Not only will the unsaved be profoundly moved, but the saved can be even more arrested and moved by the Spirit into the path of God's will as they recognize with awe the holy presence of God. God manifestly among you; God Himself speaking through the hymns, prayers, and message; God's hand upon the service—this must be your goal.

Only the Spirit's holy ministry in a service will bring the refreshing water of the Spirit to slake spiritual thirst. This may be manifest in various ways. It will bring special life and joy to the singing. It will add a holy hush in much of the service. It may result in quiet tears of joy as the Word of God is read or as you lead during the pastoral prayers. It will add a special sense of God's anointing upon your message and upon you as God's messenger. It will help God's Word come alive and speak personally to the hearts of the hearers. It may result in a special awareness of God's presence. It may add a special liberty to respond when, at the close, you challenge the congregation to commitment.

THE SHEPHERD AIDS SPIRITUAL RESTORATION

It is a fact of church life that from time to time one member or other needs spiritual restoration (Ps. 23:3). Satan is ever present to tempt Christians to spiritual negligence, to cool off and relax spiritually, or to yield to the allurements and spirit of the world. Satan is always ready to accuse one Christian to another, to cause a person to misunderstand another's actions or motives. Satan appeals to the carnal nature to break fellowship, wound believers and, if possible, to lead into open sin. If he does not succeed in leading people into sin, he tries to get wounded people to withdraw from fellowship with other Christians and thus more easily become his prey.

You as shepherd must always be on the watch for signs of spiritual coldness, defeat, or the beginning of backsliding among your people. The exhortation of Galatians 6:1 ("Brothers, if someone is caught in a sin, you who are spiritual should restore him gently") is for all Christians, for we are each one our fellow Christian's keeper. But it is the special duty of the shepherd to restore the defeated in a spiritual and gentle way. This is one way to enter into another's burden and help him carry it; this is Christ's law for the church (Gal. 6:2; 2 Cor. 2:7–8).

Even those who oppose you are to be treated with kindness, avoiding quarreling, but rather showing kindness in the hope they will become repentant (2 Tim. 2:24–26).

Barnabas restored John Mark after he had failed in Crete, and later Paul found Mark a great help to him (2 Tim. 4:11), and to Mark we are indebted for his writing the Gospel that bears his name. Peter was restored after he denied his Lord and became the early leader of the church. Jonah was restored after he ran away from God's will. David was restored and again greatly used by God, even though he had sinned tragically.

148

You as shepherd must be always on the alert for any sign of discouragement, weakness, or temptation. The ministry of encouragement is a most important duty of the shepherd. God told Moses to encourage Joshua (Deut. 1:38) and strengthen him (Deut. 3:28). It is even necessary to strengthen and encourage yourself in the Lord at times, like David did (1 Sam. 30:6). Josiah encouraged the priests in their ministry (2 Chron. 35:2). Isaiah exhorted, "Encourage the oppressed" (Isa. 1:17).

Judas and Silas had a ministry of encouragement in Antioch (Acts 15:32). Paul sent Tychicus to encourage the Ephesians (Eph. 6:22) and the Colossians (Col. 4:7–8). He sent Timothy to strengthen and encourage the church in Thessalonica (1 Thess. 3:12). He urged Thessalonian believers to encourage one another (1 Thess. 5:11) and especially those who were timid (5:14). He prayed for God to encourage them (2 Thess. 2:17). One of the qualifications for an elder, said Paul, was the ability to encourage others with sound doctrine (Titus 1:9). Young men are to be encouraged (Titus 2:6). He urged Titus to encourage those to whom he ministered (2:15). In his last letter before his death he urged Timothy to exercise the ministry of encouragement (2 Tim. 4:2).

Obviously, Paul considered this ministry of encouragement a special role for a spiritual shepherd. But it was an encouragement with substance, with solid doctrinal teaching given in a meaningful and encouraging way (2 Tim. 4:2; Titus 1:9). It must at times be the balance for discipline which you as a shepherd must also exercise (2 Tim. 4:2; Titus 1:9; 2:15). Keep alert to any of your people who need spiritual restoration or encouragement.

THE SHEPHERD MUST GIVE GUIDANCE TO HIS PEOPLE

As a spiritual leader, the shepherd is so closely watched and his words and example so often followed that he leads or misleads in many aspects of living. The principles he proclaims and the biblical standards of conduct he teaches can have a profound effect upon his people. Their righteous attitudes and actions then affect society and government. The shepherd must help them to lead such righteous lives that they become the salt of society and the Christian light in the secular and pagan darkness around them. This is the meaning of "He guides me in the paths of righteousness for his name's sake." "For his name's sake" means both "in accordance with His holy nature" and "for the honor of His name."

Bible standards teach hard work, integrity in employment and all of life, frugal expenditures, and assistance to the needy. This not only helps the church make a wholesome impact upon society, but also brings reward from the Lord. God blesses believers with peace, spiritual and physical blessing, and sometimes with personal prosperity also.

Just as counseling is one of the primary roles of the Holy Spirit, so counseling is an important aspect of the shepherd's ministry. The Greek word *parakletos,* which Jesus used as a name for the Holy Spirit in John 14:16, 26; 15:26; 16:7, can be translated Comforter, Helper, or Counselor. In fact, some Bible translations prefer "Counselor." The Holy Spirit is given to us to guide us into all truth (John 16:13) and in many other ways. He loves to lead each Christian (Rom. 8:14).

The Holy Spirit is the Counselor of every believer, but he is specially available to equip you as a shepherd to guide in counseling God's people who are under your leadership. If you have a shepherd heart, you will constantly see needs for loving, wise, and biblical teaching and counseling. You need constantly to pray and ask for the Spirit's counsel and anointing in this aspect of your ministry. You become the trusted friend and advisor of your people. They often put special weight on your counsel because they recognize you as God's representative to them. How careful you must be that you yourself are being led by the Spirit as you in turn lead and advise them.

THE SHEPHERD MUST BE WITH HIS PEOPLE IN THEIR TIMES OF NEED

Just as David knew that God his Shepherd was near him ("you are with me"—Ps. 23:4), especially in every time of need, so your people must know that you, their shepherd, are always available and ready to share their hours of need. In times of sickness, death, family problems, or other crises of life, you as shepherd must get to your people as quickly as possible. Often you can help meet their need, but always your presence with them is reassuring. That is what a shepherd is for. David was strengthened because, as he said to God, "You are with me."

Often you as shepherd may hardly know what to say; you cannot provide answers they so much long for. But you can be with them. Then is the time to show Christ's understanding love. Then is the time to rejoice with those who rejoice and to weep with those who weep (Rom. 12:15).

Such moments of need take priority over almost all else. You as shepherd may not be able to stay as long as you would like. In fact, it may not be wise for you to make a long visit at such times. But at least you must go, touch their lives with blessing, and pray with them. There are times you may be able to sit quietly for a longer time beside a hospital bed, just to be with them. If not, drop by for a moment; prayer is often the most important blessing you can leave. If you are known as a person of God and of prayer, your intercession will be all the more desired, meaningful, and depended on.

Sometimes a spiritual crisis of an unsaved person unrelated to the congregation, or long prayed for by the congregation, may take precedence over a health crisis in a member of the congregation. This will normally be understood if you as shepherd have prepared your people by teaching them constant concern for the unsaved. They will understand why such a crisis in an unsaved person takes priority over all else. The shepherd leaves the ninety-nine in the fold to aid the one who is lost.

Some of the blessings David received from God his

Shepherd are such that only God can give. Only He can anoint with the Spirit (symbolized by the anointing oil). Only God is the source of the divine goodness and love. But if you as a shepherd of God's people follow the preceding five roles patterned after God's own shepherding, you will be the constant blessing to His people that God expects you to be. It was for this that God called you to be a shepherd.

Chapter 22

The Shepherd's Accountability

The shepherd is always accountable for all who are in his flock. Zechariah warned that God's anger burns against unfaithful shepherd-leaders. "My anger burns against the shepherds and I will punish the leaders; for the LORD Almighty will care for his flock" (Zech. 10:3). You as shepherd are always responsible to God for the condition of His flock and of His individual sheep. God is the Great and Sovereign Shepherd, and you are an under-shepherd directly responsible to God.

Zechariah pronounces a special woe on a shepherd who deserts his flock. "Woe to the worthless shepherd, who deserts his flock!" (Zech. 11:17). A shepherd does not have the same right to flee from danger that an ordinary person does. The captain has no right to abandon his ship as long as there is one passenger in danger. A policeman has no right to flee from a criminal when he is endangering people. The police are responsible to die in the line of duty if need be while protecting others. A parent has no right to desert his child in the face of danger. A shepherd has no right to desert his flock when danger comes. When the armed temple police came to Gethsemane, Jesus faced them and told them to leave His disciples alone (John 18:4–8).

UNFAITHFUL SHEPHERDS

Ezekiel 34:1–10 is a prophecy on the accountability of the shepherd leaders of Israel. God pronounces woe on them for their failures.

1. *They take care of themselves rather than the flock.* They are more concerned with their personal interests and the welfare of their own families than with the welfare of God's people. "Woe to the shepherds of Israel who only take care of themselves! Should not shepherds take care of the flock?" (Ezek. 34:2). Woe to the leader who is more concerned about where he can receive the most salary or what is best for his family rather than where he is most needed.

2. *They get their living from the flock but are not adequately concerned for the flock.* "You eat the curds, clothe yourselves with the wool and slaughter the choice animals, but you do not take care of the flock" (v. 3).

3. *They fail to give sufficient care to the weak, the sick, and the wounded.* "You have not strengthened the weak or healed the sick or bound up the injured" (v. 4).

4. *They have failed to restore backsliders and to evangelize the unsaved.* "You have not brought back the strays or searched for the lost" (v. 4).

5. *They have been harsh and unsympathetic with the people.* "You have ruled them harshly and brutally" (v. 4).

6. *They are to blame that the flock is scattered.* "So they were scattered because there was no shepherd" (v. 5). When a shepherd does not truly shepherd his congregation, the people suffer spiritually and many drop out and are scattered.

7. *God will hold shepherds accountable for what hap-*

pens to the flock. The condition of the flock is the direct responsibility of the shepherd. "O shepherds, hear the word of the LORD. This is what the Sovereign LORD says: 'I am against the shepherds and will hold them accountable for my flock'" (vv. 9–10).

QUESTIONS YOU WILL FACE BEFORE GOD

God is very clear in His words. You as shepherd are awesomely accountable. You have spiritual responsibility for every person in your group. You are also in large measure responsible for every former member, especially if he is now unshepherded. Before God you will one day give account of your shepherd role, answering such questions as:

1. How well fed and spiritually strong was each member?
2. How well indoctrinated in Bible truth was each member?
3. What efforts did you make to heal those who became spiritually ill?
4. To what extent did you exhaust all efforts to restore backsliders?
5. To what extent did you search for lost sheep outside your flock?
6. To what extent did you intercede for your flock name by name?
7. To what extent did you as a shepherd lay down your life for the flock?
8. To what extent did you put the interests of the flock ahead of your personal interests?
9. To what extent did you as shepherd keep assertive members of your flock from discouraging or discriminating against more passive members?

Isaiah 56 combines illustrations of watchmen and shepherds (vv. 10–11). "Israel's watchmen are blind, they all lack knowledge; they are all mute dogs, they cannot bark; they lie around and dream, they love to sleep. They are dogs with mighty appetites; they never have enough. They are shepherds who lack understanding; they all turn to their own way, each seeks his own gain." Several new points of exhortation to shepherds are added here:

10. Are you as shepherd blind to danger? You dare not be blind to false teachings, new groups who may come and try to divide the church and mislead some of the people. It may be too late to warn people after false teachers arrive. You must have your people so grounded in truth that they are not willing to listen to new false teachers.

11. Are you as shepherd fearless and faithful in warning of spiritual and doctrinal danger? You must not be a silent watchdog. You must bark loud and long (v. 10).

If you as shepherd have fed your people deep spiritual and theological truth and the full range of Bible doctrine, then when false teachings are brought in by strangers your people will already have answers or will have such confidence in you as leader that they will first check with you. Shepherds, says Isaiah, must not "lack knowledge."

12. Do you as shepherd have a reputation for a big appetite (v. 11)? A shepherd who does not exercise self-discipline is a poor example for his people and gives a bad image to the public. Too many Christian leaders are over-weight. Too many jokes are told about ministers loving to eat, or wanting expensive foods. Isaiah calls such leaders "dogs with mighty appetites; they never have enough" (v. 11).

You as shepherd today need to set the example of fasting rather than feasting. How can the one who does not discipline his own appetite call his people to fasting? God's people today need frequently to hear God's call to this spiritual discipline. But a non-fasting leader cannot give such a call to his people. Can you?

13. Do you as shepherd have the reputation of always wanting your own way? It is easy for a person in authority to grasp for more and more authority. Be more aware of the needs and desires of your people than of your own. Learn to solicit and give careful consideration to the suggestions of your people. Don't act as though you always know all the answers yourself.

If you always seek your own way and are inconsiderate of

your people, you will not become known as a person of God or for your Christness. Isaiah warns of shepherds who "turn to their own way" (v. 11).

14. Do you as shepherd have the reputation of always looking out for yourself? Isaiah condemns those who seek their own gain (v. 11). No one retains a name for spirituality who always seeks his own benefit. Holiness is contrary to self-seeking. A holy person is always thinking of the interest and welfare of others. Holiness is love. Once William Booth sent a brief message to The Salvation Army around the world; it was one-word: OTHERS. That was his challenge to them. This was to summarize their ministry and their lives: OTHERS.

This is the Spirit of Jesus. He came not to be served but to serve and give his life for others (Mark 10:45). Jesus said that Christian leaders should not always be showing their authority. That is the way of the world. He said, "Not so with you. Instead, whoever wants to become great among you must be your servant, and whoever wants to be first must be slave of all" (vv. 43–44).

You as shepherd are to serve the sheep. The sheep are not primarily to care for you. Of course, as shepherd you deserve to be supported (Luke 10:7). You deserve adequate food and shelter. You have some rights. But in many respects you are called to forget your own interests for the sake of your people. Your calling is to self-sacrifice: God first, others next, and self last.

Chapter 23

Your Accountability
as a Leader, Part 1

Acts 20 contains Paul's final exhortations to the leaders at Ephesus. First Paul testified. He called them to witness how he had lived and served among them as their founding pastor. He challenged them to remember his service from the first day on (vv. 18–27).

1. He served the Lord with great humility (v. 19).
2. He served the Lord with tears (vv. 19, 31).
3. He willingly faced danger for their sake (v. 19).
4. He gladly preached anything which might help them (v. 20).
5. He taught publicly and in all their homes (v. 20).
6. He proclaimed the whole will of God (v. 27).
7. For three years he never stopped warning night and day with tears (v. 31).
8. He did not covet their financial help (vv. 33–34).

9. He set an example of hard work (v. 35).
10. He set an example in helping the weak and in giving (v. 35).

In the middle of this testimony Paul urges upon them their tremendous responsibility as leaders. Not only are they to follow his example in these ten ways, but he specially urges them to:

1. Keep watch over themselves (v. 28).
2. Keep watch over the flock (vv. 28, 30).
3. Shepherd the church (v. 28).

Paul is reminding them of their accountability to God.

The writer to the Hebrews also emphasizes how leaders will have to give an account to God. "Obey your leaders and submit to their authority. They keep watch over you as men who must give an account" (Heb. 13:17).

Twice Paul says that all Christians will stand before God's judgment seat (Rom. 14:10–12; 2 Cor. 5:10–11). Hebrews repeats the warning: "Man is destined to die once, and after that to face judgment" (Heb. 9:27). This is as true for the Christian as for the non-Christian. No Christian will face final judgment for sins of which he repented, made confession, and as far as possible made restitution. But every Christian will be judged for the way he lived after his conversion.

What teaching have you given to prepare your people for the time when they must kneel at Christ's judgment seat to hear Him evaluate their lives and announce their rewards?

But what I am specially concerned about is that you be prepared when Christ judges your role as a leader. You and I as leaders will stand before Christ's judgment seat for two reasons (Heb. 13:17):

a. We will be held accountable as spiritual leaders. Therefore, we lose sleep (v. 17) to fulfill our responsibility to watch over our members (the Greek word *agrupnousin* means to be sleepless). The same word is used in Mark 13:33; Luke 21:36; and Ephesians 6:18—"With this in mind, be alert (sleepless) and always keep on praying for all the saints."

b. We will be witnesses concerning what we saw in our members as we led or pastored them (Heb. 13:17).

Have you prepared a list of things which you expect God to ask you when you stand before Christ's judgment throne and are judged for your leadership role? As surely as you are alive today, you will stand there to give your account.

Let me suggest items on which Christ will judge your faithfulness as a leader. Undoubtedly there are many more. If you want to prepare yourself for the judgment day, make your own list.

YOU WILL BE ACCOUNTABLE FOR YOUR SLEEPLESSNESS AS A WATCHMAN

A sleepy watchman is a danger. The last thing he dare do is to sleep. A soldier on guard who goes to sleep can be sentenced to death. Why? He is a danger to everyone in the army.

You as a leader are a spiritual guard for your people. It is spiritually dangerous for your people for you to become spiritually drowsy. Guard duty is no laughing matter. It is a solemn responsibility to be a leader.

a. *You are responsible to guard the children.* 1. Make sure they understand all essential spiritual truth. Train and supervise Sunday school teachers; make gospel truth interesting and understandable to children. 2. Monitor their obedience to Christ. 3. Pray for them by name in private. 4. Join parents in praying for their children.

b. *You are responsible to guard the youth.* 1. Be sure they understand essential spiritual and moral truth. 2. Give special instruction in areas of concern to them. 3. Be available to counsel youth. 4. Involve youth in the services and in church-related activities (music, singing, reading Scripture lessons in worship services, ushering, helping the needy, literature distribution, gospel distribution or selling). 5. Pray by name for your youth.

c. *Guard the homes of your church.* Help to protect them by 1. planning Sunday school classes on the relationships of husbands and wives; 2. preaching sermons on the Christian home; 3. providing classes for parents on children's problems; 4. being available for counsel for family members; 5. visiting from house to house; 6. holding home prayer meetings; 7. praying daily for the homes.

d. *Help guard the community.* 1. Prepare your people for effective citizenship. 2. Watch for opportunities for your people to help the needy. 3. Lead your people in praying for national and local leaders (1 Tim. 2:1–3), for schools and universities, for the nation and its needs, for national issues, for local needs, and for local witness and activities by members. 4. Urge your people to be salt and light in their communities. 5. Lead your people to meet local needs. In all these areas you will be accountable for your sleeplessness as a watchman.

YOU WILL BE ACCOUNTABLE TO WARN OF DANGERS

God made clear to Ezekiel that his role as a prophet made him responsible for the eternal destiny of those he contacted.

a. *You are responsible to see as God sees.* At the very beginning of Jeremiah's ministry God gave him a vision and then asked him, "What do you see?" (Jer. 1:11). When Jeremiah answered correctly, God commended him and said, "You have seen correctly." Berkeley translates this, "You are a close observer."

The leader must have eyes to see. Your eyes must always be open. Be a close and accurate observer. God's ability to use you depends first of all on constant close and correct observation on your part.

Many a leader has missed opportunities to help in a moment of need because he was spiritually insensitive, because he did not have eyes to see. There are moments when a person is overwhelmed by a problem. If at that moment you show Christian concern and love, you have your best opportunity to influence that one or win him for Christ. There are moments when a person faces a special temptation.

Do you have eyes to see the moment of need? How can you pray effectively and warn if you do not have eyes to see?

Every leader should repeatedly pray, "Lord, give me eyes to see what You see; give me eyes to see correctly today." Some have been lost to the church and to Christ because in the hour of need the leader was spiritually and personally unprepared to see.

b. *You are responsible to hear what God says.* Every leader needs a listening ear. Every morning you should pray, "Lord help me to hear Your voice today. Guide me throughout the day."

When you see a person or situation as God sees, you next need to hear what God has to say to that person or group. God always has a word for each need. Have a listening ear to sense quickly His guidance or His voice.

King Zedekiah asked Jeremiah, "Is there any word from the LORD?" "Yes," he replied, and immediately gave the king a message of warning. On another occasion the people came to Jeremiah and asked him to pray for God's guidance for them. "I have heard you," Jeremiah answered. "I will certainly pray to the LORD your God as you have requested; I will tell you everything the LORD says" (Jer. 42:3–5). "Ten days later the word of the LORD came to Jeremiah" (v. 7), and he had God's word for them. You too on some occasions may need to pray for some time about a situation before you have God's guidance concerning what to say and when and how to say it.

You are not called to be a prophet and give inspired, infallible answers to people. But you are responsible to have eyes to see and ears to listen for the word of the Lord for your people.

Ezekiel was told, "I have made you a watchman for the house of Israel; so hear the word I speak and give them warning from me" (Ezek. 3:17). Later this was repeated word for word in Ezekiel 33:7. This is God's sequence for you: see, hear, pray, and then speak.

Ezekiel was reminded of his awesome responsibility in these words, "When I say to a wicked man, 'You will surely die,' and you do not warn him or speak out to dissuade him from his evil ways in order to save his life, that wicked man will die for his sin, and I will hold you accountable for his blood. But if you do warn the wicked man and he does not turn from his wickedness or from his evil ways, he will die for his sin; but you will have saved yourself. Again, when a righteous man turns from his righteousness and does evil, and I put a stumbling block before him, he will die. Since you did not warn him, he will die for his sin. The righteous things he did will not be remembered, and I will hold you accountable for his blood. But if you do warn the righteous man not to sin and he does not sin, he will surely live because he took warning, and you will have saved yourself" (Ezek. 3:18–21).

There are no more solemn words for a Christian leader in all of Scripture. When I was a child I was tremendously impressed by these verses. The words of the King James Version are "His blood will I require at your hand." I could not forget them. Whenever another minister would visit our home (my father was a pastor) I would, after a few minutes, ask what these words meant. When I had just entered high school, I was permitted to sit in several sessions of a ministers' conference. When they announced that in the next session there would be time for questions and answers, I went to a minister and said, "When the question period comes don't tell who asked, but could you ask for me what these words mean in Ezekiel 3:18?" I have never yet heard an answer that fully satisfied me. I ask you what it will mean for you if God holds you accountable for someone you fail to warn.

When you see a careless youth, a straying husband or wife, an unrepentant sinner, and you fail to give the warning in a loving yet clear way, what difference will it make in your life in heaven if God holds you accountable for your sin of omission, your failure to let God use you?

Chapter 24

Your Accountability
as a Leader, Part 2

We continue our discussion of leaders' responsibility to
God and their people.

YOU WILL BE ACCOUNTABLE TO PRACTICE
WHAT YOU SAY

Jesus commanded us not to be like the Pharisees. "They
do not practice what they preach" (Matt. 23:3–4). Bishop
Ryle comments, "So long as the world stands, this chapter
ought to be a warning and a beacon to all ministers of
religion. No sins are so sinful as theirs in the sight of Christ."

Paul adds, "You, then, who teach others, do you not teach
yourself? You who preach against stealing, do you steal?"
(Rom. 2:21).

There is no greater hindrance to the cause of Christ, no

164

greater insult to the name of Christ than the lives of Christians not measuring up to the teachings of Christ and the Bible. This is, above all, true for Christian leaders. The world has every right to demand that we practice what we teach or preach. If we don't we are hypocrites, and no hypocrite deserves public respect.

It is all too easy to be more strict with others than we are with ourselves. It undermines parental respect when parents require of children what they themselves do not practice. It undermines respect for the church if people can point to flaws in leaders' lives. It destroys the power of the truth when we do not live up to the Bible or to what we say to others.

Jesus said, "Be on your guard against . . . hypocrisy" (Luke 12:1). Peter urges us to rid ourselves of all hypocrisy (1 Peter 2:1). Beware lest you overstate the Bible standard. There is only one way you have a right to preach a higher standard than you live. You may need to say, "This is what the Bible teaches. I confess I do not yet live up to it. Pray for me that by God's grace I will from this day on."

Many a leader has preached himself under the conviction of the Holy Spirit as the truth became even more clear to him as he spoke. If you do, humble yourself before God and your people. Confess your need. If you give an invitation to people to come forward and seek God's help in obeying the truth you have preached, be the first to go to your knees and ask for the prayers of your people. Then you will maintain their respect.

YOU WILL BE MORE ACCOUNTABLE THAN YOUR PEOPLE

James warns us, "Not many of you should presume to be teachers, my brothers, because you know that we who teach will be judged more strictly" (James 3:1). In the very next verse he adds that we all stumble in many ways. Are you stumbling "in many ways"?

Jesus reminds us of the danger of judging. This is a special danger to a leader. We easily get into the habit of judging because in the eyes of the people we become authorities on the meaning of Scripture, and they so often trust our opinions as the only answer. Remember how imperfectly you really understand the whole of God's truth.

Jesus said, "Do not judge, or you too will be judged. For in the same way you judge others, you will be judged, and with the measure you use, it will be measured to you. Why do you look at the speck of sawdust in your brother's eye and pay no attention to the plank in your own eye? How can you say to your brother, 'Let me take the speck out of your eye, when all the time there is a plank in your own eye? You hypocrite, first take the plank out of your own eye, and then you will see clearly to remove the speck from your brother's eye" (Matt. 7:1–5).

Why did Jesus imply that our brother's problem is like a speck of sawdust in the eye but in our own eye the problem is as large as a plank? Because others' faults seem larger to us than our own do and because we leaders are held more accountable and our role as leaders makes our defects loom large in others' eyes.

It is a human characteristic to minimize our own mistakes but to maximize the mistakes or sins of others. Jesus says we must do just the opposite.

After James states that as Christian leaders we will be judged more strictly He gives three illustrations of areas where we will be strictly judged:

1. *You will be judged strictly for boasting.* James says the tongue is a small part of our body but it makes great boasts (James 3:5). So often the more you repeat an incident, the more you embellish it and the larger your story grows. Your mind can easily play tricks on you. Beware of exaggerating. "Evangelistically speaking" has become an unfortunate expression which implies that preachers' stories are more vivid and the number of people converted often larger than the facts warrant.

Many a leader boasts of how hard he is working when actually he is wasting a lot of time and works no harder than any of his people. James says we will be judged more strictly than others concerning our boasting.

2. *You will be judged strictly for your influence on others.* James illustrates this by showing that a small spark can set a whole forest ablaze. One slight remark of suspicion, of doubt, of accusation, of resentment, or anger can set a devastating fire ablaze in a church.

Because of your position, what you say will be taken more seriously, will be believed more unquestioningly, and will be quoted more often to more people than you think. What you tell confidentially will rarely be kept confidential. What you state as a possibility will be quoted as a fact. What you say will often be quoted out of context.

If anyone needs to watch his tongue it is a leader. If anyone can easily kindle a fire which will burn and destroy some in the church, or some outside the church who need to be reached, it is the leader. Remember, you will be judged more strictly by God for the way you use your tongue than your people will be.

3. *You will be judged more strictly for poisoning the minds of others.* What? Leaders poison the minds of their people? Yes, that is a constant danger. James says (3:8) that the tongue is like a wild animal which cannot be tamed, like an evil which cannot be brought under control, like a poison with power to kill. Remember, this is said in explaining the accountability of Christian leaders.

Just one remark by a leader in public or in private can poison the minds of many. James says it can be deadly. One remark can destroy unity. One sermon, even one statement, can poison the atmosphere of the church, the community, a home. If anyone needs to control his tongue at all times it is a leader.

That is why James pleads with Christian leaders to remember that we will be judged more strictly than others. Constantly we use our tongues with their tremendous potential for good or evil. With them we bless or curse; we praise God or destroy people.

YOU WILL BE ACCOUNTABLE
FOR YOUR EXAMPLE

Jesus lived His life as an example to us. He deliberately acted in a certain way to set an example.

1. He was an example in restraining His tongue. "Christ suffered for you, leaving you an example, that you should follow in his steps. 'He committed no sin, and no deceit was found in his mouth.' When they hurled their insults at him, he did not retaliate; when he suffered, he made no threats. Instead, he entrusted himself to him who judges justly" (1 Peter 2:21–23).

2. Jesus was an example in humble service of others. When He washed the feet of the disciples He said, "Do you understand what I have done for you? . . . I have set you an example that you should do as I have done for you . . . Now that you know these things, you will be blessed if you do them" (John 13:12–17).

Three times Paul urged his converts to follow his example:

1. "Follow my example, as I follow the example of Christ" (1 Cor. 11:1). The literal Greek is "continue to be my imitator as I continuously imitate Christ." The immediate context in which Paul specially wanted the Corinthians to follow him was (a) in not causing anyone to stumble; (b) in seeking as far as possible to please others; and (c) in seeking the good of others rather than his own good.

2. "Join with others in following my example" (Phil. 3:17). Literally, the Greek is "continue to be fellow-imitators of me." The immediate context Paul was emphasizing was his beautiful description of how he pressed on in following Christ (vv. 7–16). (a) He considered all else loss compared to knowing Jesus better in all His lordship. (b) He considered all else as rubbish that he might gain Christ and be righteous by faith in Him. (c) He wanted to know Christ and His resurrection power, gladly sharing in Christ's sufferings in the extension of the gospel and eventually being raptured at the second coming of Christ. (d) He made this his one

overwhelming priority, forgetting what was past and straining every effort for what lay ahead. This is what Paul wanted all Philippian believers to join him in doing. Are you pursuing Christ and His priorities so whole-souledly that you are a constant example?

3. "You ought to follow (Greek, imitate) our example" (2 Thess. 3:7). The immediate context is Paul's not being idle but working day and night to support himself and not be a burden on others. He had done this "in order to make [himself] a model for you to follow" (v. 9). Paul knew that one of the besetting sins of the Thessalonians was idleness. So during visits to Thessalonica, he deliberately supported himself. To Paul it reflected poorly on Christ for Christians to be idle. He was entitled to support from the church, but he purposely chose to forego his rights to emphasize the example he was trying to give them. God forgive you if you have a reputation of not being a hard worker.

In 1 Timothy 4:12 Paul exhorts Timothy to "set an example for the believers," especially in five items which he lists: speech, life, love, faith, and purity. The Greek is literally "continue becoming a model."

Peter writes the same thing "to the elders," i.e., the pastor-leaders: "Not lording it over those entrusted to you, but being examples to the flock" (1 Peter 5:3).

Nothing is more important in a leader's life and ministry than to lead an exemplary life in all things. His leadership can be no more effective than his life. His manner of living prepares the way for the reception of his words. This is true both among his own people and among the unsaved.

The example of your life validates or invalidates your ministry. You have no more credibility in any community than your life warrants. You must incarnate what you say. You must demonstrate that the gospel is true.

God may even permit you to pass through difficult experiences in order to prove to non-Christians that Christ is real and that you are genuine. Setting an example can be costly. Nothing is more urgent.

YOU WILL BE ACCOUNTABLE
FOR YOUR PRAYER LIFE

The foundation on which all ministry and leadership is built is your prayer life. Your leadership is never greater than your prayers. Successful leadership requires much more than prayer, but no leadership can ever be ultimately successful apart from much prayer. Measure your ministry not by the praise you receive, not by the size of the congregation, not by the amount of the offerings of the church, not by the number of activities centering in the church, but by the amount of prayer that is invested in all the above. Other things being equal, a praying leader with a praying people will be blessed of God.

Every leader gives lip service to prayer. However, many have a deplorably ineffective prayer life. It is not enough to have a praying people. The leader is to be a person of God and a person of prayer. You cannot be a person of God without being a person of prayer.

An essential element of leadership is praying for your people. When the Israelites in effect rejected Samuel as they clamored for a king, they nevertheless begged for him to pray for them. They recognized that they needed his prayers and probably realized that they owed more to his prayers than to all else he did for them.

Samuel's immediate reply was, "Far be it from me that I should sin against the LORD by failing to pray for you" (1 Sam. 12:23). He knew that it would be a sin against God to fail to pray for his people. Probably leaders sin more against God and against their people by failing to pray enough for them than in any other way. Do you? It is always a sin to fail to pray for those for whom you are spiritually responsible.

A parent is responsible to pray for his children. A pastor is responsible to pray for his people. A superintendent is responsible to pray for all the ministers and churches under his jurisdiction. The head of a denomination is responsible to pray for the whole denomination, but specially for all the leaders of the denomination. A teacher is responsible to pray for all his students. Oh, how greatly we all fail in our prayer responsibilities!

Paul wrote to the Ephesian believers, "Pray in the Spirit on all occasions with all kinds of prayers and requests. With this in mind, be alert and always keep on praying for all the saints" (Eph. 6:18). If this is the responsibility of each member of the church, how much more for the pastor. Jesus says the shepherd calls his own sheep by name (John 10:3). As previously urged, each leader must pray regularly by name for all his people.

Surely the most sleepless way you watch over your people (Heb. 13:17) is in prayer. In the Bible the words *pray* or *prayer* and *watch* are often associated together. You cannot spiritually watch without praying. Shepherding and watching involve much more than praying, but prayer is central to your work. You can be sure that you will give account before God of your prayers for your people.

Measure your love for your people by your prayer life. Measure your concern for your people, your vision for your people, and your leadership by your prayer. So important is this that chapters 31 to 34 are specially given to this.

Chapter 25

Prepare Your People
for Eternal Reward

God intended that Israel should be a kingdom of priests (Exod. 19:6). Israel's people were to be God's means of blessing to the whole world (Gen. 12:2–3). They were also to be God's witnesses (Isa. 43:12). Israel tragically failed God's purpose in both. Other than some psalms, we see no record of their praying for the salvation of the nations.

Then God raised up the church to fulfill His plan for the world. We are now to be exercising the role which Israel failed to fulfill. We in the church are now to be God's kingdom of priests (1 Peter 2:5, 9; Rev. 1:6; 5:10), God's means of blessing the world (Rom. 12:14; 1 Cor. 4:12; James 3:9). We are to be God's salt (Matt. 5:13), light (Matt. 5:14, 16; Eph. 5:8), and witnesses (Luke 24:48; Acts 1:8).

GOD'S GREAT PLAN

God is the Supreme Planner. Before the beginning of creation, God planned for creation, earth, time, eternity, humankind, the atonement, and His people (Matt. 25:34; Eph. 1:4; 1 Peter 1:20; Rev. 13:8).

God's plan is that of all creation His special care relates to this earth. Of all beings He created, God chose a unique role for humankind. He created us in His own image, sending His Son to be eternally incarnate as man and in no other form. He planned for only one group of beings to share eternally in closest personal relation to His Son as the Son's bride—the church. The angels of God are assigned to assist and care for redeemed humanity (Heb. 1:14). None other is to be God's deputy ruler of earth (Gen. 1:26, 28; Ps. 115:16).

We are to be God's witness on earth and God's evidence to help the angels understand God better (Eph. 3:10; 1 Peter 1:12). Only we can lead people to Christ. The Holy Spirit works with and through us. Only we share Christ's present priority ministry of intercession (Heb. 7:25; 1 Tim. 2:1).

Christ perfectly completed the atonement. We preach the finished work of Christ in accomplishing redemption for humankind (John 17:4; 19:30; Eph. 3:11). However, He placed upon the church the responsibility of making His plan of redemption available to the world. This is the great unfinished work of the church and in that sense is the great unfinished work of Christ. It consists primarily of intercession (which He also continues with us) and witnessing-evangelism (Matt. 24:14).

A chief responsibility of all church leaders now is to prepare every member to participate in an all-out harvest crusade of intercession and witness to complete Christ's unfinished task, His great eternal plan. For all we do to this end, He will eternally reward us. This is God's priority for the church in this age.

173

TWO GREAT AGES FOR THE CHURCH

For all humankind, history is divided into time and eternity. Our state in eternity will depend on what we do with our time. We refer to time as "here," and eternity as the "hereafter." The separation point is death. For any individual life until death is his time; after death it is his eternity. Time is brief at best; eternity is endless. Time is for sowing; eternity is eternal reaping.

This all adds tremendous seriousness to our lives as Christians—to our intercession and to our evangelism. Christians who live and think primarily of today are fools, eternal fools. Throughout eternity they will never cease to regret that they made such little use of their time in sowing for Christ and His kingdom. Any Christian may be the only one who will ever pray for some people or witness to them. He may be their main hope of heaven.

But eternity is much more than the decision of heaven or hell. For those in heaven there will be great differences—differences in glory (Dan. 12:3) and reward (1 Cor. 3:8–15; Rev. 22:12). There will probably be eternal differences in closeness of fellowship with Jesus. While Jesus was on earth all 5,000 who were fed by Him listened to His voice and had fellowship with Him. But the fellowship of the Twelve was much closer to Him, and the fellowship of Peter, James, and John was closest of all.

Christ is no respecter of persons, but He is a respecter of our response to His love, His commands, and the work He assigned us. Not all Christ's disciples were chosen to see Him and fellowship with Him after His resurrection (Acts 10:41).

Undoubtedly we are determining by our obedience today the degree of fellowship with Christ we will share in heaven. Every believer will spend eternity in heaven, which will be Jesus' headquarters and home, but in what forms that fellowship will consist, how frequently each will have such intimate privileges, and the role each will have in reigning with Jesus and serving Him will be decided at the judgment before Christ's throne. That will be based on how faithfully

174

each is praying and living for Christ today. Heaven will not be the same for all. Jesus made that very clear again and again in His teaching.

One of your great responsibilities as a shepherd is to prepare each believer for the greatest possible eternal reward. The reward does not consist merely in words of commendation as the person stands before Christ's judgment throne. The reward is announced then, and everyone will have some praise from God then (1 Cor. 4:5). But on the basis of the just decision of Christ, the rewarding roles of eternity which He announces then will go on forever. Salvation is by grace alone; reward is according to our works—how fully and closely we lived for God and His kingdom.

Most Christians are daily wasting opportunities which could increase their usefulness to Christ and the degree of their reward. This is what saddens you as a Christian shepherd. This is why you must plead with your people, pray with tremendous burden for them, weep for them and, like Paul, warn them with tears. Woe to you as a shepherd-leader if you fail to prepare your people for Christ's judgment of rewards (1 Cor. 3:11–15)!

Life on earth is work time—work for Jesus. Heaven is rest and reward time. Jesus committed His unfinished task on earth into our hands to complete. Paul said that his great desire and ambition was to "complete the task the Lord Jesus [had] given [him]" (Acts 20:24). Many Christians are living as if the Lord gave them no task, as if they have no accountability for Christ's kingdom. It is your responsibility as their shepherd to teach and warn them of their responsibilities and of the questions Christ will ask them when they stand before His judgment throne.

It is not enough to avoid sin, attend church, read the Bible a bit, and pray a few minutes each day. It is how one invests time in prayer, blessing others, and extending Christ's kingdom that will decide his reward. Oh, the opportunities for great eternal reward now being thrown away by Christians! What sorrow this brings to Christ!

THE TWOFOLD ROLE OF EVERY
CHRISTIAN LEADER

You as a Christian leader or pastor have a twofold responsibility for every believer under your supervision. You have other responsibilities—the evangelism of the unsaved, representing your group before the community and government, intercession for God's plan for your denomination or organization, for your nation and for the world. But you have two special responsibilities for your own members.

A. *You are responsible for the spiritual nurture and life of each believer.* It is not enough merely to preach, lead your group, or conduct services. You must preach, teach, and counsel so that each one grows in grace and matures in Christ (Col. 1:28) and keeps faithful to the Lord and to your church or group. You are responsible for the children, the youth, the older ones. You are responsible to keep the strong saints growing and to give special attention to the weak and the wounded.

You are responsible to keep your church or group revived, the believers in harmony and unity, and the services and activities sealed by the presence and blessing of the Lord.

B. *You are responsible to prepare each believer to be effective in working for the Lord.* We are saved to serve. If we are saved but do not serve, we are disappointing and failing the Lord, and forfeiting some of the reward God had planned for us for our faithfulness.

1. *God expects each believer to bless as many people as possible.* Jesus went around blessing people (Acts 3:26). Now we are to complete His task and bless all we can in every way we can. Each believer is to show Christian love in such a way that the unsaved recognize and feel that love. Even a child can be taught to show love and be a blessing. The children of Christians should be known for their kindness, helpfulness, and love. Homemakers have a circle of neighbors they can bless. Each is to be such a loving person, such a blessing, that

it prepares the way for witness and invitation to gospel services. No Christian is excused.

2. *God expects each believer to have a prayer ministry.* We are saved to pray, and our major praying should not be for ourselves. It is not enough to be concerned only about the spiritual life of one's family. Every believer is called to an effective prayer ministry for the church, for revival, for evangelism, and for reaching the whole world for Christ.

Jesus meant it when He said we are responsible from our Jerusalem (our home, church, or town) to the ends of the earth. Any Christian whose daily prayer does not include his whole nation and the other nations of the world is disobeying Christ's last command. That demands planned prayer—not just moments each day, but a carefully planned prayer ministry for every believer. Are your believers having such a prayer ministry? How have you prepared them to do so?

3. *God expects each believer to be a witness.* Each is to be Christ's salt and light in his community, Christ's active witness by word as well as by life. Each believer is to be an ambassador for Christ (2 Cor. 5:20). Millions of Christians have never begun to be ambassadors. Who is to blame? Whom will God hold accountable? Believers? Of course! You as the pastor or leader? Yes, in many cases you will be even more accountable than the believers. Why? Because you are responsible to train them to witness and to prepare and follow a personal plan for intercession.

THE DAY OF ACCOUNTABILITY IS COMING

The most important day in the future of every believer is the judgment day. Paul makes Jesus' teaching clear—that we must each be ready for that day.

"We will all stand before God's judgment seat. It is written: 'As surely as I live,' says the Lord, 'every knee will bow before me; every tongue will confess to God.' So then, each of us will give an account of himself to God" (Rom. 14:10–12).

"We make it our goal to please him . . . . For we must all

appear before the judgment seat of Christ, that each one may receive what is due him for the things done while in the body, whether good or bad" (2 Cor. 5:9–10).

How many times a year do you include a major section in one of your sermons or Bible teaching on the judgment? How clearly have you taught your people—from the children to the adults—that all they do each day will be included in the things they face at the judgment and that they will be asked by Christ to give an account? It is not enough to preach or teach what the judgment will mean for the sinner. You must make very clear what the judgment will mean for the believer.

Paul is speaking to Christians each time he says, "We must all stand" at the judgment. He includes himself. Elsewhere he clearly emphasizes that he is comparatively unconcerned about how other people judge him, because Christ is going to be his Judge (1 Cor. 4:3–4). Both good and bad things will be judged. The book of Revelation adds that there will not only be the Book of Life at the judgment, but other books also. These undoubtedly have the complete record of each life, including yours and mine (Rev. 20:12).

How have you prepared your people for this most important day in their future? Hebrews 9:27 reminds us that "man is destined to die once, and after that to face judgment." Everyone will die—saint and sinner. And after death everyone will "face judgment"—saint and sinner. If you have failed to teach your people adequately on this subject, you may need to ask their forgiveness and immediately make the subject clear. They may already have lost great reward because they have not been living for that day.

Every leader will face many questions about his ministry when he stands before Christ. Jesus has made him responsible for every Christian under his charge. He will be responsible for what he taught them and what he did not teach them of Bible truth. If he teaches wrong doctrine, he will also have to answer for that. Hebrews 13:17 reminds us that he must watch over his people as a person "who must give an account" to God for his stewardship of their lives.

If friends and contacts of your believers go to hell because they were not properly loved, blessed, prayed for, witnessed to, and warned, who will be held accountable? Ezekiel says that your people will (Ezek. 3:18–19). But if you failed to teach your people that they will be held accountable, you too will be held accountable. Ezekiel says that this will mean blood on your hand.

Do you remember how concerned Paul was that he not be held accountable for anyone's blood? Acts 20:26 says, "I declare to you today that I am innocent of the blood of all men." What was Paul talking about? He was innocent of the blood of those he had taught and won to Christ. Why? Listen to his words: "I have not hesitated to proclaim to you the whole will of God" (v. 27). He refers to his teaching of doctrine. He would be free of blood-guilt because he had taught them clearly every essential doctrine. Will you be able to say the same? How clearly do you teach Bible doctrine? Many Christian leaders are failing Christ at this point. They will be held accountable at the judgment, not for teaching wrong doctrine, but for omitting to teach essential true doctrine. No leader dare avoid doctrinal teaching.

In the next verses, after talking of his own freedom from blood-guilt, he tells the Ephesian leaders, "Keep watch over yourselves and all the flock of which the Holy Spirit has made you overseers. Be shepherds of the church of God, which he bought with his own blood" (v. 28).

Christ's great unfinished work is the evangelization of the world. Christ's blood was shed for the whole world (1 John 2:2). God loves the whole world. God does not want anyone to perish, but everyone to come to repentance (2 Peter 3:9). His number one priority today is for each believer to do everything humanly possible to win as many of the people of the world as possible. He died for them. Cannot we try to reach them?

DO YOU LOVE THE WORLD AS GOD DOES?

Ezra wept over the sins of his people (Ezra 10:1). Nehemiah mourned for some days over Jerusalem's need

179

(Neh. 1:4). Daniel mourned and fasted for three weeks (Dan. 10:2–3). Jesus wept over Jerusalem (Luke 13:34). Paul was in heart anguish for unsaved Jews (Rom. 9:2–4). He wept night and day for three years as he evangelized Ephesus (Acts 20:31).

There are more unsaved people in the world today than ever before. If we go to the judgment seat of Christ not having wept over the lost of our city, our nation, and the other nations for whom Christ died, what will He say to us? How will we explain our lack of love and concern, our lack of burden in our daily prayer?

If your people never see you weep over the lost as you lead them in prayer in the services, how will they learn to weep as they pray for the unsaved millions of our world? Will they fail Christ and the unsaved because of your lack of example to them?

If your congregation goes to the judgment having only rarely, if ever, carried a great intercessory burden for evangelization, whom will God hold accountable? Usually it is like shepherd, like sheep.

In Luke 16 Jesus told the parable of the manager who wasted the possessions of his employer. He had to face a day of accounting for his failure. To whom was Jesus speaking when He taught this? Not the unsaved multitude but to the disciples. Are your people wasting God's love for the lost by failing to bring it to them? Are they wasting Christ's blood shed for the unreached? Are they wasting His promises which He commanded His church to appropriate in prayer? Are they wasting the opportunities He is giving them to reach the lost near them? If they are, they will have to give an account. And you and I as leaders who failed to teach them and challenge them will give an even stricter account. Jesus said a severe judgment would face those who failed to use their talents before His return (Luke 19:20–23).

Chapter 26

Prepare Your People to Pray

The reason God calls some to be prophets, some evangelists, some pastors and teachers is explained in Ephesians 4:11–12. God gives these leaders "to prepare God's people for works of service, so that the body of Christ may be built up." This building up is done in two ways—by nourishing the spiritual life of believers and by adding new believers to the body of Christ. The Hebrews writer adds, "May the God of peace . . . equip you with everything good for doing his will" (Heb. 13:20–21). How can you prepare your people for the work of service God wants each to do? How can God use you to equip them? This does not refer to spiritual gifts. Only the Holy Spirit bestows spiritual gifts. We cannot impart them or teach people to receive them. We can teach how they are to be used.

PREPARE YOUR PEOPLE TO BLESS OTHERS

"God bless you" should be one of the most common expressions on a Christian's tongue. God is a God of blessing. The high priest was to bless the people, saying, "The LORD bless you" (Num. 6:24). God wants to bless all the work of our hands, if we obey Him (Deut. 14:29; 24:19). "He will richly bless you, if only you fully obey the LORD your God" (Deut. 15:4–5). You will find similar promises in many places. Jesus was sent to bless us (Acts 3:36). Jesus went about doing good and blessing both the righteous and the sinners (Acts 10:38).

We are to bless all people, even those who persecute us (Rom. 12:14). When we are cursed, we bless (1 Cor. 4:12). God blesses actions as well as people (Ps. 33:12), the poor as well as the rich, children as well as adults (Mark 10:16). Here are steps you can teach your people to take in blessing others:

1. *Seize every opportunity to bless a person.* Watch for opportunities. Pray for God to guide you. Each morning ask God to make you a definite blessing to someone that day.

2. *Show love in the name of Jesus.* Watch for opportunities to smile at people, help people, encourage people. Seek to bring the joy of the Lord wherever you go. Ask God to pour the love of Christ through you into the lives of others—saved and unsaved whether children, young people, or adults.

3. *Pray constantly for others.* Prayer is a chief way to bless. As you pass houses, ask God to bless the people within. As you pass children, ask God to bless them. When you see angry people, ask God to deliver them. Go through your day breathing brief prayers for those you meet or those God brings to your attention. Through prayer you can bless more people than in any other way.

PREPARE YOUR PEOPLE FOR A PRAYER MINISTRY

Prayer is a form of ministry Christ desires for every believer. We are saved to pray for others. Prayer is the basis for whatever other ministry one has. Prayer can be the most important ministry in most Christians' lives. One of your greatest responsibilities is to help your people become a praying people, and to help them make their intercession effective for Christ. How much prayer time does your average believer invest in Christ's kingdom per day?

This preparation has two phases. You must prepare them to be personally strong in prayer and intercession. You must also guide your people as they develop their personal prayer plans. Nothing is more important to a ministry of intercession than a personal prayer plan.

1. *Help them deepen their personal prayer life.* Your people not only need your repeated clear teaching on prayer, they need to see in you a beautiful example of a life and ministry of prayer. A love for prayer needs to be taught, caught, and practiced.

a. *Deepen your own prayer life.* Prayer must become the life, the joy, and the passion of your own soul. Your people must see that prayer is your eager delight and your very life-breath. If you only talk about prayer and do not demonstrate the joy and power of prayer, your teaching will seem to be mere words—pious words to which everyone agrees. But they will not realize how blessed prayer can be, until they see it in you.

All Christians believe in the duty of some prayer each day. Most, however, have an ordinary prayer life except in emergencies. Too often they have never realized the thrill and excitement of communion with Jesus and prevailing in prayer for others. There are exceptions—people who pray more than others.

You are the key to the prayer ministry of your people. This assures that at the judgment you will have the most strict account to give. Don't expect your people to hunger for what they fail to see in you. They must sense your joy in the Lord, your intimacy with God, your love for Jesus and for themselves. They must sense your vibrant faith as you pray—that you really expect and get answers to your prayers. They must sense these things in your normal public praying; then they will begin to hunger to go deeper in prayer themselves.

But remember that your public praying reflects the

quality of your personal, private prayer life. God cannot mightily use public prayers and prayers in homes when you are weak, lifeless, and ineffective in your private prayer. You must be a person of God if you expect your people to become people of God. Many Christian leaders' prayer lives are inadequate for the work they are attempting to do. They are inadequate to satisfy Jesus. Is that true of you? Learn to pray if you want your people to pray.

b. *Give priority to prayer in your public ministry.* Prepare your heart as much for your public praying as for your speaking and teaching. If your heart is not melted when you pray, it will probably not be melted when you speak. If your heart is not aflame for God when you pray, it will probably not be while you preach.

You should always pray longer in private than in public, but if your heart is melted with God's love or aflame with God's fire, a longer public prayer that really leads the people into God's presence often will be welcomed by your people. Some of God's greatest preachers have been great in prayer. Do people come to your services specially to hear you pray?

Your prayer must echo the concerns, the heart cries, and the deep desires of your people. A "quickie" prayer tends to suggest that prayer is unimportant. But a long prayer that comes from a heart and lips that do not evidence God's near presence and power easily can seem perfunctory. It may seem so much a part of the routine of the service that people are relieved when you stop praying. Live and pray so that your public prayers are fragrant with God's presence and vibrant with God's power.

c. *Make prayer a natural and vital part of all private ministry.* Include a brief prayer in all your personal counseling, home or hospital visitation, farewelling, or committing a task to a person or group. Make prayer so constant and natural a part of all you do that you are known for praying about everything (Phil. 4:6). Prayer must be an ever-present part of your entire ministry. Remember, prayer adds God's benediction to anything you say, God's presence to anyone you contact, and God's power to answer any need you try to meet.

As your people see you bring God into everything by your prayers, they too will begin to bring prayer into everything they do, as Paul urged (Eph. 6:18). Your people almost unconsciously begin to become a praying people when they sense that prayer is an indispensable part of your whole life.

2. *You can guide them in developing their own prayer plans.* Every Christian needs to develop a personal prayer plan. No one will bring prayer into the full role God desires for his life unless he plans for it. We plan our times for sleep and food. When we miss our usual food or rest time we become conscious of it. We may even become uncomfortable.

In the same way, prayer must be built into the normal day's schedule of each believer. This does not happen unless definite prayer habits are formed and plans are specifically made to build prayer into the spiritual lifestyle. This will please the Lord, fulfill His will, and bring the eternal reward Christ longs to give.

a. *Guide in establishing regular daily prayer times.* Each one's circumstances vary, so general prayer principles need to be taught and then each person helped to adapt these to his or her own need. Even children and youth need regular prayer habits. How well do you know the prayer habits of your people?

A time early in the day is always preferable for at least one of the prayer times. Hours of employment, times when children are sleeping or away at school, health, and personality characteristics must be taken into consideration.

Not everyone can have his main prayer time at the beginning of the day. It may be necessary to have a briefer time before others are up or noisy, or at a planned time in the early morning, with a major time later when the person can have a longer undisturbed period.

Some are "night" people. They find it hard to be alert and at their best when they first awake. However, some of one's best time, priority time, should be given to the Lord near the beginning of each day. Help your people explore other possible times and places for meaningful prayer. As shepherd of your people, on a personal basis counsel each of your people about his prayer plan.

b. *Guide in the use of the prayer time.* Emphasize such points as:

(1) Be as fresh and alert as possible. Washing the face can help one be instantly alert as he wakes up. Praying in bed is rarely the way to get the most out of prayer time. During longer prayer periods, varying posture can make one more alert. All postures are sacred to the Lord.

When exceptionally weary, some find they are more alert if they stand when they read the Bible or pray. Some walk back and forth while praying if they are alone in a room. This may also add a sense of urgency (2 Kings 4:32–35). Sometimes a sip of water or a very small snack—a nut or two, or a small bite of bread or fruit may refresh and help one to be at his best during prayer.

(2) Begin with Bible reading. It is as important to hear God as it is to speak to God. Normally, begin with the Word and pray afterward. A good average is to spend half of the quiet time reading Scripture and half in prayer. Remember, no devotional book is a substitute for God's Word. Time with other good books should be in addition to the regular prayer time.

No literate Christian should read less than one chapter of the Bible each day. For most Christians it is wise to read at least three chapters each day and five on Sunday. In this way anyone can read consecutively through the Bible each year.

Don't read the Bible hit and miss from first one place and then another, or mainly from favorite passages. God's Word deserves more respect than that. God intended us to feed on all of it. Some prefer to read the New Testament through twice for each time they read through the Old Testament. The normal practice should be to read Scripture consecutively.

(3) Plan the normal content and outline for the prayer time. God welcomes all prayer and all forms of prayer (Eph. 6:18). Usually one begins with worship, and expresses love and thanksgiving. Many find the outline Jesus gave us in the "Lord's prayer" (Matt. 6:9–13) helpful as a guideline:

—First adoring, worshiping, and thanking God (v. 9)
—Next praying for Christ's cause (v. 10)
—Praying for situations where God's will must be done (v. 10)

186

—Then praying for personal, family, or group physical and material needs (v. 11)
—Asking forgiveness for failures, shortcomings, or sins (v. 12)
—Praying for guidance and victory (v. 13)
—Closing with further worship and love expressed to God (v. 13).

Many prayer leaders suggest this model outline: Adoration, Thanksgiving, Confession, Intercession, and Commitment.

Often personal prayer times arise out of a need or emergency situation when your usual prayer outline may be disregarded. Always trust the Spirit's guidance in the freedom of His presence.

(4) Use prayer lists for at least one major time of intercession daily. Every believer should use a major portion of his prayer time in intercession for others and for the advance of God's cause. Probably the only effective way to do this and to be sure you include all for which you should pray is to prepare several short prayer lists or a longer list with several sections.

Your permanent prayer list or lists should include government leaders and situations (1 Tim. 2:1–2); church leaders, ministries, and needs; world evangelism—missionaries, mission organizations, nations, Christian workers; lists of the unsaved; loved ones.

Temporary lists can be changed from time to time and may include current events; those ill or in mourning; problem situations.

Teach your people to prepare and use personal prayer lists.

Chapter 27

Teach the Stewardship of Time and Possessions

THE STEWARDSHIP OF TIME

Life and time are a special trust and stewardship given to us by God. Time is a portion of eternity God lent to us. Every hour we spend meaninglessly is potential blessing to Christ's kingdom unrealized and potential eternal reward lost forever. Satan wants to rob God and to rob us of our reward by robbing us of the wise use of our time. The question, "What are you doing with your life?" involves the second question, "What are you doing with your time?"

We all need time for fellowship with family, friends, and others. We do not lose time by fulfilling our normal duties. God wants us to fulfill our responsibilities to family, our employer, and our church. He wants us to have wholesome

188

fellowship, and needed wholesome recreation. This is important for physical and mental health.

However, the pastor is responsible to teach his people
how to use free time wisely. Otherwise the time is wasted,
lost forever. Ten minutes is long enough to read another
chapter or two in God's Word. A Christian who uses prayer
lists can always wisely invest ten minutes in prayer.

Do heaven's books have a record of our unused or wasted
time? Undoubtedly! Is wasted time a sin against the Lord?
Undoubtedly! We need to see time in its tremendous
potential for Christ's kingdom and for our eternal reward. We
will one day give an account to God of what we did with our
lives. That includes what we did with our days, hours, and
sometimes even what we did with our minutes. If all the idle
minutes of the members of your church during one week
were invested in prayer for your services, your ministry, and
for church outreach there would be greatly increased blessing, multiplied results, and touches of revival blessing.

We are shocked when someone dies prematurely and we
call it a tragedy. Add together the wasted minutes day after
day over a lifetime and it is the same as cutting off several
years of one's life. It is a sin to take one's own life or that of
another. It is equally a sin to kill several years of one's life
through wasted time. The effect is as great a loss as if
someone had killed you several years before the time you
would otherwise have died.

Some years ago while ministering in New Zealand, I was
introduced to a Mr. Wright, a zealous Baptist layman in Upper
Hutt. He was a subscriber to *Revival* magazine, which I was
then editing. He was deeply burdened for revival in New
Zealand and around the world and for missions, especially
OMS International. He read in the OMS monthly of the death
of an arthritic OMS prayer partner in Florida, Arthur Wood,
who spent most of his retirement days praying around the
world and for OMS's ministry.

Mr. Wright asked me, "Do you think God would let me
take the place of Arthur Wood?" I assured him I believed
God would be greatly pleased. He then showed me a room in

his house which he had set apart for his prayer room. "I rise each morning, and after breakfast I come to this room and spend much of my day in intercession. Would you like to see my prayer book?"

He showed me a large black loose-leaf notebook. In it I saw maps of the various nations where OMS works, pictures with names of missionaries, national evangelists, pastors, and others. These were his calls to prayer—his prayer maps, his prayer lists. Mr. Wright has been in heaven for a number of years now, but I am sure that throughout eternity he will thank God over and over again that when he retired he gave the last years of his life primarily to intercession.

Think of the thousands and millions of people who could be won to Christ if all Christian retirees invested heavily of their time in intercession! Their retirement years could be the happiest, most fruitful years of their lives—a great eternal investment. Retirees could become eternity's millionaires in blessings. You are responsible to train your people to be investors of intercession. But think of how they will reproach you in heaven if you fail to train them so that they can be thus rewarded.

The senior citizens and retirees of your church are your special responsibility. Have you taught them how to invest their time for maximum blessing and maximum reward? Retirement time is not theirs to squander any way they choose. It is a special trust from God.

In dozens of ways God can use portions of their time in visiting the sick, the aged, helping with duties around the church, helping in evangelistic visiting, in special work with children. Teach them the privilege of massive reading of God's Word, of major prayer investments. Make them special prayer partners of your ministry, supplying them with weekly lists for prayer.

What is more healthful than to exercise by walking? Have you ever tried investing a half hour or more a day in a health walk during which you intercede for your church, your community, your nation, missions, your loved ones? Try a prayer-walk; it can be blessed!

THE STEWARDSHIP OF LIFE

The youth of your church are your sacred responsibility. How many young people from your church will God call into Christian service? Are you equipping each of them for useful Christian living? Do you have a personal Timothy whom you are preparing for the Lord's service?

How many of your youth have no adequate goals in life? How many lack adequate parental guidance or encouragement to prepare for great usefulness? God wishes to use you to challenge them with God's possible call for some form of Christian service. If you have eyes to see the youth about you and ears to hear God's guidance to you, you may be used by God as Paul and other leaders have been, to be part of God's process of guiding many young people into kingdom service.

Wherever Paul went, he seemed to discover potential team members, found ways to involve them, and then helped them with a shorter or longer time of in-service training. Find your Timothy, Titus, Luke, Onesimus, Aristarchus, Sosthenes, Mark, Silas, Priscilla, and Aquila. God will help you find them and guide them into God's will for their lives.

As leader, you are responsible to challenge your people with God's call. Teach them to pray regularly for more workers to be sent out into God's harvest. Twice during His ministry Jesus commanded His followers to pray for Christian workers (Matt. 9:37–38; Luke 10:2). He gave the urgent parable of idle potential workers (Matt. 20:1–6). How many people will be called into His service because of you?

THE STEWARDSHIP OF POSSESSIONS

The whole earth belongs to God. He created it; He has lent it to us. He is our landlord. We are in debt to Him for everything we use or have. Our homes are made of materials on loan to us. Our clothing, our every possession is a kind of loan from Him.

Our life belongs to God. He has protected us and provided our needs. If He had not surrounded us with mercy we would have succumbed long ago to the millions of disease germs all around us. We owe Him our life and breath.

Our salvation—God's forgiveness, presence, and power in our lives and God's promise of heaven is ours through God's grace. We are in debt for Calvary. We are debtors for all we are and all we have.

God asks us to give Him a significant portion of our income and our possessions. In the Old Testament dispensation God required one-tenth of the income and produce of the people. We owe God for even more than they did. It would not be surprising if God asked a fifth, or a fourth, or even a half from some of us. The least we can do is to give our tithe and additional love offerings. Giving to God is one way of showing love to God. When they consider the rewards they could have received had they invested more in God's cause, some Christians may be shocked to find at judgment day that reward-wise and comparatively speaking they are eternal paupers.

You as the leader are responsible to train your people to give. To fail to do so is to hinder the church and the advance of Christ's kingdom. To fail to train in giving is to rob people of the reward they will have in heaven if they do give. The more they sacrifice in giving, the greater their eternal reward. Shame on you as a Christian leader if you do not train your people to give generously and thus invest in eternity.

If a person is unemployed and is producing nothing, train him to give a larger portion of his time in lieu of money. He can help keep the church building clean; he can run errands for the pastor. He can distribute gospel literature, read the Scripture to the aged or the sick, go house-to-house witnessing, or witness at recreational spots, in malls and market areas, or wherever people gather.

He can prepare prayer lists and give several hours a day in intercession. He can help the pastor pray daily for each member of the church. He can visit and pray with the sick. He can help saved and unsaved in practical ways that will demonstrate his Christian love and be a blessing to others. He can make his unemployment time an eternal investment. Let no one say he can give nothing. If he gives as he is able, Christ will reward him greatly in the ages to come.

You as leader are responsible to teach every believer the stewardship of life, time, money, possessions, strength, and the best way to invest for eternity. No one is a faithful shepherd if he robs his people of heaven's rewards because he did not teach him to give possessions, time, and self.

Chapter 28

Help Your People Discover and Develop Their Spiritual Gifts

Every natural ability God gives us is a trust which we are responsible to use. We must be good stewards or God may withdraw the ability. If we wisely use our abilities and experiences for God's glory, He often gives additional experience and abilities to use.

The Bible lists spiritual gifts in a number of places (Rom. 12:6–8; 1 Cor. 12:7–10, 28; Eph. 4:7–8, 11–13; 1 Peter 4:10–11). Twenty-one are named, some several times. Obviously, these are just samples of the manifold ways God gives special divine enablements. All ability, skill, and personal endowment is due to God's gracious goodness, His provision in our personality, and His faithfulness in our heritage and experience.

Some of these spiritual gifts are completely dependent upon God's miracle power and are therefore often referred to

194

as supernatural spiritual gifts. While they require our obedience to God in their use, they are in no way operable apart from God's supernatural enabling, power, and wisdom. Among these are prophecy, miracle powers (plural), healings (plural), kinds of languages (plural), interpretations of languages (plural), and distinguishing between spirits.

No one can produce a supernatural gift by his own choice. He cannot choose the occasion or time when it will be manifested. He can only obey the Spirit's promptings and guidance, and humbly depend on God, giving all the glory to God. The gift is the working of the Spirit and thus is under the control of the Spirit, but is manifested only as we obey and cooperate with the Spirit.

Thus no one can heal anyone he chooses, whenever he chooses, or in a manner he himself chooses. All healing is from God. One can follow the scriptural injunction to pray for healing, can be guided to pray for the healing of a particular person at a particular time, and can be given faith for a particular physical need. The healing power, however, is always God's power, and is always subject to the lordship of the Spirit and the will of God.

Another category of gifts listed in Scripture is more fully based on abilities with which we were born or which we have developed. To these gifts (sometimes called "natural gifts") God can add a special supernatural touch which supplements the natural with the divine, guides and empowers the natural skill with the supernatural supervision, and maximizes and multiplies the effectiveness by the enabling and anointing of the Spirit.

For example, many consider teaching a natural gift. Some seem to be born teachers. They have a combination of personality characteristics which enable them to be trained to become skilled teachers. However, a Christian "born teacher" can have a special added divine enabling in teaching. This then is a true gift of God. The person thus given the gift of teaching recognizes when God's hand is upon him in this special enabling and empowering way. He knows when God touches his teaching and when he is merely teaching by his own natural ability and training. He is at times aware of God's touch not only in the moment of teaching, but also in his preparation for teaching and even in the gathering and preparation of his teaching materials.

Remember, God's list includes such practical gifts as serving, administrating, encouraging, faith, giving, helps, knowledge, showing mercy, speaking, and wisdom. No mention is made of many other special ways in which God gifts people, such as special enablement for children's work, youth ministry, music ministry, song writing, and for careers as theologians, artists, poets. Note that in the Bible lists the individuals whom God uses in this way are also listed as His gifts to the church.

WAYS YOU HELP YOUR PEOPLE DISCOVER AND USE THEIR GIFTS

1. Help them realize that every natural ability is a gift entrusted to them by God for the good of others.

2. Help them realize areas of potential which they can develop or in which they can receive training.

3. Help them recognize ways in which God is using them now and putting His seal upon them. Often others realize a gift God is giving before we recognize it ourselves.

4. Help them realize that God is waiting to guide them in the use of their talents, gifts, and time. Teach them to pray for and believe for His guidance. Teach them how to develop a listening ear.

5. Help them realize that God can add His anointing, His supernatural touch, to any form of legitimate work or ministry. Teach them the importance of asking for the anointing of the Spirit every time they do something out of love for Christ, in His name, and for His glory.

6. Help them realize any spiritual supernatural gift which God seems to be giving them. Help them test the gift and guide them in using it. But teach them not to overemphasize these special gifts. In most cases God uses people by adding His special touch to their natural gifts.

7. Help them discover ways to use God's special gifts and the skills, talents, and experiences God has given them.

8. Caution them to remain humble in the use of God's gifts, to value the gifts of other Christians, and to give God the praise and glory for all.

Chapter 29

Train Your People for Witnessing and Soul-Winning

Witnessing is the responsibility of every Christian. God expects each to witness both by life and by lips. Witnessing is primarily to Christ, but also to the Father and to Bible truth. In Old Testament times God gave this responsibility to Israel. " 'You are my witnesses,' says the LORD, 'that I am God' " (Isa. 43:12). Today our witness primarily focuses on Jesus our Savior. Jesus said, "You are witnesses of these things" (Luke 24:48). "You also must testify" (John 15:27). "You will be my witnesses" (Acts 1:8). A great portion of Paul's ministry was witnessing (Acts 22:15–16; 26:16, 22).

1. *Christian testimony as witness.* One important form of witnessing is Christian testimony. This may be shared privately to fellow-Christians and to non-Christians or to Christian groups and to non-Christian groups. Testimony to non-Christians can be a powerful form of witnessing. Teach

198

your people that Christian testimony should follow these simple rules:

a. Relate your testimony personally to Jesus. Tell of His guidance, love, blessings, answers to prayer, companionship.

b. Bring glory to Jesus, not yourself. Testify in such a way that people remember what Jesus did and not what you did. Draw people closer to Jesus, not primarily closer to yourself.

c. Testify humbly. If testimony is not humbly given, people are less likely to accept it or be helped by it. As you testify humbly, God will continue to work for you and through you. If you let pride enter, God cannot trust you with continued blessings or success. Be honest in your testimony so that people sense it is genuine.

d. Adjust your testimony to the situation. In some situations you must be brief. Do not impose upon others' time. A brief, joyous testimony can open the door then or later for others to ask you to share further details.

e. Watch for opportunities to weave your testimony into conversation inoffensively. Help your people always to be ready with an up-to-date word of testimony, including personal fresh blessing, and recent answers to prayer. Your own brief word of personal testimony, humbly given, can bring life to your sermon or Bible exposition.

f. Help create opportunities for others to testify. "Isn't that similar to what Jesus did for you, John?" "Mary, you ought to share the wonderful answer to prayer the Lord just gave you." "Have you ever heard how Jesus helped Bill?" "You know, I wish everyone could have the kind of opportunity Sally had. Tell us about it, Sally."

2. *Witnessing to the unsaved.* This can be of two kinds: as part of an attempt to lead a person to Christ or as preparation for someone to become open to further soul-winning efforts later. Christ expects each Christian to be alert to both kinds of opportunities.

We are not primarily witnessing to the role of religion, defending Christianity in general, or even the Bible as true. There are times when that kind of presentation is appropriate. But witnessing is primarily pointing to Jesus. We present Jesus. People may argue with your opinions, beliefs, or even about the church. But it is more difficult to argue with a sincere, deeply personal witness of what Jesus means to you.

Prepare your people for more effective witnessing by sharing such suggestions as these:

a. Keep Jesus central. Help them realize that Jesus is a real person—alive and active today. Other questions can be dealt with later. The primary question they will have to answer at the judgment will concern what they did with Jesus.

b. Be personal. When did you meet Jesus? What has Jesus done for you? True, Jesus died on the cross, but bring that in as a part of your testimony of the reason you love Him, or trusted Him to forgive your sins, or are glad that His love reached you.

"He really changed my life." "Jesus has given me a peace and joy I never had before." "You know, when I pray, Jesus is so real, so close to me." "I never would have believed that Jesus could make such a difference in my life." Witnessing is not preaching. Remember, the two main parts in your testimony are Jesus and you.

c. Be definite. A witness in court is a person who has definite information. He saw, he heard, he was present. Your witness to Jesus must always be specific. Tell what He did for you, when He did it, and what happened in your life. "You know, I have known Jesus personally only about two years." "It was October 16, 1979, when I first met Jesus." "I know my sins were forgiven. I can never forget that day." "I had a real problem with a habit of . . . before Jesus saved me." "I have not been defeated by . . . since I met Jesus four years ago." The more personal, the more definite you make your testimony, the more the Lord can use it.

d. Be up-to-date. Be sure to include something recent and real from your present life. "You know, as I was thanking Jesus this morning . . ." "Really, this week Jesus has seemed so near to me." "Just Tuesday while I was praying to Jesus . . ." "It was really important to me this week that Jesus has been so near in my prayer time because . . ."

e. Include some form of special appeal. Let the Spirit guide you as to how direct that appeal should be. Timing is important. If the person to whom you are testifying continues to listen well and sympathetically, become even more direct. "I hope Jesus is as real to you as He has become to me." "When I think of the joy Jesus has brought into my life, I want everyone to know Him too. I hope you have that joy." "You know, it's hard to realize that all those years I struggled with (life, a problem, a particular sin) all alone, Jesus wanted to help me. If you are facing anything like that, I know He can help you." "If you would like to know how simple it is to come to Christ and receive Him as your Savior, I'd be glad to talk with you." "Would you permit me to pray with you just now?" Then include prayer for God to bless the person and meet his personal needs. Prayer is a powerful form of witness.

f. Prepare the person beforehand by intercession. Ask the Lord to place upon your heart people to whom He desires you to witness. Ask God to guide you in advance and then prepare the way by definite intercession daily for each of the people for whom the Spirit burdens you. In the meantime, use every opportunity to be friendly and a blessing. Then after some weeks or months of prayer, ask God's guidance for the right time and place, and seek to witness to and lead that person to the Lord.

A few years ago God led the leaders of the Korea Evangelical Church, the denomination there that has grown out of our OMS ministry, to call their churches and people to special soul-winning witness. At the beginning of January they asked each believer in each church to ask God to show them five unsaved people for whom they should be spiritually responsible. They were to pray for each of these as often as possible throughout each day from January 1 until Good Friday.

They were urged, "Don't try to witness to them now. Just keep saturating these people with your prayer. Show love in any way you can, but wait with your witness." In the meantime, the church prepared soul-winning lessons with flip-charts for each congregation. Each pastor trained his people in witnessing. They prepared special soul-winning tracts outlining the steps to Christ, and taught each believer in its use.

Each believer was given five tracts, one for each person he had been covering with prayer. They were not to go out and distribute these indiscriminately, but only to those for whom they had been praying, and only at the time they tried to lead them to the Lord.

On Good Friday each was to go to the five people for whom he had been praying daily. On Easter Sunday new converts were introduced at church to their new Christian brothers and sisters.

That year more than 11,000 were won to Christ. Never had the church had such a day of salvation! The next year the number rose to more than 15,000. Year by year it increased until more than 25,000 were won to Christ at this season. Could your people be trained for similar efforts?

3. *Leading a person to Christ.* Often in witnessing you do not have an obvious opportunity to lead the person to a personal experience of Christ. Look for opportunities to do so. Don't be timid about bringing people to the point of decision, especially when you sense God is near as you witness. If you help them receive Christ, in heaven they will thank God and you that you were faithful to them.

Every Christian should know the bare essentials of personal evangelism. If you happened upon an accident and a person was alert but near death, could you lead him to the assurance of salvation? You must know how to be concise and prepared for any emergency. Don't hesitate to be direct in such an emergency.

In some situations you know that the person you have been witnessing to has a definite problem or sin blocking the way. You may need to deal with that first. You may have to resolve questions or problems before the person is willing to make a personal commitment to Jesus. Know the answer or how to get the answer from another person. But remember that many things which seem like huge problems before conversion almost disappear once one experiences salvation. As quickly as you can, point the person away from his question or objection and to Jesus.

Trust the Holy Spirit to guide you in how much time you spend on each of the following points. In an emergency, go directly to the essential point: "Trust Jesus this moment to forgive you and He will save you."

a. Assure people that Jesus, His love, and His forgiveness are for them. "Jesus died for you as well as for the whole world. He loves you now. It is not too late to ask and receive His forgiveness now." Scriptures: Matthew 11:28; John 3:16; Revelation 22:17b.

b. Help them confess their need and sins now. "We have all sinned. You have sinned. Admit your need. Be ready to forsake your sins by God's help. If you need to ask forgiveness of others,

or make things right with others, promise God you will do it."
(In an emergency, have them confess their sins or admit they
need Jesus. If they cannot speak, ask them to confess in their
hearts. Or say, "I will pray aloud, and you agree in your hearts
with me." Then pray a short, specific prayer of confession,
asking forgiveness, and placing trust in Jesus as Savior, then
thanking Him.) Scriptures: Proverbs 28:13; 1 John 1:9.

c. Help them trust Jesus to forgive them. "Accept His love,
His forgiveness, and His power to change you." You may want
to quote a promise or two and then emphasize it. (In an
emergency, it is enough to say, "Jesus said . . ." "Just thank
Him.") Scripture: John 6:37; Romans 10:9.

Chapter 30

Prepare Your People by Teaching Them God's Word

One of your main responsibilities as a shepherd is to feed your flock (1 Peter 5:2). This was among the last exhortations Jesus gave before He ascended to heaven. His threefold word to Peter was to feed both the lambs and the sheep (John 21:15–17). Bible truth is compared in Scripture to food. God's Word, especially in its more simple teachings, is compared to nourishing milk (Isa. 55:1; Heb. 5:12; 1 Peter 2:2). Its more doctrinal teachings are compared with solid food (1 Cor. 3:2; Heb. 5:12–14). Jesus called His words real food (note John 6:35, 55, 63). David testified that God's Word was sweeter than honey to him (Ps. 119:103).

Spiritual health and strength depend upon spiritual food. Weak spiritual life in a congregation usually indicates that the pastor has not been feeding his people adequately. The pastor who complains that his people are not interested in deep spiritual truth tells us two things: he has not led his people into a deep walk with God, and he has not been feeding them adequate Bible truth. Only spiritually sick people lack appetite for spiritual food.

Spiritual service for God depends on spiritual health and that depends on adequate spiritual food. The basis for preparing God's people for spiritual service is to make them spiritually strong and well taught. They must know God's Word to be guided in God's service, to be able to answer questions and to lead unsaved people to Christ. Christians are always to be prepared to answer everyone who asks the reason for the hope they have (1 Peter 3:15).

Paul reminded the Ephesian elders, "I have not hesitated to proclaim to you the whole will of God" (Acts 20:27). His next words were, "Keep watch over yourselves and all the flock of which the Holy Spirit has made you overseers. Be shepherds of the church of God" (v. 28). Paul relates the two concepts. He is innocent of the blood of all (v. 26) because he has declared God's whole will. Now the elders are to do the same. That is what is involved in watching over the flock, in being a shepherd of the church of God.

What must you do to declare the whole will of God?

1. *Derive your teaching from the whole Word of God.* Use both Testaments. The Old Testament was the only Bible the apostles had; all their messages were based on it. Don't neglect it. Anyone who declares the whole will of God must be familiar with and understand every book of the Bible so that the Spirit can guide him to preach from any part and use the whole of Scripture.

2. *Over a period of several years cover every major topic in the Bible.* When God considers subjects important enough to be included repeatedly in His Word, they are important to God's people. Other types of preaching may be used at times, but only by expository preaching through the books of the Bible can the whole of Scripture be thoroughly covered. God will guide regarding the sequence you are to follow. A spiritually lazy person who is not adequately reading and studying the whole Word tends to preach most of his

messages from the same part of Scripture or on the same topic.

3. *Place your emphasis where God places it.* Give constant attention to the major emphases of Scripture. What God only mentions in one or two verses of Scripture is not a major topic for your ministry. Topics which recur again and again are obviously of great concern to God. The constant use of a reference Bible and concordance is a necessity for your Bible study.

4. *Ground your teaching thoroughly in every major doctrine of the Bible.* The Bible is not organized like a manual of systematic theology. But your systematic understanding of doctrine is essential to your knowing and preaching the whole will of God. You cannot give messages in the concise and highly organized form of a chapter in a book of theology. You must digest doctrine, preach and teach in language your people understand, and over a period of time you will ground them in every major Bible doctrine.

Occasionally you may want to give a doctrinal series for a few weeks. However, systematic doctrinal teaching can be included bit by bit in your regular messages. Continue to give doctrinal insights as well as practical applications. First, you yourself must understand the doctrine clearly. Only then can you teach it simply with illustrations and applications which will live in the hearts and minds of your people. If your heart is aflame with a doctrine, and it should be, your teaching will be full of life.

5. *Constantly include practical application.* God's Word was inspired by the Holy Spirit section by section to help people in real-life situations. It is eternal truth of relevance to all people, but not all sections are equally relevant or urgent at a given moment.

6. *Convey a clear overview of God's great plan.* Your people must be helped to realize the grandeur, glory, and significance of God's overarching plan for the ages. Help them realize the unity of God's plan and the significant role God has for them within that plan. Nothing makes the whole of Scripture come more alive or more relevant to your people

than to catch a vision of their own part in God's great plan that stretches out into eternity. Then they will thrill over both the practical impact for today and the great eschatological promise for their tomorrows in eternity.

Thus you will equip them with zeal to be involved in God's ongoing purpose, with practical direction to serve the Lord meaningfully and significantly in their daily lives, and will help them see their part in the church as it fits into God's eternal plan.

YOUR PRAYER

Chapter 31

Your Prayer Life as a Leader

"Great praying," wrote E.M. Bounds, "is the sign and seal of God's great leaders." What should be the role of prayer in your life as a Christian leader? The instant answer to this should be the answer the apostles gave. They decided to give themselves to two things: "We ... will give our attention to prayer and the ministry of the word" (Acts 6:4). For them, prayer was the first priority, and probably took the largest amount of their time. They could lead only as they prayed. They realized that their greatest responsibility was to cover the church with prayer as they ministered the Word. It was so urgent that they delegated many other duties to Spirit-filled lay people.

Bounds said that each leader "must be preeminently a man of prayer. His heart must graduate in the school of prayer .... No learning can make up for the failure to pray. No

211

earnestness, no diligence, no study, no gifts will supply its
lack. Talking to men for God is a great thing, but talking to
God for men is greater still. He will never talk well and with
real success to men for God who has not learned well how to
talk to God for men. More than this, prayerless words . . . are
deadening words."

You need audience before God before you attempt
audience with your people. Stand in God's presence before
you stand before them. You must prevail before God before
you can prevail before them. Not till you have worshiped
with the seraphim are you ready to worship with your people.
Only when you come from the presence of God can you lead
them into the presence of God.

The saintly and gifted Church of Scotland minister
Robert Murray McCheyne said, "In general it is best to have
at least one hour alone with God before engaging in anything
else. I ought to spend the best hours of the day in communion
with God." In an ordination sermon he exhorted: "Give
yourself to prayers and the ministry of the Word. If you do not
pray, God will probably lay you aside from your ministry, as
He did me, to teach you to pray. Remember Luther's maxim,
'To have prayed well is to have studied well . . . . Carry the
names of the little flock upon your breast like the High Priest.
Wrestle for the unconverted.'"

You as a Christian leader today must not only follow the
apostolic example, but you must be an example of prayer to
all your people. Charles Spurgeon said, "Of course the
preacher is above all others distinguished as a man of prayer.
He prays as an ordinary Christian, else he were a hypocrite.
He prays more than ordinary Christians else he were dis-
qualified for the office he has undertaken."

When Spurgeon was asked the secret of his success he
responded, "Knee work! Knee work!" Finney explained, "In
regard to my own experience, I will say that unless I had the
spirit of prayer I could do nothing. If even for a day or an hour
I lost the spirit of grace and supplication I found myself
unable to preach with power and efficiency, or to win souls
by personal conversation."

Andrew Murray asked, "What is the reason why many thousands of Christian workers in the world have not a greater influence? Nothing save this—the prayerlessness of their service ... It is nothing but the sin of prayerlessness which is the cause of the lack of a powerful spiritual life."

To learn how to pray and be empowered and guided through prayer is the most important task of your preparation as a leader. To establish a leadership lifestyle of prevailing prayer is probably the most decisive element in your spiritual success. You will never be a greater leader than your prayers. You may have some apparent success without a strong prayer life. However, the eternal value of it and your eternal reward for it will be heavily dependent on your prayer life. All success apart from the spiritual dimension is a house built on sand.

If you as leader should be ahead of your followers in anything, you should above all be the model and leader in prayer. May God make every leader a praying Elijah. Spurgeon's cry was, "Oh, for five hundred Elijahs, each one upon his Carmel, crying unto God, and we should soon have the clouds bursting into showers. Oh, for more prayer, more constant, incessant ... prayer."

Your prayer life is a clear revelation of how much a person of God and how much a spiritual leader you are. You will never be more important in God's sight than your prayer life. No part of your ministry will be more greatly rewarded in eternity. The eternal value of all else you do depends on this.

YOU ARE RESPONSIBLE TO KEEP STRONG AND BLESSED THROUGH PRAYER

Spiritual ministry demands spiritual power. The Holy Spirit is the source of all power, and He is given in answer to prayer. "If you then, though you are evil, know how to give good gifts to your children, how much more will your Father in heaven give the Holy Spirit to those who ask him" (Luke 11:13). That promise is given by Jesus immediately after He had given the great command-promise: "Ask and it will be given to you; seek and you will find; knock and the door will be opened to you." Then for fear that Satan might tempt you to think this promise is for some specially chosen ones and not for you, Jesus added, "For every one who asks receives; he who seeks finds; and to him who knocks, the door will be opened" (Luke 11:9–10).

This tremendous promise is available as you pray according to the will of God for many kinds of things. But as Jesus pointed out in verse 13, it is specially given in reference to the Holy Spirit. Spiritual ministry is dependent upon the Spirit. There is no other way. You can never minister effectively unless you are filled with the Spirit and daily anointed, led, and empowered by the Holy Spirit.

Your greatest need if you desire to see the conviction of sin among the unsaved and the growth and blessing of your people is the powerful presence of the Holy Spirit. Our teaching and our sermons, unless empowered by the Spirit, may hinder rather than bless. Truth in itself does not transform. Truth applied by the Spirit changes lives.

"He has made us competent as ministers of a new covenant—not of the letter but of the Spirit; for the letter kills, but the Spirit gives life" (2 Cor. 3:6). Your words of truth may only deaden hearers unless accompanied by the power of the Spirit.

The effectiveness of your leadership is dependent upon your spiritual life. E. M. Bounds emphasized years ago, "Men are God's method. The Church is looking for better methods; God is looking for better men." Again he wrote, "The Holy Spirit does not flow through methods, but through men. He does not come upon machinery, but on men. He does not anoint plans, but men—men of prayer."

Dr. A. J. Gordon urged, "Our generation is rapidly losing its grip upon the supernatural; and as a consequence the pulpit is rapidly dropping to the level of the platform. And this decline is due, we believe, more than anything else, to an ignoring of the Holy Spirit as the supreme inspirer of preaching."[1]

Why is it that so few leaders are continually anointed

with the power of the Spirit? Because most depend more on their study, work, and plans than on prayer which is the main channel for the flow of the Holy Spirit into your life. You become saturated and covered with the presence of God only as you remain long in His presence. It was after Moses absorbed the close presence and glory of the Lord for eighty days on Sinai that his face became radiant with the presence of God. Prolonged daily prayer adds a Christlikeness to your personality and His spiritual fragrance lingers wherever you go.

You keep blessed as you speak words of love, communion, praise, and thanksgiving to Jesus throughout the day. You thus live in God's presence. You are a continuous blessing as you continuously ask God to bless others. Being constantly a blessing grows out of being constantly blessed.

In communion you constantly see Him who is invisible. This Moses did (Heb. 11:27). The Greek here suggests that Moses beheld without wavering. This was the secret of his whole life. At times he was face to face with God in a way no other human being had ever known (Deut. 34:10). But even when not on Sinai or in the tent of meeting, Moses kept the unseen face of God before him in prayer.

You as leader must maintain constantly a communing heart. You must live in God's presence and "under his wings" (Ps. 91:4), "in the shadow of" His loving wings (Ps. 36:7). Closeness to God and refuge in God are implied by these metaphors. You are not only to come close to God (Heb. 7:19; 10:22; James 4:8), but are to live close to Him throughout your days.

In the Hebrew of the Old Testament the concept of being in God's presence is literally being where you can see His faces (always in the plural and probably suggesting all the various emotions and attitudes of God). It is essential that you as a leader be this close to God, where you can constantly see on God's face His joy or displeasure, His encouragement or His restraint.

Just as Moses went back and forth daily from his time of communion in the tent of meeting with the Shekinah presence of the Lord to his manifold ministry and responsibilities among the people, so you as leader of your people are to come from the presence of the Lord to your people, and then return from your people back to the presence of the Lord to present their needs before Him. Is this your experience?

A New Testament leader has to be God-made. God makes him during prayer. Many leaders are hypocrites in their prayer life. They urge others to pray and fail to do so themselves. Power in prayer has a direct relation to time spent in prayer. A short public prayer that prevails can be prayed only by one who has prevailed at length in private.

The local church is made or destroyed by its leaders. It is usually like leader like people. Only praying leaders have praying followers. A godly, dynamic, praying leader is God's gift to the people. A leader weak and careless in prayer is often a hindrance to God and the people. Leaders who know how to pray are God's greatest gift to the church and to earth.

Your task as a Christian leader is too big for you. Its immensity and awesomeness must drive you to prayer. Your vocation is too large for you and your calling too sacred for you. But God is available for your ministry if you are willing to pay the price in prayer.

Chapter 32

Your Prayer Controls
Your Work

As a leader your usefulness is dependent upon your prayer. Nothing brings more blessing and effectiveness as you visit your people. Nothing puts more of the seal of God upon you before the community. Nothing does more to win the hearts of your people or give you more spiritual stature and respected leadership than your prayer life. Nothing else can keep you spiritually refreshed, with messages constantly from the heart of God. Nothing does more to bring the anointing of God upon your leadership.

It was the insistence of E.M. Bounds, apostle of prayer, that prayerless leaders hinder God's cause. "God wants consecrated men because they can pray and will pray ... As prayerless men are in His way, hinder Him, and prevent the success of His cause, so likewise unconsecrated men are useless to Him, and hinder Him carrying out His gracious plans, and in executing His noble purposes in redemption."

Your people need to feel God's power upon you, God's voice speaking through you, God's touch as you touch their lives. God's power in your ministry comes not from the fluency, loudness of voice, or your ability to express your ideas. Anointing is difficult to describe, but once the people see the real anointing of the Holy Spirit upon you, from then on they know when you have it and when you don't.

Prayer prepares you for every aspect of your work. Prayer brings the divine additive that makes a recognizable difference in your life, your words, and your work. Prayer makes you the person of God who is loved and respected.

PRAYER PREPARES GOD'S BLESSING
FOR EACH SERVICE

When many people pray intensely for the same thing, a massive prayer power is built up which will bring outstanding blessing. This is important for the church services. Whether lay person or minister, you can help make each service a maximum blessing.

1. *Amassed prayer is required to fill the building with God's presence.* There are times when God's presence is brought so near and into such manifestation, that as people enter they feel a special hush, reverence, or awareness of God's sacred nearness. This rarely happens except when the leader, some of his godliest people, or both have been spending much time in prayer and fasting.

Sometimes an awareness of God's presence is recognized by people when the leader enters the pulpit or as he begins to speak. This special seal of the Holy Spirit can come only when the leader has been truly living in God's presence. It can be greatly aided if he has taught his local church leaders to gather early and to spend the time in intercession. Others meet Saturday nights for prevailing prayer. Some have trained their people to arrive before daylight on Sunday morning and spend several hours in prayer for the services.

Dr. John Maxwell at Skyline Wesleyan Church, Lemon Grove, California, has 200 men who are his special prayer partners. They are divided into four groups so that each one prays during the morning worship one Sunday each month. They meet for prayer on Sunday mornings from 8:00–8:30. The church uses prayer chains also.

Abundant prayer fills the atmosphere with the presence of God. This holy sense of God's presence prepares the people to be blessed by God and to obey God.

2. *Amassed prayer helps bring the needy to the services.* When prayer has prepared the way, neighbors and friends are more likely to accept an invitation to attend services. When prayer has prepared the way, God has brought people who were not invited by others, but who were drawn by the Spirit into the building.

In special times of revival in Wales and in Scotland, God has on occasion brought people to the church at a time when a service had not even been announced. But people from all directions began to gather at the same time.

During the revival in the Hebrides in 1949 when God was so mightily using Rev. Duncan Campbell, there had been no initial response to the services in one place. Around midnight after a time of prayer in an elder's home, a young man offered a prayer of faith that seemed to release the power of the Spirit. As they went outside they found people leaving their homes and arriving from all directions at a central spot in the village. There they waited. As Rev. Campbell spoke, a mighty work of the Spirit began which transformed the village and closed the drinking house.

Amassed prayer makes people willing to attend special services. During the revival of the United Prayer meetings in the 1850s in the United States, daily noon prayer meetings were held in hundreds of cities. Thousands upon thousands of unsaved people were drawn into the services, and hundreds of thousands were saved in one year.

3. *Amassed prayer can anoint the singing.* Why do we have congregational singing at the beginning of our public worship? To lead the people into the presence of God and to

prepare our hearts for worship. We sing of His greatness, His holiness, His goodness and power to draw our attention away from earthly things and focus our hearts on God. Singing is primarily "unto the Lord."

Secondarily, we sing to one another as we praise God and sing our testimony of personal joy in the Lord and His blessing and grace to our souls. This aspect of worship may come later in the service and on other occasions. Such singing has been much used of the Spirit in times of evangelism and revival. Singing was greatly blessed of the Lord during the Reformation, in the time of awakening under the Wesleys, and at other times of widespread revival.

We do not begin a service with singing with the primary purpose to "sing the people in," to awaken the people from listlessness, or to create a warm, friendly atmosphere. Unfortunately, some song leaders seem to feel they are conducting a pep rally rather than leading worshipers into the presence of God. They even interject humor to capture the attention of the people. Such leadership does not bring overwhelming awareness of God's sacred presence and His awesome power into the service.

Often when prayer has prepared the way of the Lord, the congregational singing has led to awareness that God in His nearness and holiness has come. It is as if God comes close to us as we draw close to Him (James 4:8).

Vocal numbers can also be specially used of the Lord to bring an awareness of His nearness and presence. Usually this can be done only when the singers are godly, Spirit-touched, and prayer-prepared. A fifteen- or thirty-minute prayer time by the singers just before the service, added to adequate prayer preparation by the members of the congregation before the service, can wonderfully prepare the way for God's blessing on the singing.

4. *Prayer can make the public reading of Scripture speak to hearts.* How seldom is God's Word read with the anointing of the Spirit! How rarely it is read with the reverence due the very Word of God! The reading of Scripture had a prominent role in the Jewish synagogue and the early church.

When Ezra opened the Scripture to read, the people stood (Neh. 8:5). This same reverence was otherwise reserved for royalty. The opening of Scripture for public reading was the equivalent of God entering the service and being welcomed. As court attendants stood in the presence of the king, so the people stood in honor of God, for the Word of God represented God Himself.

No doubt from this comes the practice in some churches for all to stand in reverence as the Word is read. If the Word is to be honored in this way, it should be read reverently and with skill. A reader should familiarize himself with the passage by reading it in advance several times, being sure to pronounce each word correctly. He must read it with such distinctness that everyone can hear and understand. He should pray specially for God's help and anointing in the reading of the Word.

If the congregation stands while the Scripture is read, it helps keep them alert and attentive as they should be. Probably more time should be given to reading the Word, that is, longer passages should often be read, than is sometimes done in our services.

5. *Much prayer needs to prepare the way for the pastoral prayer.* It is a sacred responsibility to lead in public prayer. One time Spurgeon was to speak in a united service. The platform party was instructed about each person's part. A would lead the meeting, B would pray, C would read the Scripture, D would take the offering, Spurgeon would preach. He spoke up, "If there is only one thing that I may do tonight, then I want to offer the prayer." To him the pastoral prayer was the most important part of the service.

The pastoral prayer has a blessing, teaching, and intercessory function for everyone present. Everyone must realize that you are really in touch with God. Everyone should be helped to revere God, love God, and obey God by the prayer which he Amens (1 Cor. 14:16). All should be hushed as you speak to God on their behalf.

Your public prayer should be loud enough that all can hear, but should not be shouted as if God were deaf. The gods of the heathen cannot hear, so they shout before them. We pray to a God who hears even silent prayer. There are times of deep heart cry and soul desperation when we, like Jesus, may pray with loud cries and tears (Heb. 5:7). However, that is more usual for our private prayer times than in the leading of the church in prayer.

Your pastoral prayer can do more to prepare your people for your message than perhaps any other aspect of the service. Your pastoral prayer can help bring the awareness of God's nearness and heartbeat.

You must not only prepare your heart for your sermon, but you must prepare it for your prayer. You must prepare it with heart hunger, heart humility, and heart purpose. You must carry a daily prayer burden if you would have power with God when you intercede in the pulpit. You must daily commune in the intimacy of God's secret presence if you are to lead the church in public adoration, worship, and praise.

Chapter 33

Your Prayer Must Saturate Message Preparation

Teaching God's Word or giving God's message must be a joint work of God and the speaker. God's part is as important as yours. God's preparation of the speaker is both long-term and immediate. There is a sense in which every God-guided, God-anointed message has been a lifetime in preparation. Your heart-preparation builds upon your entire spiritual life and walk with God since your conversion.

Dry sermons grow out of starved souls. Lifeless messages come from empty hearts. Jesus said that it is "out of the overflow of the heart the mouth speaks" (Matt. 12:34). A full heart always has more to say than can possibly be said; there is always a remainder left over, like the twelve basketfuls when Jesus fed the five thousand.

God must make you before you can make your sermon. An effective message comes only from an effective person.

You must live what you preach. Your sermon will be the exposition of your soul. A great message comes only from a great heart. The sermon is your heart up to that date.

When your heart is flooded with God, floods of living water will stream from your soul. If your heart is a spiritual desert, your ministry will be dry and barren. Only a God-saturated soul has a God-saturated message. You can share no more life than you have received. Your sermon reveals your innermost being or else it is hypocrisy.

To the extent that heaven touches your soul, to that extent will your hearers feel heaven in their souls. Only a prophet can have a prophetic ministry, and prophets must get their vision and message from God. A person without a burning message is a person who is not living enough in the presence of God. A minister or Bible teacher without a God-given message is a tragedy. The people need to see God's Spirit in your life, to feel God's touch in your ministry.

He said through Jeremiah, "I did not send these prophets, yet they have run with their message; I did not speak to them, yet they have prophesied. But if they had stood in my council, they would have proclaimed my words to my people and would have turned them from their evil ways and from their evil deeds" (Jer. 23:21–22).

God condemns those who speak their own ideas, thoughts, and dreams instead of His message:

> "Let the prophet who has a dream tell his dream, but let the one who has my word speak it faithfully. For what has straw to do with grain?" declares the LORD. "Is not my word like fire," declares the LORD, "and like a hammer that breaks a rock in pieces?
>
> "Therefore," declares the LORD, "I am against the prophets who steal from one another words supposedly from me. Yes," declares the LORD, "I am against the prophets who wag their own tongues and yet declare, 'the LORD declares.' . . . "They do not benefit these people in the least," declares the LORD (Jer. 23:28–32).

Each time you as the leader stand before your people you stand as the representative of God. You may not be called a prophet, but you must fulfill a prophet's role for your people. Each time you speak you are responsible to present the message God wants His people to have at that hour. There is no possible way you can do this except as you live constantly in the presence of God. You must be a person of God even more than a person of the people.

John Wesley asked his ministers, "Have you any days of fasting and prayer? Storm the throne of grace and persevere therein, and mercy will come down." The only way to put God in your sermon is by prayer. How long your sermon has an impact on your people is usually in direct proportion to how much you have prayed.

Preparation of your heart must precede the preparation of your message, must continue during its preparation, and must continue until your message is delivered. Prepared hearts prepare fruitful messages. It is dangerous to put more thought than prayer into your sermon. The more talented, the better trained you are, the more you need to be a person of prayer lest you have more self-confidence than power.

1. *Receive God's guidance as to the Scripture passage and the subject through prayer.* Robert Murray McCheyne said, "Give yourself to prayers . . . Get your texts from God, your thoughts, your words."

How blessed it is to have no knowledge of a specific need and then to have people come and tell how your message was exactly what they needed. One of the most important steps in sermon preparation is getting God's guidance in the subject to be prepared.

2. *Saturate with prayer your study of the passage on which you speak.* There are times when God opens up the passage and the thoughts and words come almost faster than you can write them down. At other times it takes hours of Bible study, tracing references, studying the context, and praying over which illustrations will be most effective. The passage or passages to be included in the message must be prayed over, meditated upon, and lived in your soul until you catch afire with the truth.

Finney emphasized that truth by itself will never produce spiritual results. It takes the Spirit of God setting truth aflame, empowering truth, and applying truth to the hearers.

Luther, who believed to pray well was to study well, spent three hours daily in prayer. Prayer is not a substitute for study, but neither is study a substitute for prayer. From prayer you share the heartbeat of the writers of Scripture. From prayer you catch the vision, the soul-passion, the emphasis which God intended in inspiring the Scripture.

"The LORD confides in those who fear him" (Ps. 25:14). Bishop Quayle pointed out that this can be translated "the whisper of the Lord." We can get so close to Him in prayer that He whispers the deep things of God to us. The casual, unprayerful Bible student never understands or shares with God's people these deep truths.

"The Spirit searches all things, even the deep things of God. For who among men knows the thoughts of a man except the man's spirit within him? In the same way no one knows the thoughts of God except the Spirit of God. We have not received the spirit of the world but the Spirit who is from God, that we may understand what God has freely given us. This is what we speak, not in words taught us by human wisdom but in words taught by the Spirit, expressing spiritual truths in spiritual words" (1 Cor. 2:10–13).

Genuinely to minister the deep things of God requires not only that you study your Bible carefully, but that you be filled with the Spirit, illumined by the Spirit, guided by the Spirit, and anointed by the Spirit. Remember, all the ministry of the Spirit is yours through prayer. You as leader have no alternative to constant prayer—living, studying, and ministering in the spirit of prayer. In the words of Quayle, "[The minister] does not stop to pray; he simply does not stop from prayer." No ministry can be a spiritual one without much prayer. No prayerless leader can interpret the mind of God aright.

3. *Powerful praying secures and keeps the anointing of the Spirit on your message and on your leadership.* There is never a time when you can relax your prayer life. It is not enough to have a God-given message. It must then be

delivered with the anointing and power of the Spirit upon you as you speak.

Anointing is the gift of God given at the moment of your ministry. There are several prerequisites to God's anointing upon you. There must be commitment to God, obedience, total dependence, and prayer. Anointed ministry prevails. God's anointing enables the Spirit to grip hearers with the truth of your message, clothes you with the authority of God, and is His seal upon you and your message.

Unanointed messages do not bring lasting transformations in lives. It takes more than the power of words to change people. Satan is always ready to snatch away the seed sown in the minds (Luke 8:12). Anointed words burn their way into hearts until they are not easily forgotten and pierce to the innermost nature. They are the sword-thrust of the Spirit (Eph. 6:17), and bring sweetness to the saint, faith to the believer, and courage to the warrior.

God's anointing is available to every leader including you—for a price. Primarily that price is prayer. Perhaps the most frequent failure in every form of leadership is the failure to be anointed. Earnestness is essential but earnestness is not anointing. Anointing is God's crown on earnestness in answer to prayer.

God's anointing separates God's prophet from a lecturer or speaker. It is His power flowing through a personality, quickening the thoughts, adding freshness and new insights, quickening the emotions, and adding a divine dimension to one's love, hunger, passion, and zeal. In anointing, God takes charge and speaks powerfully through your words. It makes your words God's voice to the souls of the people.

Anointing adds a divine richness to your thought, a divine originality to your speaking, a divine sweetness to spiritual food, a divine illumination to insight, a divine benediction, a divine power, and a divine seal upon you as a person.

Chapter 34

Your Responsibility to Intercede for Your People

God has given you no greater responsibility than that of interceding for your people. It is as urgent to bring your people before God in prayer as it is to bring God before your people in your messages. You must intercede for your ministry, the services, and the outreach. But you must also intercede for your people family by family and person by person.

Every believer is called to be a priest of God. "You are a chosen people, a royal priesthood" (1 Peter 2:9). "You also . . . are . . . to be a holy priesthood, offering spiritual sacrifices acceptable to God through Jesus Christ" (1 Peter 2:5). Your twofold priestly role is to offer spiritual sacrifices and to intercede.

Your spiritual sacrifices consist of praise (Heb. 13:15), your body (Rom. 6:13, 16, 19; 12:1), good deeds (Heb. 13:16), and financial gifts (Phil. 4:18; Heb. 13:16). Your constant priestly role is prayer. Personal communion with God is your daily privilege and need. Personal intercession is to be your daily ministry and work. This is true for every Christian; it is even more true for you as a spiritual leader.

The role of the high priest in Old Testament times was to offer sacrifice and make intercession. The intercessory role was symbolized by his official garments. He wore the priestly ephod over his robe. The ephod was like an apron, with two onyx stones—one fastened to each shoulder. On each stone were the names of six of the tribes of Israel. The breastplate was fastened to the ephod over the heart of the priest by gold chains, so it would never swing away from his heart. It had twelve jewels in four rows of three stones each. On each stone was engraved the name of one of the tribes.

Thus, symbolically, every time the high priest entered the tabernacle (and later the temple) to officiate in the presence of God he bore on his shoulders and close on his heart the names of the tribes. This spoke of his responsibility for the people and love for the people (see Ex. 28). Similarly, the New Testament minister must carry invisibly upon his shoulders and heart the people to whom he ministers. This is his responsibility before God. He must carry a burden for them and he must love them.

Christ completed the work of sacrifice in His work of atonement on the cross. But Christ's unfinished ministry is the ministry of intercession. Every Christian is to be a partner-priest with Christ. How much more every minister and leader is to share a partnership with Christ in intercession for His people! Jesus lives to continue His ministry at the side of the Father. He is reigning by prayer. John 17, the great high priestly prayer of Jesus, expresses the kinds of concerns always on His heart for His people.

Israel would never have reached Canaan but for the intercessions of Moses. He was great in administration and in leadership. But Israel would have been wiped out as a people but for the intercession of Moses.

Paul is the great New Testament example of the priestly

role of Christ's leaders. We know more about the prayer life of Paul than of any other Bible character except, perhaps, Moses. His ministry grew out of his unceasing life of prayer. He was the great New Testament example of a prayer warrior. He wrote no book on prayer, but prayer is woven into all of his writings. Prayer and fasting were the foundation of his whole ministry. He pioneered the expansion of the church by unceasing intercession, labor, and unbelievable suffering. He was the apostle of godly, whole-souled intercession.

He evangelized through love, tears, toil, and suffering. His zeal was unstoppable. But the fire was kept constantly burning in his soul by his day and night prayers of intercession. Paul's three great testimonies were (1) how Christ won him; (2) his love for the church; and (3) his prayer for Christ's cause.

In ten of Paul's letters, he spoke of his prayer for those to whom he was writing. In eight of his letters, he pleads for the prayer help of his converts and friends. Paul was such a model of prayer that he developed a praying people. Every evangelical leader should look to Paul as his example of what ministry can be by the grace of God. Paul the intercessor is the model of what you and I should be today.

No leader is greater than his prayers. If we want to see the church revived and become a mighty force for God we must have a new generation of Pauline prayer giants. Probably the greatest weakness of the ministry today is the lack of intercession by the leaders for the people. At least forty-one verses in Paul's writings refer to his prayer and subjects for prayer, but only one verse refers to his praying for himself or his personal needs. He was always praying for others. One of the ways to measure the role and scope of your prayer life is to note the proportion of the time you spend praying for your own needs and interests as compared to the time you spend praying for others.

When we pray in the Spirit, we pray primarily for others. When we seek first Christ's kingdom, God will take care of all our personal needs (Matt. 6:33). The prayer Jesus taught as a model indicates that normally we do not begin our prayer time praying for personal needs. First we pray for Christ's name, will, and kingdom. Then we turn to our own needs. We do not pray a "me" or "my" prayer, but rather an "us" and "our" prayer.

You as the leader have such a heavy responsibility of daily prayer for your people that you may have to limit the amount of time you pray for yourself and your own family. But as you bear the burdens of others God will, in turn, put your personal burdens on the hearts of your people, especially if you have taught them to be a praying people. When you fulfill your prayer role for the flock for which you are accountable, Christ Himself will intercede for you. Weep for others, and God will uphold you with the loyal love and prayer of your people.

SUGGESTIONS FOR YOUR PRAYER ROLE

Regardless of your leadership role—pastor, teacher, Sunday school leader, lay leader, youth leader, missionary—adapt this to your situation.

1. Plan your intercession for your people. You will be sure to fail God and your people unless you have a regular prayer plan for your intercession times. If anything in life is worth planning, surely this is.

a. *Reserve a special daily time for your intercession.* This is as important as setting apart time for preparing your messages or for visiting your people. This should be daily time, choice time, when you are physically alert and able for intensive intercession.

In addition, God will bring your people and their needs to your attention at special times at the particular moment when someone needs your prayer. When God thus specially prompts you, as far as possible put other work aside instantly and pray. God will also bring your people to your prayer attention as you work, travel, as you have moments when your mind is comparatively free. As their leader, your people should constantly be on your heart, even as they were on the heart of Paul.

Paul said of Epaphras, pastor of the church at Colossae, "He is always wrestling in prayer for you, that you may stand firm in all the will of God, mature and fully assured. I vouch for him that he is working hard for you ..." (Col. 4:12–13). Epaphras was with Paul at the time. Paul's testimony of the intense burden Epaphras carried for his people—"wrestling in prayer" and "working hard for you" though he was miles away—portrays the prayer life of an ideal leader. Could you be said to be "always wrestling in prayer" for your people? Could your regular prayer for your people be correctly called "hard work"?

b. *Have a place where you intercede for your people.* If you have a private room, you can make that your prayer closet. It is an added blessing when you have a special place to pray. When I visit John Wesley's house in London, I always treasure the time I can spend praying quietly in his prayer room at the top of the stairs.

c. *Have prayer lists of your people.* God greatly blesses the use of prayer lists. There is strong evidence that Paul used them. You will also want special lists—of unsaved people you are seeking to win, of leaders of your nation, of missions needs (nations, people, ministries), a prayer-partner list (people in whose ministry you want to share by prayer), a family list. Your major responsibility, as shepherd, is your prayer list or lists for your own people.

John Welch, godly Scots minister, as far as possible spent eight to ten hours each day or night praying for His people. He kept a cloth to wrap around himself when he arose in the night to pray, but his wife complained whenever she found him on the floor weeping. His reply was, "O woman, I have the souls of 3,000 to answer for, and I know not how it is [spiritually] with many of them." Three thousand lived in the area around his church.

Jesus said the good shepherd calls his sheep by name (John 10:3). If a shepherd knows the name of each sheep, how much more should the spiritual shepherd pray by name for each one of his flock. Hudson Taylor, founder of the China Inland Mission, used to pray for every mission station, every missionary by name, and every specific need and circumstance of which he was aware. His prayer lives on in China today. Bishop Azariah, sweet-spirited leader of the church in South India, prayed by name for every pastor and leader under his jurisdiction in his large area. It may be that the greatest change that could come in your life and ministry would be for you really to learn to pray for your people and for your ministry among them.

d. *Plan how you will cover with prayer the needs of your people.* If your congregation is too large to pray for each one personally each day, plan ways to include regularly all for whom you are spiritually responsible and accountable to God (Heb. 13:17). You may need to segment your list so that you pray for a portion of your congregation each day of the week. Perhaps you will want to have a list of family names so that you do pray each day for each family by name. On your more detailed family list you will want to have the names of each member of the family and the approximate age and perhaps birthdays. You may want to have a birthday prayer list. You can promise your people that you will spend special time praying for them on their birthdays.

You will want a constantly changing "need list" on a separate sheet of paper with the special needs of your people as they arise. This would include sickness, accidents, bereavement, unemployment, special discouragement, or trial. You can truly bear the burdens of the people on your heart only as you know what those needs are. As your people begin to realize how personally you pray for each of them, they will gladly share their needs as they arise so you can more effectively be their prayer shepherd.

e. *Have a prayer plan for major needs of your people and community.* Special concerns and major needs weigh heavily on the heart of every pastor. If your congregation is small, perhaps you can pray for them all each day. If it is large, you will need to plan your prayer with separate topics for each day of the week.

Among your major prayer concerns for your people as a whole are unity, integrity, godly living, a praying people, a witnessing people, revival, a growing church impact, a worldwide church impact, God's presence in your services.

Among the church groups for whom you must carry prayer concern are:

The Youth. Maintain a special prayer burden for the youth and your ministry to them even though you may have a youth pastor. Pray for (1) an adequately planned ministry to them; (2) the salvation of each; (3) an expanding ministry to youth outside the church; (4) God's call to Christian service for youth of His choosing; (5) training or employment for needy youth; (6) strength to withstand the special temptations of youth.

God can give you your own Elisha, Timothy, or Titus from your own community. When God seems to be raising up such a person, pray daily for him and often with him. Take whatever steps are needed to disciple and counsel him.

The Men. Every church needs spiritually strong men, active in the prayer and witness of the church. Every home needs a spiritually strong father to set the example and take the spiritual responsibility for the home. Too often this has to be done by wives and mothers. Your men need your prayer.

The Women. They have their special concerns and needs. They can be a tremendous spiritual strength to the church. Many wives carry a heavy burden for the salvation of their unsaved companions, and the pastor should help them by sharing this prayer burden.

The Singles. How our single people need our prayer these days! Do they hear you praying for them in your public prayer? Single parents need special prayer for their responsibilities and concerns.

Civic and Government Leaders. All Christians are commanded by Scripture to put priority on praying for government leaders (1 Tim. 2:1–3). We owe it to our government to pray for God to give wisdom, integrity, and right decisions to our rulers whether in nation, state, or city. Key government figures should be on the leader's daily prayer list, and he should regularly pray for them in his pulpit prayers and train his people to pray for them. But at times when crucial issues are facing the government it is right to schedule special times of personal and church prayer.

Revival and Harvest. God depends upon Christian leaders to call their people to prayer for revival and for a great harvest of souls, just as He depended on prophets to call the people in Old Testament times to prayer. The leader should frequently include this in his public prayers and in his requests at prayer meetings. Groups within the church may schedule special times of united prayer. The entire church may be led to spend half-nights in prayer (from six or seven in the evening till midnight), or nights of prayer (from 9 p.m. till 4 or 5 A.M.). All leaders must carry this burden.

To prepare your own heart for leading others in this hungering and seeking God's face, you need to set apart personal half-days or days of prayer, or a personal night of prayer, or a special hour or two daily for prayer for revival and harvest for a week, month, or even longer.

God greatly honors such preparation of the way of the Lord, though we must beware that we do not think we can earn God's blessing. The more we pray the deeper our heart hunger becomes until finally we prevail over the powers of darkness and see God's great victory.

2. *Set apart special prayer times for special burdens the Holy Spirit places upon your heart.* Not only may the Spirit guide you to set apart special times of prayer for revival or harvest, He may guide you to seek new special blessing on your own heart. Greatly used people of God have often found it necessary to get alone with Him for a longer time for a new anointing, new spiritual refreshing for their own soul, or God's special guidance concerning their ministry or their people. This was Finney's personal prayer habit.

A building project which needs funding may be God's call to a special half-day of prayer. Critical illness of a member of your church or group may call for special prolonged prayer. Keep a listening ear for the whispers of the Lord calling you to prayer or perhaps to prayer and fasting.

God may guide you as leader to take steps to multiply prayer for the needs He has put on your heart. You may be led to call your people to make a commitment of a given number of hours of prayer for a need—five hundred or a thousand hours of prayer for revival, or for a special evangelistic campaign. Almost anyone should be willing to pledge an hour of prayer, especially if you permit them to divide it into two half-hours or four fifteen-minute periods. Many may be willing to commit themselves to an hour a day, or five hours in a week, or some similar pledge.

Another approach is to ask people to commit themselves to as many ten-minute or fifteen-minute periods of special prayer as possible. By careful use of their time they may be able to find an extra ten minutes or more for this special, definitely focused prayer in the morning, at noon, and at night. The more times they stop their work and give God a love offering of intercession for the special need, the more God will be able to place the burden on their hearts, and the more their faith will begin to rise.

Spurgeon said, "If any minister can be satisfied without conversions, he shall have no conversions." We are too satisfied to carry on in our ministry with little or no outpourings of God's Spirit and with few regularly coming to the Lord. God gives souls only to those who cannot live without them. The leader who is not hungry for souls is in serious need of a revival in his own heart. But there is no limit to what God can do if we are hungry enough and take specific steps to enlist the prayer of God's people.

Chapter 35

Your Ministry of Tears

Yearning intercession for your people often enables God to anoint your heart with tears. Tears in your heart as you intercede alone, as you speak of Christ personally to the spiritually needy—inner tears as you minister publicly and as you look out upon your community and your world—these can add spiritual power to your leadership and ministry. Tears so deep in your heart that they are also noticed in your voice as you pray or speak, and noticeable in your eyes on special God-anointed occasions—these can add a whole dimension of unusual influence and spiritual authority to your role as a person of God.

How much do you know in your own life of a ministry of tears? How deeply have you shared the heartaches of God? Dr. Bob Pierce, founder of World Vision, was deeply moved by the physical and spiritual needs of the world. He was known for his oft-repeated statement: "Let my heart be broken with the things that break the heart of God."

Our world can be moved Godward only by leaders who have shared to a deep degree His heartbreak as He looks in compassion and love on the world. Until you sense the suffering tears in the heart of God, until you share to some extent our Savior's suffering passion in Gethsemane, until you come close enough to God to enable the Spirit to yearn within you with His infinite and unutterable yearning, you are not prepared to minister about the cross.

The shortest verse in the Bible is also one of the deepest in its terse expression of the reality of the Incarnation, the divine identification with sin-destroyed humankind in their need, and the measure of Christ's unending empathy: "Jesus wept" (John 11:35).

Jesus is supremely anointed with the oil of joy (Ps. 45:7; Heb. 1:9). Yet He so identified with the Father's will and the world's need that He became our Man of Sorrows, familiar with our suffering (Isa. 53:3). "Surely he took up our infirmities and carried our sorrows" (Isa. 53:4). The tears that were visible at the tomb of Lazarus were not mere tears of human sympathy. They were the external distillation of the heartbreak of God.

The lament of Jesus over Jerusalem during the third year of His ministry was not a momentary outcry. It was the abiding yearning of His all-consuming love. "O Jerusalem, Jerusalem ... how often I have longed to gather your children together, as a hen gathers her chicks under her wings" (Luke 13:34).

Ceaselessly He weeps as He looks out across our world. As He weeps over our cities and villages, our nations and races of people, our families and our suffering people from our children to our aged—how constantly He longs to save, bless, and deliver! The Jesus who wept is the Jesus who still weeps. Do you share His tears?

As a Christian leader you, too, know the joy inexpressible and glorious that comes from the heart of Christ to you (1 Peter 1:8). You, too, rejoice with heaven when sinners

238

repenting come back to the Father (Luke 15:7, 10). You know how to rejoice with those who rejoice (Rom. 12:15). Do you know also how to mourn with those who mourn?

While ministering in Manchester, England, forty years ago I wrote these words:

Where Are Your Tears?

There are tears in the sinner's eyes.
Habits of sin binding heart, hand, and feet;
Broken with shame at his sin and defeat,
Hot burning tears coursing down his hot cheek—
There are tears in the sinner's eyes.

There are tears in the suff'rer's eyes.
Long weary hours of disease, weakness, pain,
Praying that health be restored once again,
Waiting for healing, but waiting in vain—
There are tears in the suff'rer's eyes.

There are tears in discouraged eyes.
Misunderstood by the ones who should know;
No one to love, to compassion bestow,
Fainting, discouraged, with hope burning low—
There are tears in discouraged eyes.

There are tears in non-Christian eyes.
Calling to idols of wood and of stone,
Calling in vain, Christ and Savior unknown,
Comfortless, helpless, without God, alone—
There are tears in non-Christian eyes.

There are tears in the Savior's eyes.
Tears for those sinning, discouraged, and ill,
Tears for the straying ones, out of His will,
Tears for the millions unreached by us still—
There are tears in the Savior's eyes.

But where are the tears in your eyes?
Can you not weep with the millions who weep?
Have you no tears for the other lost sheep?
Jesus is weeping! Are you still asleep?
OH! WHERE ARE THE TEARS IN YOUR EYES?

MEN WHO SERVED THE LORD WITH TEARS

Paul testified to the Ephesian elders, as he looked back over his several years of ministry among them, and now bade them farewell, "You know how I lived the whole time I was with you, from the first day I came into the province of Asia. I served the Lord . . . with tears" (Acts 20:18–19).

Any tear shed in sharing the heartbeat of God, any tear shed through Christlike loving empathy with our fellowmen, any tear born of the yearning constraint of the Holy Spirit is a tear by which we serve the Lord. Nothing pleases Christ more than for us to share with Him His burden for the world and its people. Nothing so weds us to the heart of Christ as our tears shed as we intercede for lost ones with Him. Then truly we become people after God's own heart. Then we begin to know what it is to be Christ's prayer partners.

There were those in Old Testament times who served the Lord with tears:

Job. Job was able to testify, "Have I not wept for those in trouble? Has not my soul grieved for the poor?" (Job 30:25).

David. David wept and fasted when men insulted God (Ps. 69:9–10). When his enemies were ill, he fasted and mourned as if for his brother and wept as if for his own mother (Ps. 35:14).

Isaiah. Isaiah, echoing the heart cry of God, wept when enemy Moab suffered in drought and famine; his eyes flooded with tears (Isa. 16:9, 11).

Josiah. God heard Josiah's prayer for the nation as he fasted and wept before God for his people (2 Kings 22:19).

Ezra. When Ezra realized how deeply his people had sinned and brought the judgment of God upon themselves, he so prayed and wept before God that a large crowd of men, women, and children gathered around him (Ezra 10:1–2). This is ever the pattern. A weeping leader results in a weeping, praying people. A leader who takes on himself the sins of the people, praying and repenting vicariously for them, will have a people who are led to repentance. A dry-eyed leader with a heart not really broken, who knows no

240

tears in his heart, may denounce the sins of the people, but seldom leads them to the confession of sin that brings God's mercy.

Nehemiah. When Nehemiah heard of the tragic condition of Jerusalem and his people, he recorded, "I sat down and wept. For some days I mourned and fasted and prayed before the God of heaven" (Neh. 1:4). For days he kept praying and fasting as he served the Lord with his tears. Thus God was able to use Nehemiah to bring revival to Jerusalem.

Jeremiah. Jeremiah is often called "the weeping prophet." What an example he set of burden-bearing and brokenness for his people! No doubt from the human standpoint it was the prayers and tears of Jeremiah and the vicarious prayers and tears of Daniel that brought a portion of Israel back from captivity. Listen to Jeremiah:

> Since my people are crushed, I am crushed; I mourn, and horror grips me. Is there no balm in Gilead? Is there no physician there? . . . . Oh, that my head were a spring of water and my eyes a fountain of tears! I would weep day and night for the slain of my people (Jer. 8:21–9:1).
>
> If you do not listen, I will weep in secret because of your pride; my eyes will weep bitterly, overflowing with tears, because the LORD's flock will be taken captive (Jer. 13:17).
>
> Let my eyes overflow with tears night and day without ceasing (Jer. 14:17).

See also Lamentations 1:16; 2:11; 3:48–51.

Daniel. For more than sixty years Daniel was a statesman in the court of the dominant world power of his time; he was also a man of God and a man of prayer. We read of some of his prayer times:

> I turned to the LORD God and pleaded with him in prayer and petition, in fasting, and in sackcloth and ashes. I prayed to the LORD my God and confessed . . . While I was speaking and praying, confessing my sin and the sin of my people Israel and making my request to the LORD my God for his holy hill—while I was still in prayer (Dan. 9:3–4, 20–21).

At that time I, Daniel, mourned for three weeks. I ate no choice food; no meat or wine touched my lips; and I used no lotions at all until the three weeks were over (Dan. 10:2–3).

From what we know of Jewish mourning and Daniel's vicarious burden and confession, we can be sure the mourning included his weeping.

Paul. Paul was both the Isaiah and the Jeremiah of the New Testament. He preached the greatness of God's grace, the amazing blessedness of the atonement, and the judgment and final triumph of Christ. He also went among the people pleading, weeping, and leading the lost to salvation.

He served the Lord with his tears as well as his sufferings (Acts 20:18–19), and that ministry was given both publicly and house to house (v. 20). He testified, "For three years I never stopped warning each of you night and day with tears" (v. 31). Not only did he preach with tears and do his personal evangelism with tears, he also wrote with tears to the churches he loved so dearly: "I wrote you out of great distress and anguish of heart and with many tears . . . to let you know the depth of my love for you" (2 Cor. 2:4).

We can also be sure that his praying was anointed with his constant tears. Repeatedly in his letters to the churches, he tells how he prays for them night and day. If all his other ministry was made fruitful by his tears, we can be sure his praying was also. There is no more mighty praying than that from a heart which longs so deeply that it pours forth its pleadings with tears.

Our Lord. Of Jesus we read, "During the days of Jesus' life on earth he offered up prayers and petitions with loud cries and tears" (Heb. 5:7). Undoubtedly this included Jesus' prayer in Gethsemane. The words, however, seem to imply that this was a characteristic often repeated.

While the crowds were shouting their "Hosannas" in praise of God, we learn that "as he approached Jerusalem and saw the city, he wept over it" (Luke 19:41). No doubt His breaking heart was convulsed with His tears of agonizing love. Probably He wept similarly when He called out, "O

Jerusalem, Jerusalem," as He expressed His longing, heart-broken love (Matt. 23:37; Luke 13:34).

GOD DESIRES THAT WE LEADERS WEEP

God spoke through Joel at a time of His imminent judgment upon the nation because of its sins: "Let the priests, who minister before the LORD, weep between the temple porch and the altar. Let them say, 'Spare your people, O LORD' ". (Joel 2:17). The religious leaders of the nation were responsible to intercede with weeping for the nation.

Similarly Isaiah, at a time of national calamity, said to the leaders, "The Lord, the LORD Almighty, called you on that day to weep and to wail . . . to . . . put on sackcloth" (Isa. 22:12). But instead they feasted and enjoyed themselves in revelry (v. 13). So guilty did this make them that Isaiah adds, "The LORD Almighty has revealed this in my hearing: 'Till your dying day this sin will not be atoned for,' says the Lord, the LORD Almighty" (v. 14).

When those who should bear the spiritual burden for a people by mighty intercession and tears are so indifferent spiritually that they sense no prayer burden and take it easy and enjoy themselves, carrying on their leadership with an attitude of "business as usual"—this is scandalous in the sight of God.

What was Samuel's attitude as God's appointed judge and prophet for the people? "As for me, far be it from me that I should sin against the LORD by failing to pray for you" (1 Sam. 12:23). Every leader is responsible to God to fulfill a mediatorial role for His people. Christ is the only Mediator between God and man in redemption. But because of that mediation we are now responsible to be the intercessor-mediators for our people. We must so identify with those we lead, both by love and by commitment, that we carry them on our hearts every day of our leadership. Even as the high priest did symbolically, we must do this day by day as we enter God's holiest; we must touch His throne constantly for our people. We sin against the Lord if we fail to do so.

When that commitment to our people is as deep as God wants it to be, when we love them with a Christlike love as Christ's under-shepherds, a mediatorial intercessory role is inescapable. The more we mediate in intercession of our people, the deeper our love becomes and the more certain it is that our hearts will be crying out to God in tears, whether they are visible or not. Our people will recognize the love and tears of our hearts by the tone of our voices and the power upon our prayers.

Dr. R.W. Dale of Birmingham, England, co-worker of Moody while he was campaigning in the British Isles, said that Moody never spoke of the possibility of one being lost without tears in his voice. "He turned from fiery denunciation of sin into quiet, plaintive, tearful, heart-broken constraint." R.C. Horner said, "There is nothing that tells so much as the tears in Christian work . . . but when your tears are dried up, the people may perish and die and go to hell around you and you don't seem to know it."

Oswald J. Smith wrote in his diary, "I must experience God's power no matter what it costs. Oh, that He would break me down and cause me to weep for the salvation of souls!"[1] Many places in his diary record answers to his prayer for tears. Of John Welch, son-in-law of John Knox, it is written that he "often in the coldest winter nights was found weeping on the ground and wrestling with the Lord on account of his people." Jonathan Edwards knew the deep soul hunger that added tears to his prayer time. Finney, in his memoirs, repeatedly mentions praying with tears.

Spiritual harvest demands wholeness of soul, intensity of desire, and Christlike love. Spiritual harvest results from costly sowing, sowing with a love that weeps as it cries out to God. Gethsemane travail of soul leads to Pentecost harvest.

Said John Henry Jowett in his classic *The Passion for Souls:*

> My brethren, I do not know how any Christian service is to be fruitful if the servant is not primarily baptized in the spirit of suffering compassion. We can never heal the needs we do not feel. Tearless hearts can never be the heralds of the Passion. We

must pray if we would redeem. We must bleed if we would be the ministers of the saving blood. We must perfect by our passion the Passion of the Lord, and by our own suffering sympathies we must "fill up that which is behind in the suffering of Christ." "Put on, therefore, as God's elect, a heart of compassion" . . . If the prayer of the disciple is to "fill up" the intercession of the Master, the disciple's prayer must be stricken with much crying and tears. The ministers of Calvary must supplicate in bloody sweat, and their intercession must often touch the point of agony . . . . True intercession is a sacrifice, a bleeding sacrifice, a perpetuation of Calvary, a "filling up" of the sufferings of Christ. St. Catherine told a friend that the anguish which she experienced, in the realization of the sufferings of Christ, was greatest at the moment when she was pleading for the salvation of others. "Promise me, dear Lord, that Thou wilt save them. O give me a token that Thou wilt." Then her Lord seemed to clasp her outstretched hand in His, and to give her the promise and she felt a piercing pain as though a nail had been driven through the palm . . . She felt the grasp of the pierced hand."[2]

George Whitefield was one of the most eloquent evangelists in the history of the church. He often preached to crowds of up to ten and even twenty thousand. Once in Scotland it is estimated that he preached to 100,000. Ten thousand professed conversion in that one service. He was mightily anointed by the Holy Spirit. Dr. Martyn Lloyd-Jones records that Whitefield almost invariably preached with tears streaming down his cheeks. He was moved so greatly and deeply that he moved thousands to Christ.[3] He said, "Whole days and weeks have I spent prostrate on the ground in . . . prayer."[4]

It takes more than tears to win souls. I am not referring to carnal tears of self-pity. I plead for Christlike tears of love for our people and for the lost convulsing our hearts in mediatorial intercession. Whether or not you have tears visible in your eyes, at least your heart should weep. God always knows how deep our longing and our heart cries are. He measures the depth of our loving concern and the compassionate brokenness of our intercession for others. Do not seek emotion for emotion's sake. Do not try to work up emotion in an attempt to move God or man. Yet emotion is an inseparable part of our being. We cannot separate emotion from holy love for God or people. Our primary place of weeping should be our secret place of prayer, for that is where we should be daily interceding for our people (Jer. 13:17).

How can we be so unmoved by the story of the cross if we have really understood how our Savior loved us and died for us? How can we be so dry-eyed as we intercede for a lost world, and as we preach the gospel of Calvary? A missionary was telling the love of Christ to an unsaved pagan, how Christ left the glories of heaven, shared our life, our sufferings, but was rejected and crucified by sinful men. As the pagan listened to the story of the cross he began to weep. Then he turned to the missionary and asked, "Did this same Jesus die for you?" "Yes," replied the missionary. The pagan looked at him in amazement and asked, "Then why don't you cry?" Pardon me if I ask you, "Why don't you?"

Wanted: More brokenhearted leaders like Hosea, crying to God for the sins and failures of their people! Wanted: More heartbroken prophet-leaders like Jeremiah, prevailing for their people! Wanted: More flaming-hearted Pauline evangelists and leaders, weeping as they plead for their people, as they plead with them, as they proclaim Calvary love!

Give Me Tears

Give me tears in my eyes, loving Lord, I pray!
Give me tears when I intercede.
Give me tears when I kneel at Your throne each day;
Give me tears when I learn to plead.

Piercèd Lord, break this cold, stony heart of mine;
Melt my heart with Your holy fire!
Flood my soul with the passion of love divine;
May I hunger with Your desire.

Take the callousness all from my heart again
Till I hunger and thirst and yearn,
Till the longings for souls of sin-ruined men
All-consuming within me burn.

Your Ministry of Tears

Fill my heart with your tears; there unveil Your cross
Till all else of this world has died,
Till all else in my life I shall count but loss,
Save the cross of the Crucified.

May my heart be a crucified heart alway
That it bleed for the souls of men.
May the burden for souls melt my soul each day
Till I share Your travail again.

Give me tears when I preach of Your dying love;
Give me tears when I plead with men.
Give me tears as I point to Your throne above;
Love of God, melt my heart again.

Wesley Duewel

YOUR ANOINTING AND INTEGRITY

Chapter 36

You Can Be an Anointed Leader

In Old Testament days kings, prophets, and priests were anointed with oil to set them apart in a special sense for God and His service. The oil symbolized the Holy Spirit coming upon them both to set them apart and also to give them special divine enablement.

The word *Christ* is the counterpart Greek term for the Hebrew "messiah." Both words mean "anointed one." "God anointed Jesus of Nazareth with the Holy Spirit and power, and . . . he went around doing good and healing all who were under the power of the devil, because God was with him" (Acts 10:38). The term *Christian* identifies us as followers of Jesus Christ, the Anointed One.

Scripture applies the term "anointing" to all who belong to Christ. We are not only following the Anointed One; we are ourselves anointed. Every Christian, whether lay or ordained, has the scriptural privilege to appropriate the spiritual content of the term for himself. God wants every Christian to live an anointed life.

J. Elder Cumming writes:

> The anointing is the Holy Ghost Himself . . . He comes to be the anointing oil upon us and within us. Jesus of Nazareth was anointed—not by Him, but with Him. . .
>
> How striking, then, is the thought that we are the anointed ones of God! Messiahs of the new dispensation! Christs of God! "Ye have an anointing"; the same anointing as the Lord had. And we bear it in our names, as He did. He was called Christ, and we are called Christians. The anointed followers of the Anointed One.[1]
>
> He anointed us, set his seal of ownership on us, and put his Spirit in our hearts as a deposit, guaranteeing what is to come (2 Cor. 1:21–22).
>
> He that anointed us is God (2 Cor. 12:1).
>
> You have an anointing from the Holy One (1 John 2:20).
>
> The anointing you received from him remains in you, and you do not need anyone to teach you. But as his anointing teaches you about all things and as that anointing is real, not counterfeit—just as it has taught you, remain in him (1 John 2:27).

If you lack the realization and benefits of the Spirit's anointing you are living a subnormal, spiritually deprived life. You are living below your privilege as a Christian. No Christian has the right to lower the average level of church life by living an unanointed life. Certainly no Christian leader dare demean and debase Christ's cause or Christian leadership by living an unanointed life and exhibiting an unanointed leadership.

THE ANOINTING IS FOR YOU

When the Holy Spirit gives you new birth, you receive His abiding presence. "If anyone does not have the Spirit of Christ, he does not belong to Christ" (Rom. 8:9). The Spirit witnesses to your salvation (Rom. 8:16; 1 John 5:6, 10). But you also have the Spirit's ministry in many other ways. One of these ways is His anointing of your life and service.

The degree to which any Christian receives this anointing and is conscious of it depends on the closeness of his walk with the Lord and the extent to which, by faith, he appropriates it. It already remains in Him, but may not be powerfully active. As in all of Christian experience, faith is the appropriating means.

You as a leader have been chosen by God and His people to lead your fellow-believers. You are, in a special sense, set apart to represent Christ, the Anointed One. You need a special and discernible anointing properly to represent Christ and bring glory to Him. You are a marked person. Of all people, you can bring honor or dishonor to Christ. Of all people, you are to be Christlike and anointed in your life.

You must also be anointed in your leadership. Since Christ has provided the anointing for you by His grace, He expects you to be constantly anointed by the Spirit in all aspects of your leadership role. Your responsibility as His leader for His people is so great that you dare not function without constant experience and repeated renewals of His anointing upon you. You are also responsible to your people. They look to you above all else as their spiritual leader. You owe it to them to keep anointed for your responsibilities by repeated new touches of the Spirit of God.

The anointing of the Spirit, in the words of Bounds, "is heaven's knighthood given to the chosen true and brave ones who have sought this anointed honor though many an hour of tearful, wrestling prayer." He terms it the "one divine enablement" by which a leader of Christ's people is equipped for his leadership. Without it, he says, "there are no true spiritual results accomplished."

God has provided divine enabling for you. Scripture gives repeated examples of His leaders receiving this special equipping. This is the age of the fullness of the Spirit. Any lack of the Spirit's role in your leadership is not due to God's unwillingness. God longs to make you all that you can be by His grace, a leader clothed, anointed, guided, and empowered by the Holy Spirit. He longs to make you a far more effective leader of His people than you have ever dreamed possible. By His special touch, He can draw out the outstandingly important potential that He sees within you. His anointing in all its fullness is for you.

I quote Bounds again: "The unction, the divine unction, this heavenly anointing is what the pulpit needs and must have. This divine and heavenly oil put on it by the imposition of God's hand must soften and lubricate the whole man— heart, head, spirit—until it separates him with a mighty separation from all earthly, secular, worldly, selfish motives and aims, separating him to everything that is pure and Godlike."

THE OLD TESTAMENT SIGNIFICANCE

The prophets (1 Kings 19:16), priests (Ex. 28:41), and kings (1 Sam. 10:1), set apart by anointing in the Old Testament period, were considered "God's anointed." The thought of anointing was closely associated with consecration. By the act of anointing they were consecrated (Ex. 28:41; 30:30; Lev. 8:12), i.e., set apart for God's purpose and use. It was also an act of appointment or ordination (Lev. 21:10). The symbolic pouring of oil in some profusion ("poured" is often used) indicated God's abundant endowment and enablement by the outpouring of the Holy Spirit. David points out that in the anointing of Aaron, the high priest, the precious oil was poured on his head so abundantly that it ran down on his beard and even on the collar of his garments (Ps. 133:2).

Anointing was always for a sacred purpose and done on behalf of God, indicating God's favor. It sealed visibly the special endowment of the Holy Spirit for the responsibilities of the office and conferred the divine enablement needed for the service. It made a significant difference in the one anointed (1 Sam. 10:6, 9–10). Of David's anointing we read, "From that day on the Spirit of the LORD came upon David in power" (1 Sam. 16:13). Anointing in the will of God meant an induction into a continuing experience of the outpouring of the Spirit to empower for sacred responsibility

THE ANOINTING IS KNOWABLE

A number of Bible terms and descriptive phrases point out God's special enabling through the Holy Spirit. Among these are the following: "the Spirit of the Lord came upon," "the hand of the Lord came upon," "the power of the Lord came upon," and the "anointing" of the Spirit. Each of these adds to the fullness of our understanding of the important enabling ministry of the Spirit. In a sense, perhaps all could be considered as aspects of the Spirit's anointing.

Every Spirit-filled leader is one of God's anointed, and he experiences aspects of the anointing in his leadership. But many place so little emphasis upon God's anointing, express so little desire for it in their praying, and exercise so little faith for its appropriation that they experience only occasionally and minimally the dynamic difference that the anointing of the Spirit can make in ministry.

Dr. Martyn Lloyd-Jones emphasized the necessity of the Spirit's anointing. He called it the greatest essential in connection with preaching. He insisted, "Careful preparation, and the unction of the Holy Spirit, must never be regarded as alternatives, but as complementary to each other .... Do you always look for and seek this unction, this anointing before preaching? Has this been your greatest concern? There is no more thorough and revealing test to apply to a preacher."[2]

Are you one who has been all too casual about the Spirit's anointing? Has it been largely a nominal experience on your part? Would you have to confess that you neither expect nor depend on any significant difference in your ministry through God's supernatural endowment? Don't measure God's hand upon you in your tomorrows on the basis of your past. God wants to give you a new dimension of His divine enabling so that you can have an ever more effective and God-glorifying leadership. May you more fully than ever become "the Lord's anointed!"

God's anointing is real and knowable. Usually the one anointed can recognize it; often other spiritually discerning people recognize the difference. One day I asked Dr. Ezra Devol, missionary medical superintendent of a hospital in India, "Ezra, is there such a thing as the anointing of the Spirit in surgery?" His instant reply was, "You bet there is, and I know when I have it and when I don't have it!"

Jesus was supremely aware of the Spirit's anointing. He said, "The Spirit of the Lord is on me, because he has anointed me" (Luke 4:18). David knew it (2 Sam. 23:2). Ezekiel testified to it repeatedly. Ezra (Ezra 7:6) and Nehemiah (Neh. 2:18) knew when the hand of the Lord was on them. Paul knew it in his experience (2 Cor. 1:21–22). You can know it too.

Chapter 37

God's Anointing Confers Blessings

Anointing is the divine enabling for activity and ministry done in Christ's name and for Christ's glory. It rests upon the life and ministry and specially crowns and blesses Christian ministry. But it is not reserved exclusively for so-called "spiritual" activities. It is God's extra touch upon your mind, skill, effort, memory, emotions, and strength.

Anointing will aid the mechanic to determine problems and solve them, a student taking examinations, an author as he writes, the Christian as he speaks or teaches, the cabbie negotiating traffic, the musician in his playing, the singer in his singing, the artist in his painting, and the poet in his writing.

The anointing of the Spirit is for Christian living, but specially for Christian service in whatever form. It is yours for the asking. It is God's gracious provision for you. Let me first describe how the anointing affects your living, and then its great effect on your ministry.

1. *The Spirit's anointing helps you physically.* He can anoint your body so that you are physically strong, refreshed, and adequate for your task. The Spirit is available to help you be at your best. Do you need extra strength? The Spirit is available.

Do you remember how in the spiritual conflict on Mt. Carmel Elijah, seemingly alone, faced the 450 prophets of Baal and the 400 prophets of the Asherah who ate at Jezebel's table? When their deception was proved, Elijah slew them as God had commanded for false prophets in Old Testament days. Then came Elijah's prolonged prayer battle on the summit of Mt. Carmel with seven periods of strenuous intercession until God sent the first cloud to the sky. Before night ended he had run thirty miles ahead of King Ahab to Jezreel (1 Kings 18). Where did Elijah get that amazing strength? From the anointing of the Spirit (v. 46).

Remember Isaiah 40:29–31. "He gives strength to the weary and increases the power of the weak. Even youths grow tired and weary, and young men stumble and fall; but those who hope in the LORD will renew their strength. They will soar on wings like eagles; they will run and not grow weary, they will walk and not be faint." Francis Asbury testified in his journal for February 24, 1772, "My labours increase, and my strength is renewed. Though I came here weak, yet after preaching three times I felt myself strong."[1]

Prayer, trust, and waiting on the Lord remove weariness, and renew physical and spiritual power no matter how weak you are in yourself. Many a minister of the gospel has experienced freshness of body and a special sense of God's blessing and presence on the service and particularly upon the ministry of the hour.

How well I remember a busy day of ministry in Monaghan, Eire. One Sunday morning we drove from Belfast, Northern Ireland, to County Armagh and across the border into Eire to Monaghan. I preached in the morning service in the Presbyterian church, had lunch with the Presbyterian minister, was taken to the home of relatives of our OMS British home director, and shown the family agricultural plant. Then came visiting with the family and very little time to get alone for prayer and quiet. In the early evening I spoke at a Methodist church, and immediately after was taken to a Baptist church for my final message of the day before we drove back to Belfast.

As I sat behind the pulpit in the last service of the day I felt weary, emotionally exhausted, and spiritually empty and dry. As the service began I bowed my head in my hands and prayed, "O Lord, you have been so gracious with me and used me today. But now I feel so empty and dry. I have many things I could say, but how do I know what You want me to say to these people? I am like the man whose friend came at midnight who had nothing to set before him. O Lord, I have nothing fresh to give to these people. You have anointed me today. I bow my head for You to place Your hand upon me again. I need a new anointing."

As I raised my head I saw, to my surprise, a godly Irish farmer, his wife, and daughter from Armagh enter the church and take their seats in the well-filled building. I was amazed that they had driven there and were in the service. I looked at them, and they smiled and nodded.

As I stepped behind the pulpit, a fresh anointing came upon me from heaven. Instantly my weariness was gone, I was refreshed and alert, my thoughts began to flow rapidly, and from the first words I sensed the anointing of the Lord upon me. I gave a missionary challenge and plea for prayer for India. God came mightily and took charge of the service.

Just before the benediction the pastor said to the people, "This is not an ordinary service. God has spoken to us tonight. I do not want you to leave this service in the ordinary way. Don't speak to one another. Go silently to the door. I will have Brother Duewel stand at the door. If you are going to pray for him and his ministry in India, just grip his hand as you go out the door. Don't say a word to others. Go home, get down on your knees beside your bed, and ask God what He would have you do."

259

As I stood by the door, person after person had tears in his eyes as he gripped my hand. Then came the Mulligans. Mr. Mulligan squeezed my hand so forcefully that I almost winced. The daughter, Bertha, about twenty, barely touched my hand and almost ran out to the car. Mrs. Mulligan gripped my hand, looked with tears into my eyes, and said, "I'll just say this. Our family spent the entire afternoon on our knees praying for you and for this service!" Then I understood the gracious anointing!

Later I found that they drove all the way back to their farm in Northern Ireland without saying one word. When they reached home, Bertha ran upstairs to her room and did not come down till late the next morning. When she appeared, she said, "Daddy, Mama, last night Jesus called me to be a missionary." She later enrolled in Bible college, married a young Methodist minister, and they served some years in the West Indies. They now pastor a church in Ulster.

That family's obedience to God in prayer had brought God's special anointing on me anew and on that missionary service, and brought their daughter into missionary service. Included in that anointing were God's physical, emotional, and spiritual touches.

2. *The Spirit's anointing enables you mentally.* The Holy Spirit can add alertness, aptness of expression, creativity, and the ability to say with unusual clarity what God wants said. Jesus promised that the Holy Spirit would bring to your remembrance the things He had told them (John 14:26). This special enablement of memory was not reserved for the apostles and the writers of Scripture. It is available to everyone who ministers in Christ's name to bring Scripture passages, the exact words needed, expressions, and illustrations to your memory even while you are on your feet speaking or while you are writing. It is God's special touch on your mind for your ministry.

Bounds, in trying to describe how the Spirit's anointing benefits one mentally, said, "It clarifies the intellect, gives insight and grasp, freedom and fullness of thought, and directness and simplicity in expression."

3. *The Spirit's anointing touches your emotions.* The Spirit can so pour God's love into your heart and mind (Rom. 5:5) that you are given a special tenderness as you seek to express the love, comfort, and heart of God reaching out to the unsaved, the hurting, and those who grieve. The Spirit can give you a ministry of tears when God sees it will add effectiveness to your pleas in His name (Acts 20:31; 2 Cor. 2:4; Phil. 3:18). This anointing with tears is available not only for your messages, personal evangelism, counseling, and writing as Paul experienced it, but it can add special strength, intensity, tenderness, and power to your ministry of intercession, especially in your private intercession (Rom. 9:1–3; 10:1).

The Spirit, on the other hand, can add special firmness, solemnity, holy boldness, or righteous indignation when you as a prophet of the Lord preach against sin. "But as for me, I am filled with power, with the Spirit of the LORD, and with justice and might, to declare to Jacob his transgression, to Israel his sin" (Mic. 3:8).

Isaiah shows that the Spirit of the Lord can anoint you to proclaim God's judgment and vengeance as well as God's comfort (Isa. 61:1–2). It was such an anointing that enabled Old Testament prophets to thunder the justice, holy anger, and judgment of God against sin. Any minister who preaches only the blessings and beauty of God's grace and love and never proclaims the holiness, justice, and anger of God against sin and injustice is neither fully biblical nor fully anointed.

Jeremiah, "the Weeping Prophet," clearly presented God's alternative when God's mercy was refused (Jer. 4:4). The Spirit's anointing then made him "a fortified city, an iron pillar and a bronze wall to stand against the whole land— against the kings of Judah, its officials, its priests and the people of the land" (Jer. 1:18). He could say, "I am full of the wrath of the LORD, and I cannot hold it in" (Jer. 6:11).

Such an anointing was on Peter when he faced the Jerusalem crowd (Acts 2:23–24) and the sullen and angry Sanhedrin (Acts 4:8–12). Paul stated the balance between the two types of ministry clearly: "Consider therefore the kindness and sternness of God" (Rom. 11:22).

4. *The Spirit's anointing enables you spiritually.* While the anointing of the Spirit provides God's special enabling for you physically, mentally, and emotionally, its greatest significance in your ministry is spiritual. Among the blessings involved are these:

a. *It makes you aware of God's presence with you and His touch upon you.* What a blessedness when you realize, like Jacob, "Surely, the Lord is in this place" (Gen. 28:16). He added, "How awesome" (v. 17). There comes sacred awe upon you as you realize that in spite of your humanness and unworthiness God's hand is upon you and using your words and ministry.

When God met Moses at Sinai at the burning bush, Moses said to Him, "Who am I?" He felt so unable and unworthy for God to use him. When God revealed to David all that He planned to do for him and his family, David exclaimed, "Who am I, O Sovereign Lord . . . that you have brought me this far?" (2 Sam. 7:18). Then David began to worship God for His greatness (vv. 22–29).

Many a minister or writer, as God's anointing has come upon him during the preparation of messages, has gone to his knees and lifted his eyes to the Lord and called out, "Who am I, O Lord, that I should speak this message for You?" Almost instantly, I have found, comes the additional prayer, "O Lord, help me to tell this, to share it as I should! Help me to express it—it is so overwhelmingly beyond what I can say or express!" Thank God for the anointing of His Spirit!

Often you will be strongly aware of God's hand upon you as He specially uses you during your message, teaching, counseling, personal evangelism, or writing. After you finish you will long to get alone with Him to fall upon your knees or face before Him, thanking Him for so graciously using you, giving Him all the glory, and then joining the seraphim in worshiping: "Holy, holy, holy is the Lord Almighty; the whole earth is full of his glory" (Isa. 6:3); "You are worthy, our Lord and God, to receive glory and honor and power"

(Rev. 4:11); "Worthy is the Lamb, who was slain, to receive power and wealth and wisdom and strength and honor and glory and praise!" (Rev. 5:12).

b. *It gives you fragrance of Christian character.* God prescribed a special fragrant holy anointing oil for the high priest and the lower order of priests (Ex. 30:22–33). They and their clothing were to be anointed with it before their priestly duties. They carried with them this holy fragrance. Christ our High Priest is the holy fragrant One. Christlikeness, the sweet fruit of the Spirit in our lives, makes us fragrant with the holiness of Christ's character.

The fruit of the Spirit is a collective noun in singular form suggesting the many-sided yet interrelated qualities of the life of Christ. It is not a "work" resulting from our own effort or self-discipline. It is primarily a fruit of the Spirit's working. It is the nature of Christ reproduced in us.

It is described in the ninefold graces of the Spirit which the Holy Spirit produces within us (Gal. 5:22–23). The fruit is developed as we live by the Spirit (Gal. 5:16, 25), having crucified the sinful nature (v. 24), and then sow to the Spirit (Gal. 6:7–8). Although the origin is in God, we have a Christian responsibility to make every effort to grow in these aspects of mature Christlikeness (2 Peter 1:5–8). It is the harvest of the Spirit in our personal life. It is increased as we walk closely with God (Eph. 4:1–3; 5:15–20; Col. 1:10), remain in Christ (John 15:4–5), obey God (Rom. 6:13, 19, 22; 12:1–2; 1 Peter 1:22), walk in the Spirit (Rom. 8:4–5, 13), respond to the discipline and pruning of the Spirit (John 15:2), and commune with Christ (1 John 1:7). It is the loveliness of Jesus making us beautifully and fragrantly Christlike. It marks us as a person of God.

c. *It gives you joy.* It was said of Jesus, "God, your God, has set you above your companions by anointing you with the oil of joy" (Heb. 1:9). The passage from Isaiah from which Jesus quoted when He spoke of His anointing by the Spirit (Isa. 61) is messianic prophecy where, in verse three, He tells that the Spirit is also anointing Him to give to others "the oil of gladness."

Jesus was a joyous Savior as well as the Man of Sorrows. He entered into our joys and He wants us to rejoice. The first fruit of the Spirit is love and the next is joy (Gal. 5:22). David, after speaking of the Lord his Shepherd, said, "You anoint my head with oil." Then he added, "My cup overflows" (Ps. 23:5).

The anointing of the Spirit gives spiritual refreshing. Times of refreshing were promised following Pentecost (Acts 3:19). The Spirit gives new freshness, new variety, new adequacy. He gives joy and freshness to the prayers we pray, the worship and meditation we share, and to all aspects of our ministry. He gives us new promises, shows us new depths in the Word, and gives us new assurances of His love. He is creative, original, and makes all things new.

The Holy Spirit is the Spirit of joy, and when He fills us with Himself He fills us with an inner joy which Peter calls inexpressible and glorious (1 Peter 1:8). One of the rivers of the Spirit is certainly joy (John 7:38–39). It causes us to rejoice even in the midst of the sorrows we must share (2 Cor. 6:10). Any leader who would attract others must be basically a person anointed with joy supplied by the Spirit.

Dr. Martyn Lloyd-Jones wrote, "This 'unction,' this 'anointing,' is the supreme thing. Seek it until you have it; be content with nothing less. Go on until you can say, 'And my speech and my preaching was not with enticing words of man's wisdom, but in demonstration of the Spirit and of power.' He is still able to do 'exceeding abundantly above all that we can ask or think.' "[2]

Chapter 38

You Can Be Anointed
for Service

The Holy Spirit is given you to anoint you for effective living and for effective service. These can be real, and they are interrelated.

1. *The anointing gives you liberty and skill.* The Spirit's anointing frees from any kind of fear—fear of failure, of the future, and of your overwhelming task. He frees from fear of Satan and of people, which is always a snare (Prov. 29:25). He gives strong confidence in God, His Word, and in His wisdom and power.

As He touches and anoints, giving added skill and guidance, we begin to realize that our task is really more His responsibility than ours. The church is His church, the cause is His cause, the name that must be exalted is the name of Jesus. The Spirit enables us to cast our anxiety on God

(1 Peter 5:7), and depend on God for all we need to make our ministry effective.

As we prove the Spirit's faithfulness and power, our ministry becomes in a new and wonderful sense not only a solemn duty but a holy joy. We begin to anticipate with eagerness how He will help us in the next aspect of His work. This frees us to be at our best and to receive His best. The anointing thus brings out our natural skills and God's gifts in us, and adds to them His supernatural "extra"—extra blessing, extra wisdom, extra power. He teaches us the "immeasurably more" than He is able to do with our efforts (Eph. 3:20).

2. *The anointing illumines God's Word.* The anointing of the Spirit may bring special illumination upon the Scripture both while you prepare and while your are speaking, teaching, or explaining Scripture.

Finney tells us, "I almost always get my subjects on my knees in prayer; and it has been a common experience with me, upon receiving a subject from the Holy Spirit, to have it make so strong an impression on my mind as to make me tremble, so that I could with difficulty write. When subjects are thus given me that seem to go through me, body and soul, I can in a few moments make out an outline that enables me to retain the view presented by the Spirit. I find that such sermons always tell with great power upon the people."[1]

Jesus loved to illumine the minds and understanding of the Scriptures as He taught His disciples. After Jesus revealed Himself to Cleopas and his companion at Emmaus, they said, "Were not our hearts burning within us while he talked with us on the road and opened the Scriptures to us?" (Luke 24:32). An hour or so later when Jesus met the disciple group in the Upper Room we again read, "Then he opened their minds so they could understand the Scriptures" (Luke 24:45). Today Jesus opens His Word to you through the Holy Spirit.

Jesus promised concerning the Spirit, "He will bring glory to me by taking from what is mine and making it known to you. All that belongs to the Father is mine. That is why I said the Spirit will take from what is mine and make it known to you" (John 16:14–15). He also said, "He will guide you into all truth" (v. 13). The Spirit answers the prayer, "Open my eyes that I may see wonderful things in your law" (Ps. 119:18). He shows us that beautiful unity of Scripture and how one verse shines light on another. He inspired the Scripture originally, so He is the One now to help us understand its depths. There are whole dimensions of meaning that we will miss unless He illumines us.

"Oh, the depth of the riches of the wisdom and knowledge of God! How unsearchable his judgments, and his paths beyond tracing out! Who has known the mind of the Lord?" (Rom. 11:33–34). Who but the Spirit! What deep things of God the Spirit wants to reveal to us here and now! " 'No eye has seen, no ear has heard, no mind has conceived what God has prepared for those who love him'—but God has revealed it to us by his Spirit. The Spirit searches all things, even the deep things of God. . . . We have . . . received . . . the Spirit who is from God, that we may understand what God has freely given us" (1 Cor. 2:9–10, 12).

He is the One to help us experience the sweetness of God's Word. "How sweet are your words to my taste, sweeter than honey to my mouth!" (Ps. 119:103) "They are sweeter than honey, than honey from the comb" (Ps. 19:10). He brings holy thrill to our hearts as He blesses us with wonderful truths.

The Holy Spirit guides us in how to apply the Word to our own hearts and to the needs of others. This is the aspect of His ministry that strikes home like the blows of a hammer (Jer. 23:29), that effectively pierces the heart like a sword, and penetrates the thinking of the hearer (Heb. 4:12). This also makes the encouragement of the Scriptures blessedly real (Rom. 15:4).

3. *The anointing teaches*. The teaching ministry of the Spirit as He anoints is closely related to His illumination. "The anointing you received from him remains in you, and you do not need anyone to teach you. But as his anointing teaches you about all things and as that anointing is real, not

counterfeit—just as it has taught you, remain in him" (1 John 2:27).

Jesus is your great Teacher. He was called Master, i.e., Teacher, during His earthly ministry. His teaching included interpretation of Scripture, impartation of new truth, application of Scripture to the daily lives and ministry of the disciples, and practical instructions for their ministry.

The Holy Spirit was sent to continue the teaching ministry of Jesus (John 16:12–15). This is an important aspect of His anointing. He guides us into all truth (John 16:13). His leading us is part of His teaching ministry (Rom. 8:14). He reminds us of what Jesus said and of biblical truth (John 14:26). He teaches us what to pray and when to pray (Rom. 8:26–27). He teaches us by both guiding and restraining us.

Isaiah had promised that all believers would be taught by the Lord (Isa. 54:13). Jesus said this would be the ministry of the Spirit. "The counselor, the Holy Spirit, whom the Father will send in my name, will teach you all things" (John 14:26). This, says John (1 John 2:27), is what the anointing within us does.

No Christian leader knows enough in himself to do the work of God. We can but exclaim with Paul, "Who is equal to such a task?" (2 Cor. 2:16). "Not that we are competent in ourselves to claim anything for ourselves, but our competence comes from God. He has made us competent" (2 Cor. 3:5–6). Every Christian leader must be constantly and totally dependent on God. We have no alternative but to be taught continually by the anointing of the Spirit.

The Spirit must not merely guide and teach us in our goals, strategies, and action; He must guide us in our attitudes, our positions on issues, and even in our words (1 Cor. 2:10–14). Not only when we are standing before civic authorities; but in many leadership activities we must be given answers by the Spirit (Matt. 10:19–20).

4. *The anointing confers spiritual authority.* The Spirit enables you to exercise the authority in prayer which you have as a child of God (Eph. 3:12). This includes confident boldness in coming to the throne of grace and a holy

confidence and boldness in claiming the promises of God (Heb. 4:16; 10:19–22). We have a tremendous responsibility to intercede for our people and to use our authority in prayer for them again and again.

The anointing enables you to use your authority in resisting Satan. The shepherd must defend the flock of God. Christ gave us authority to overcome all Satan's power (Luke 10:19). He gave His disciples authority to drive out demons and to cure diseases (Luke 9:1). Today this is not our major ministry, though it is needed in many mission situations and in facing the occult. We need not run from situations which suddenly confront us. God the Spirit may at any time use you to rebuke Satan, to claim the authority of Christ. At times He leads us to resist Satan strongly and all his powers of darkness (James 4:7). God's Word promises that then the Devil will run from us. We are to resist him, standing firm in the faith (1 Peter 5:9).

The Spirit confers great authority in using the name of Jesus whether in prayer (John 14:13–14; 15:16; 16:23–27) or in confronting demons (Mark 16:17). He gives us authority to give the command of faith (Matt. 17:20). In fact, He gives us authority to do everything in the name of Jesus (Col. 3:17). Satan fears that Name. Let us use it wisely but authoritatively.

We do not minister on our own; we are ambassadors for Christ (2 Cor. 5:20), fellow workers of God (1 Cor. 3:9; 2 Cor. 6:1). When we proclaim God's Word we do it in the name of God. When we offer the forgiveness of sins through Christ we do it in the name of God. When we minister to God's people we do so in the name of God. The anointing gives us a love and an authority beyond our own.

5. *The anointing clothes with God's power.* Micah testified, "I am filled with power, with the Spirit of the LORD . . . and with might" (Mic. 3:8). Jesus commanded His disciples (both the apostles and the laity and both men and women) to delay the beginning of their witness and ministry and wait on God "until you have been clothed with power from on high" (Luke 24:49).

Thomas Payne, British writer at the turn of the century,

attributes the great results of the ministry of George Whitefield not primarily to the effect of his sermons as being that extraordinary, but rather to the spiritual tone and powerful anointing as he preached.

Samuel Chadwick, noted British leader, testified, "The fire of Pentecost is a blaze of moral and spiritual enthusiasm. It is a passion for God that sets personality ablaze. Every part of the man is aflame. I can speak for myself. Pentecost came to me in my twenty-second year. I had been a Christian from boyhood; and a very serious and earnest Christian as best I knew, but Pentecost was a miracle of power. The fire of God quickened my mortal body, it vitalized every faculty, it gave me a new mentality, and opened to me a new world of spiritual reality. The fire kindled to a flame."[2]

A close relationship exists between the anointing and the empowering of the Spirit. The anointing usually includes to some degree the empowering of the Spirit—yet it includes much more. Divine enabling involves guidance, assistance in prayer, illumination, the reminding, restraining, and sealing ministries of the Spirit.

On the other hand, the empowering of the Spirit is available for much more than anointing. There is empowering for holy living, for overcoming temptation, for imparting courage, for strength to suffer in Christ's name—even unto death at times, for general suffering, and for militant, mountain-moving faith. God gives us power both to be and to do. Power to do is more often related to anointing; power to be is more often related to grace. I discussed the empowering of the Spirit in chapters 4–13.

6. *The anointing places God's seal upon you.* It is the evidence of divine approval. The Spirit gives this for the sake of the ones ministered to, but it is also God's affirmation of you as His representative and of your ministry on His behalf. The fruit of the Spirit confers Christlikeness of personality and character and is a seal of your relationship to God. It is a God-given trademark. It is a ministry evidence of His presence and endorsement. The anointing declares to those you lead and those who see you that God is with you, that He

owns you as His ambassador, that He has called and sent you, and hence they are responsible to respect and accept your ministry.

The Spirit's anointing confers among those you serve an openness to your leadership and message. It stamps genuineness on your role and urgency on your words and actions. It separates your leadership from that which is merely man-appointed or self-appointed.

7. *The anointing brings results.* The anointing does not guarantee your acceptance, that crowds will attend your ministry, or that multitudes of people will be led to Christ. But God does not always measure success as we do. The anointing will produce the Spirit's intended results. God has many purposes for the ministry of His Spirit-filled servants. God's purpose may be new comfort for His people, new faith and expectancy, new vision of responsibility, new burden for evangelism and world evangelism, new burden for revival, new financial support for God's cause, new compassion for the needy, new sense of divine call to Christian service, new unity of the Spirit. God always has multiple holy purposes to accomplish. He may fulfill many of these in one service, one visit, one conversation, or one gathering.

If the Spirit anoints in chairing a committee, there will be a special sense of clarity and efficiency in the handling of business. If He anoints in teaching a class, there will be special attentiveness, clearer understanding, and real learning. If He anoints in the singing of a hymn, there will be a special sense of God's blessing and the words will constitute a real message. If the Spirit anoints a sermon, it ceases to be a lecture and becomes God's message. People know God has spoken to them and touched them. If He anoints in prayer, there will be a special sense of God's hand upon the one who prays, a sense of blessed communion, or deep concern, or real faith, and of prevailing before God.

Writing from the viewpoint of a pastor, Oswald J. Smith said:

271

Boast no more of your anointing if you love not souls. Oh, my brother, tell me; nay! tell God: Have you the burden? Do you know the passion of which I speak? Are you haunted day and night with the thought that millions are going down to the regions of despair . . . . Does the Holy Spirit awaken you during the diligent hours of sleep, to intercede on behalf of lost men and women? Have you ever agonized over the perishing? Do you know anything about soul-travail? When last did you wrestle with God for dear ones out of Christ? For, mark you, if you have been truly anointed of the Holy Ghost, such will be your experience.

. . . Ah, that burden, that burden for souls—how it has characterized God's anointed ones all down the centuries! Paul, Carvasso, Oxtoby, Whitefield, Stoner, McCheyne, Brainerd, Bounds, Hyde, and a host of others, mighty wrestlers with God. Theirs, my brethren, is the experience I crave above all other, for they had God's seal. There was no doubt about their anointing; they were Spirit-filled, every last one of them, for they travailed in soul for the perishing."[3]

Spurgeon wrote, "It is extraordinary power from God, not talent, that wins the day. It is extraordinary spiritual unction [i.e., anointing] not extraordinary mental power, that we need. Mental power may fill a chapel but spiritual power fills the church with soul anguish. Mental power may gather a large congregation, but only spiritual power will save souls. What we need is spiritual power."[4]

THE ANOINTING IS FOR YOU, IF . . .

The anointing of the Spirit is God's provision for you as His child and even more for you as a leader of His people. God knows your need and delights to meet your need. We do not deserve such a boon, but it is ours to ask for, seek, and receive. It is not automatic; it is not for the spiritually indolent, careless, or disobedient. It is God's supernatural extra added to your best.

Bounds taught that the anointing "is a conditional gift, and its presence is perpetuated and increased by the same process by which it was at first secured; by unceasing prayer to God, by impassioned desires after God, by estimating it, by seeking it with tireless ardor, by deeming all else loss and failure without it." He added, "Prayer, much prayer, is the price . . . prayer, much prayer, is the one, sole condition of keeping this unction. Without unceasing prayer the unction never comes."

Charles Finney said, "I would repeat, with great emphasis, that the difference in the efficiency of ministers does not consist so much in difference of intellectual attainments as in the measure of the Holy Spirit they enjoy . . . Until he knows what it is to 'be filled with the Spirit,' to be endued with power from on high, he is by no means qualified to be a leader in the Church of God. A thousand times as much stress ought to be laid upon this part of a thorough preparation for the ministry as has been."⁵

Oswald J. Smith wrote, "I am perfectly confident that the man who does not spend hours alone with God will never know the anointing of the Holy Spirit. The world must be left outside until God alone fills the vision . . . God has promised to answer prayer. It is not that He is unwilling, for the fact is, He is more willing to give than we are to receive. But the trouble is, we are not ready . . ."⁶

BOTH ABIDING AND RENEWABLE

The anointing of the Spirit is both abiding and renewable. It abides only upon those who are filled with the Spirit. To be filled with the Spirit does not mean merely to have spiritual interests. To be filled with the Spirit, to be under the Spirit's full control, is the result of a definite crisis of total surrender and appropriation by faith on the part of a true believer (Rom. 12:1–2). We must offer ourselves as living sacrifices, alive from the dead.

To be filled with the Spirit is more than consecration. Consecration is the necessary condition. The infilling of the Spirit is the divine response to total surrender of ourselves, our present and our future—our all. We are not filled till we have the divine response. Then we will be living our spiritual

273

life on a higher, deeper, more victorious plane, life fully in the Spirit, life controlled by the Spirit.

Is it possible to be refilled with the Spirit? Certainly, if we maintain our consecration and obedience we may receive new outpourings, new infillings of the Spirit as we have need. See chapter 11 on the need for repeated empowerings.

Some Christians use the term "anointing" as the equivalent of the fullness of the Spirit. It is far more precise to speak of the anointings as those special enablings of the Spirit, usually given only to the Spirit-filled, and given for times of need especially in ministry.

Note this word from Oswald J. Smith: "The question is: What new anointing did I receive last week? Is my experience up-to-date? So many testify to something wonderful that occurred years ago, but their lives are so barren and dry that it is clear they long ago lost the freshness of what they received. We should be anointed again and again, a fresh anointing for each new service."[7]

CAUTIONS! Do not presume on the anointing of the Spirit.

1. *Do not presume that because He anointed you in the past He will anoint you now.* Live so He will not hesitate to anoint you afresh. Ask for His anointing repeatedly. You need it for your life and ministry.

2. *Do not presume on His anointing and fail to do your part to keep blessed and ready.* He is more desirous to anoint you than you are to be anointed, but you dare not become careless spiritually and fail to walk close to God.

3. *Do not presume on His anointing and fail to do your part in preparation and diligence for your ministry.* If you are a singer or musician, you dare not be negligent in practice. If you are a speaker or writer, you dare not be negligent in preparatory study. Don't ask God to anoint your second best.

Chapter 39

You Must Be a Person of God

Your highest goal as a Christian leader must be to be a person of God. Only a few people in Bible times were given this title—Moses, Samuel, David, Elijah, Elisha, Timothy, and some others. Undoubtedly the term could have been appropriately used for leaders like Isaiah, Daniel, and Paul. Perhaps there is no higher honor to be given to anyone than to be considered to be a man or woman of God.

None of us would feel worthy of this term. At times in the Old Testament it seemed to be used for a prophet of God or one specially sent by God. Some well-meaning people have sometimes used this as an honored term for all Christian leaders, pastors, and missionaries. But no leader is automatically a person of God just because his ministry relates to the church, includes sacred duties, or because he has dedicated his life to Christian service.

275

Who is a true person of God? Perhaps we feel more free to note personality traits which should not be in persons of God than to define who is one. Yet all of us recognize those aspects of godliness that place the stamp of God upon one. Each of us desires more of God's seal upon one's own life. What does this include?

MARKS OF A PERSON OF GOD

1. *A person of God lives a consistently righteous and holy life.* Only God is perfect in holiness. Only God is infinitely and eternally righteous. Each of us has sinned (past tense) and falls (present tense) short of the glory of God (Rom. 3:23). But God can give us an unwavering commitment to His will, His truth, and His glory. We can live in present victory and blessing moment by moment. We can walk in the light as He is in the light and experience the continuing cleansing from all sin (1 John 1:7).

We all stumble in many ways and find often that we are at fault (James 3:2). But the set of the soul, the habit of the walk with God can be a life of consistent righteousness and holiness. And if we sin, we have one who speaks to the Father in our defense—Jesus Christ, the infinitely Righteous One (1 John 2:2). By God's grace we can live in holiness and righteousness before Him all our days (Luke 1:75). Any sin or moral defect in a Christian leader brings instant scandal to the name of Christ and to the church of Christ. Every person of God must live in holiness and righteousness.

2. *A person of God lives a life of love.* God is love, and the more godly we become the more the love of God will be manifest in us. "Live a life of love" (Eph. 5:2). "Do everything in love" (1 Cor. 16:14). "The fruit of the Spirit is love" (Gal. 5:22). There is no commandment greater than to love (Mark 12:31).

If there is anything that adds beauty to character and personality, it is love. If there is anything that marks a Christian leader as a person of God, it is the love of the Spirit flowing constantly out of his life to others. Our love for God is no greater than our love for those about us. This marks us as Christlike. This alone can make our leadership Christian.

3. *A person of God serves others.* We must serve one another in love (Gal. 5:13). Loving service added to the other Christian graces places a special seal upon a person. Love always serves. Love expresses itself to others by blessing them, helping them, and gladly serving them. Jesus tolerates among His followers no lording it over others (1 Peter 5:3). No one is too good to serve. No one is a follower of Christ unless he is willing to serve as the Master did, who girded Himself with a towel and washed the feet of His followers.

For Jesus' sake we are servants of others (2 Cor. 4:5). As shepherds of God's flock we are to be eager to serve (1 Peter 5:2). There is no place in a person of God for pride of leadership, methods, ministry, organization, or accomplishments. We must have the servant heart and manifest the servant attitude of the One who humbled Himself as described in Philippians 2:5–8.

4. *A person of God manifests the beautiful fruit of the Spirit.* Jesus assured us that if the tree is good the fruit will also be good (Matt. 12:33). If the Spirit controls us, He will manifest His holy fruit through our attitudes, moods, words, and deeds. All people, said Jesus, are recognized by their fruit (Matt. 7:16).

The person of God has godly fruit, godliness of disposition, godliness of emotions, godliness of spiritual lifestyle. Paul outlines the fruit of the Spirit in Galatians 5:22–23. The Christian leader carries with him the fragrant aroma of Christ (2 Cor. 2:15). The Holy Spirit imparts the loveliness, the beauty, the very spirit of Jesus. This is an essential element of the Spirit's sealing of a man or woman of God.

5. *A person of God is filled with the Spirit:* "Filled to the measure of all the fullness of God" (Eph. 3:19), "fullness in Christ" (Col. 2:9), "filled with the Spirit" (Eph. 5:18), "filled with the fruit of righteousness that comes through Jesus Christ, to the glory and praise of God" (Phil. 1:11). Surely the Bible holds an amazing vision before us! But of all the terms

the Bible uses to describe this holy reality, "filled with the Spirit" is by far most frequently used.

To be filled with the Spirit means to be saturated with the Spirit, overflowing with the Spirit, fully possessed by the Spirit, controlled and dominated by the Spirit, and transformed by the Spirit. To be filled with the Spirit implies that one is fully available to the Spirit, fully influenced by the Spirit, and made beautiful with the grace and fruit of the Spirit.

To be filled means that the whole personality is so imbued by the Spirit, pervaded by the Spirit, and saturated with the Spirit that the person is not only spiritual but Spirit-full. For you to be Spirit-filled implies that the presence and power of the Spirit rests upon your person, clothes you, and is manifest through you. It makes a decided difference in you, a new God-given dimension and a new transforming fullness in your life and leadership. You recognize it and others recognize it. It adds a God-given Christlikeness to your personality and a God-given might to your witness, ministry, and leadership. It marks you as a person of God.

OTHERS RECOGNIZE A PERSON OF GOD

When God puts His seal upon you, not only do God's children often recognize it, but the unsaved may discern something different about you. Even Satan recognizes a person of God.

David, who was himself called a man of God, said, "Know that the LORD has set apart the godly for himself; the LORD will hear when I call to him" (Ps. 4:3). One way God sets us apart is by putting His seal on our prayer life and giving us many answers to prayer. When God answered Elijah's prayer so outstandingly and repeatedly, the widow of Zarephath called out, "Now I know that you are a man of God and that the word of the LORD in your mouth is the truth" (1 Kings 17:24).

On Mt. Carmel Elijah felt God's seal was essential to his ministry if the nation was to be turned back to God. So he prayed, "O LORD, God of Abraham, Isaac and Israel, let it be known today that you are God in Israel and that I am your servant . . . . Answer me, O LORD, answer me, so these people will know that you, O LORD, are God, and that you are turning their hearts back again. Then the fire of the LORD fell . . . . When all the people saw this, they fell prostrate and cried, 'The LORD—he is God! The LORD—he is God!'" (1 Kings 18:36–39).

Later, when challenged and called a "man of God," Elijah replied, "If I am a man of God, may fire come down from heaven" (2 Kings 1:10). It did. God is ready to place His seal upon you when He sees that you need it, and others will recognize it. Your prayer life has much to do with your being a person of God and others' acceptance of you in that role.

After Elisha had eaten several times in their home, the woman of Shunem said to her husband, "I know that this man who often comes our way is a holy man of God" (2 Kings 4:9). She prepared a room for the prophet's use whenever he passed by. Why did she go to that trouble? Hungry-hearted people want to be near a person of God. My mother tells me that when I was a small child and a visitor began to talk about the Lord I stood as near to his chair as I could. Even a child can sense spiritual reality in a person of God.

When Saul's mules were lost his servant said to him, "Look, in this town there is a man of God; he is highly respected, and everything he says comes true" (1 Sam. 9:6). Yes, people respect a person of God, but they lose respect if a Christian leader does not prove by his life, his prayer, and his words that he is truly a person of God.

When Sadhu Sundar Singh, beloved Indian Christian Sadhu, was staying with a friend in the Himalayan mountains, he would go out and sit in the snow for hours in the dark to pray. One night his friend looked out and saw a wild animal approach the Sadhu. It lay down beside the praying saint. After some time the Sadhu became aware of it, stretched out his hand, and petted it. Even the ferocious beast seemed to recognize God in him and did not harm him.

A PERSON OF GOD BRINGS BLESSING

When Charles Trumbell, evangelical writer and journalist, was a small boy playing on the street, he saw Adoniram Judson walk by. He was so gripped by God's presence in Judson's face that he followed him to his hotel and had his pastor visit him.

When Robert Murray McCheyne died, a letter addressed to him was found in his desk. In it was written, "It was nothing that you said that first made me wish to be a Christian—it was the beauty of holiness which I saw in your very face."

Rev. Duncan Campbell hungered for the presence of Jesus more than anything else, till at times Jesus was more real to him than his earthly friends. Ministers, students, fishermen, homemakers who came to know him were seized with an awareness of his love for Jesus. Said one young man, "If you didn't [already] believe in God, you could no longer be an atheist after meeting that man. You could see Jesus in his life and touch Jesus in his ministry."[1] Again and again others saw the Shekinah radiance of God in his face.

Dr. Martyn Lloyd-Jones reports that when Robert Murray McCheyne walked into his pulpit, often before he even had time to open his Bible, the people would begin to weep. He carried the very presence of God with him.

A person of God brings blessing wherever he goes. He takes with him God's presence. He can live normally, have a happy home, attend joyous occasions and mix with the people—Jesus did. But the person of God leaves holy impressions behind. Those he speaks with soon sense the benediction of God from their contact with him.

THE COST OF BEING A PERSON OF GOD

No one becomes a person of God by accident. No one becomes a person of God overnight. We become children of God in a moment; we become people of God over a period of time. A casual commitment to Christ will not make you godly or Christlike. No one becomes a person of God except by a deliberate set of the soul. You cannot earn nearness to Christ, but there is a price to pay.

1. *Maintain a supreme commitment to Jesus.* It costs priority commitment to Jesus. He must become your Alpha and Omega, your supreme desire. It costs the giving of your time to Him, lavish self-giving, the setting of yourself apart for Jesus. It costs flaming love for Jesus, sacrificial devotion to Him, and unabashed expressions of your love to Him.

There must be determined, unwavering seeking to please Jesus above all else, a "Jesus first" attitude of your soul. There must be a waiting in His presence, not merely a willingness, but actual quality time alone with Jesus. He must be your supreme joy, your transcendent passion, your uneclipsed glory as you share His undisturbed and unbroken communion, bask in His presence, and delight in His love.

Then with unveiled face you will reflect the glory of Jesus and be constantly transfigured (the actual Greek word) into His likeness from glory to glory (2 Cor. 3:18). This is what Paul calls pursuing godliness (1 Tim. 6:11). It requires continuing effort, eagerness, persistence, and inflexibility in the pursuit. Regardless of what else needs to be sacrificed, with Paul you must say, "This one thing I do."

2. *Train yourself to be godly.* Paul contrasts physical training with spiritual training (1 Tim. 4:7). The Greek word Paul uses is the root for our word "gymnasium." It implies disciplined, regular, strenuous exercise. Just as an Olympic athlete training for the event of his life sacrifices all else and disciplines himself early and late to toughen and train his body, so you are to spend your energies and your hours, as far as possible, investing your time and making whatever sacrifice is required to be more truly a person of God.

And what is the purpose of your making this holy training, this spiritual discipline your supreme priority? It is to know Jesus, become one in spirit with Jesus, and identify with Jesus so that you are transfigured into His likeness (2 Cor. 3:18). Your supreme priority is not what you do for Jesus, but to be like Him. Then all you so passionately do for

Him will flow out of this deepest of all commitments. To make this possible two more steps are required:

3. *Saturate your soul in the Word.* Immerse yourself in the Word from Genesis to Revelation, but specially in everything relating to Jesus, including the whole of the New Testament and Psalms. It is the most tangible means at your disposal. Feed on God's Word, drink in God's Word, bathe your soul in God's Word. Read it—read all of it. Read it over and over and over until it penetrates the fiber of your spiritual being.

You cannot be a person of God without being a person of the Word. If you are an authority on anything, be an authority on God's Word. If you have a hobby of any kind, make God's Word your hobby. If you spend time with any reading, read God's Word. Store it in your heart. Think on it, meditate on it, memorize it, dream of it. Apply it in your heart and life. Spend major time each day with the Word.

The Word will feed you, nourish you, and strengthen you. It will enlighten you and guide you. Make it your priority guide and your final authority. When God's Word speaks, that settles it for you. Paul points out in 2 Corinthians 3:16 (Greek) that the Holy Spirit takes away the veil that covers the hearts of the unsaved when they read the Bible. The Spirit through the Word transfigures us into the likeness of Jesus from one degree of glory to another. This is what makes us persons of God. You should spend approximately as much time with the Bible itself (not just books about the Word) as in prayer.

4. *Give Jesus your prayer time.* Prayer is the greatest, most eternally beneficial way you can invest your time. Prayer is the most Christlike activity you can engage in, for He today lives to intercede. Prayer is the greatest, most lasting, most rewarding investment you can make while alive on earth. Prayer is the most precious gift you can give to Jesus.

Moses was closer to Jesus and spent more time alone with Jesus, as far as we know, than any other Old Testament leader had ever done. When the Israelites saw Moses after his forty days on the mountain they did not seem to have been specially impressed. But after his eighty days on the mountain, they were overawed by the glory on his face.

Spend much time with Jesus both in communion and in sharing His intercessory burden for the world and the church. When husbands and wives love each other and grow together over many years, it sometimes almost seems as though they begin to resemble each other. They often have similar attitudes, gestures, vocabulary, and even at times similar facial features. When a child idolizes a parent, you may begin to note a resemblance in mannerisms, attitudes, and words.

To become a person of God we must spend much time with Jesus. The more you love Him, the more you will want to spend time with Him. A weak prayer life always testifies to a weak love of Jesus. You cannot have a merely nominal or casual prayer life when you are passionately devoted to the Lord. The more you are with Him, the more you will think and speak like Him, respond and resemble Him. You will be a person of God.

> Take time to be holy, speak oft with thy Lord.
> Abide in Him always, and feed on His Word . . .
>
> Take time to be holy, the world rushes on;
> Spend much time in secret with Jesus alone.
> By looking to Jesus like Him thou shalt be;
> Thy friends, in thy conduct, His likeness shall see.
> W. D. Longstaff

Chapter 40

The Person of God
and Holy Integrity

God wants integrity in His people (1 Chron. 29:17). A person of God must be known for holy integrity. Nothing is more important in a Christian leader. Godliness is more than total mental commitment to the authority of God's Word and the doctrines of Scripture. We need that mental commitment, but that is not enough. Godliness is also more than emotions of joy and love as we sing songs and choruses of the greatness, goodness, and faithfulness of God, of the love of Jesus, and of the power of the Spirit. We do need to be moved by Calvary until our hearts and eyes are filled with tears, but godliness is more than the holiest of emotions.

Godliness includes a commitment of the will that results in righteous actions and holy living. The eye must be clear and good before the body can be flooded with light (Matt.

6:22). The heart must be pure before the attitudes, thoughts, and words are consistently pure.

According to the Bible the faith that saves us also sanctifies. Personal commitment to Christ brings the indwelling of the Spirit, and the fruit of the Spirit in its totality brings Christlikeness. The Spirit applies the lordship of Christ to all of life. There is no alternative to Christian holiness of life with its full ethical implications.

The character of a person of God is manifest in holy attitudes and holy actions. Unless holy words come from a holy heart they are powerless. And unless holiness results in total integrity it is a pseudo holiness. There is no person of God who can be careless about integrity.

Until the actions and manner of life are righteous and holy we know the heart is not holy. And until the heart is holy the person is not a person of God. The only true holiness is that which is manifested in consistent holy living. We are to "serve him without fear in holiness and righteousness before him all our days" (Luke 1:74–75).

This standard of holiness of life is not impossible for us because when the Holy Spirit fills us He conforms us to God's holiness by divine enablement. God's standard of holy living for His holy people is awesomely complete and high. We are to be holy as He is holy (1 Peter 1:15–16).

He has called us to a holy life (2 Tim. 1:9). We are being made holy (Heb. 10:14). We are to be holy (Heb. 12:14). We are to be holy in all we do (1 Peter 1:15), i.e., holiness is not just theoretical: it is to be practical. We are to live holy and godly lives (2 Peter 3:11).

Only with such holiness can we always live above reproach (1 Tim. 3:2). Since a Christian leader is "entrusted with God's work, he must be blameless" (Titus 1:6–7). Paul summarizes his meaning in the words "upright, holy and disciplined" (v. 8). We are to be "without stain or wrinkle or any other blemish, but holy and blameless" (Eph. 5:27).

Our holy ethic is both positive and negative. Having become dead to sin we become alive to God. Our holy ethic is deadness to sin and the world—a negative ethical separation in heart and life. It is also life to Christ and in Christ. It is a positive ethic of godliness, righteousness, and holiness of life. We offer our bodies, and thus our whole beings, as living sacrifices to God, holy and pleasing in His sight (Rom. 12:1). We refuse to offer the parts of our body to sin (Rom. 6:13) and we deliberately offer ourselves freely and positively to God for the ethic of holiness (Rom. 6:13, 19). We do not let sin reign in the body or through the body, but we let Christ reign on the throne of the heart; and His Spirit then lives out His reign in our practical living in righteous and holy ethical practice rising from holy character.

This makes us constantly concerned to maintain holy integrity in the eyes of all people. "Be careful to do what is right in the eyes of everybody" (Rom. 12:17). "We are taking pains to do what is right, not only in the eyes of the Lord but also in the eyes of men" (2 Cor. 8:21).

INTEGRITY IN WORD

The person of God must be a person of his word. His holiness, love, and integrity must be evident in his speech. All our statements, reports, and writings must be open, honest, and kind. Both God and man judge us by our words. "I tell you that men will have to give account on the day of judgment for every careless word they have spoken. For by your words you will be acquitted, and by your words you will be condemned" (Matt. 12:36–37).

1. Say nothing for which you are not willing to accept full responsibility. Say nothing about an absent person which you would be unwilling to repeat in his presence.

2. Beware of a compulsion always to comment or say something about matters under discussion. Be willing to delay your comments. You do not need to tell everything you know unless your information is essential to the discussion. Speak when your comments are needed; be silent when they will not be beneficial.

3. Be positive in as many of your comments as possible. Avoid the reputation for being a negative person.

4. Beware of flattery and exaggerated praise. These will cause you to lose the respect of those who hear you.

5. Express full and cordial credit to all those to whom you are indebted for ideas and help.

6. Avoid plagiarism in speaking or writing.

7. Do not assume the attitude of an authority in areas where your information, experience, and training are incomplete.

8. Be as careful and understanding in your remarks about others as you would be if it were a member of your own family.

9. Be slow to give credence to negative reports and continue to believe the best as long as possible. Be specially careful to avoid casting any reflection or aspersion on a fellow-Christian or a Christian leader.

10. Never criticize the motives of others. You rarely can put yourself in their position and so fully understand their motivation. Always give the benefit of the doubt. Remember, you only hear words and see acts; you do not know the full motives.

11. Be totally honest in intention in everything you say. Speak to bless, help, and guide.

12. Be accurate in every detail in reporting statistics and descriptions. Beware of over-generalization, understatement, or exaggeration.

13. Be faithful in characterization. All statements must be so fair, equitable, and uncolored in description that your comments could be repeated without hesitation regardless of whoever is present.

14. Avoid statements which can be understood two ways. Avoid all duplicity; let your positions be clear-cut. If you change your position, say so, but beware of appearing to equivocate. Watch lest people feel they cannot depend on what you say.

15. Daily ask the Holy Spirit to guide or restrain you in your speech.

INTEGRITY IN PERSONAL ETHICS

The person of God must maintain such integrity in his personal ethics that others can safely make him their role model. Jesus was constantly setting a pattern for His disciples, establishing the standard of what a Christian life and ministry should be. He illustrated this by His attitudes (Phil. 2:5) and by His actions (John 13:15; 1 Peter 2:21).

Paul was conscientious in setting an example which he could commend to his converts as a role model:

> You yourselves know how you ought to follow our example (2 Thess. 3:7).
> We did this . . . in order to make ourselves a model for you to follow (2 Thess. 3:9).
> I became your father through the gospel. Therefore I urge you to imitate me (1 Cor. 4:15–16).

As a Christian leader you are responsible to be a role model for God's people. No word, no attitude, no action of yours should be unworthy for your people to emulate and follow. Whether we deserve it or not, we, our companions, and our children are marked people. The public holds higher standards for us than they do for themselves.

Our lives can honor Christ and be powerful sermons only when we live in the holy integrity that always reflects Christ and always points others to Him. Our personal ethical goal must be Christlikeness. The Holy Spirit must constantly guide us so that our integrity is above reproach and so that our lives commend the gospel. I give only a few examples:

1. Be above reproach in all your personal actions and leadership duties. You always represent God and the church. You are a marked person wherever you go. Your priority commitment is to Christ and your ministerial responsibilities.

2. In every ethical decision make Scripture the standard for your action. If there is no clear scriptural statement to guide you, base your decision on the general tenor of God's Word. You can always ask the question, "What would Jesus do? What is the Christian thing to do?"

3. Keep your speech, dress, habits, hobbies, and lifestyles in balance between what is appropriate in your leadership role and that which is appropriate for you as a Christian in a world of great spiritual and physical need.

4. Be an example in your person and home in cleanliness, orderliness, harmony, and godliness.

5. Be an example of consideration, fairness, sensitivity to the feelings and rights of others. Always show respect in all interpersonal relations.

6. Be an example of gentleness and maturity in your reactions to the thoughtlessness, affronts, insults, opposition, and hostility of others. All must be responded to with forgiveness and prayerful Christian love.

7. Be an example in circumspection and discretion in all relations with the opposite sex. Be particularly watchful of the latent snares in your role as a spiritual counselor. Be vigilant to keep your thought life pure as in the sight of God.

INTEGRITY IN FINANCE

The person of God must maintain total integrity in his stewardship of possessions and finance—in his handling and accounting for personal finances, and in his handling and accounting for all finances that pass through his control.

1. Be an example in maintaining a comparatively simple lifestyle in accord with a deep commitment to the need for the extension of Christ's kingdom worldwide and for the meeting of human need.

2. Exercise all appropriate economy in your personal expenditures and of all funds entrusted to your use. Don't get a reputation for free-spending.

3. Be faithful in expending funds according to the request of those who gave them.

4. Be accurate in all your reporting. Financial reports must have adequate detail, be prompt, and meticulously correct. Reporting of what is accomplished through funds donated must be regular, detailed, and strictly factual.

5. Pay your bills on time. Do not leave unpaid bills behind when you leave to take up a new ministry.

6. Keep free of debt and keep your ministry free of debt. Debt is always a snare and often a reflection on Christ. It is always better to save money in advance than to borrow and then pay the continuing interest. A credit account can easily become a slave-master which handicaps your ministry and sullies your name. Avoid the snare of the philosophy: "Do now" or "Buy now and pay later."

INTEGRITY IN MINISTERIAL ETHICS

A person of God must maintain the highest level of integrity in all aspects of his ministry and leadership. The ministry, like every profession, has its code of ethics, and Christian workers need constantly to manifest the highest ethics in their interrelations as well as in their work.

1. Be more careful, more courteous and kind, and more professional in your duties than any other professional person could be expected to be. The name of Christ and His church is at stake in all you do.

2. Recognize that you are always on call to represent God and to meet the needs of your people.

3. Give full time to your leadership and ministry. The only exception is when you have the agreement of your board or superintendent. Beware of a reputation for indolence and dawdling waste of time. You will repeatedly be requested to accept other responsibilities, all praiseworthy, but which can erode your primary calling.

4. Be loyal to your church or organization and its doctrine and heritage. Any deviation on your part from your original commitments must be reported to the church or group.

5. Guard the reputation of Christ's church and your fellow Christian workers. The good name of all must be safe in your hands.

6. Avoid all unwholesome competition with other churches, ministries, or Christian leaders.

7. Respect the leadership of other Christian leaders and do not serve their members except in emergencies or with the consent of the other leader.

8. Keep confidences inviolate.

9. Endeavor constantly to strengthen the unity of the Spirit within your group and among Christians in general. Avoid being a part of any divisive group or church clique.

10. While seeking to please your people, keep your final priority on pleasing God.

11. Model and build loyal respect for government and active Christian citizenship.

12. Regard your service as primary and remuneration for service or financial advancement as secondary.

Always remember that even when you are not in a leadership role, you are always perceived as a Christian leader. You have a right to private relaxation and personal and family time. But even then you are a representative of Christ and His church. You are never off duty as a person of God. Maintain your integrity in all that you do and wherever you go. Then God's seal can continue to rest upon you and His power can continue to clothe you.

YOUR INFILLING

Chapter 41

Be Filled With the Spirit

There is no more blessed command in the Word for you as a Christian, and especially as a Christian leader, than "be filled with the Spirit" (Eph. 5:18). It parallels and flows from Christ's command to His disciples not to begin their ministry until they had been clothed with power from on high (Luke 24:48). They were to wait till they were baptized with the Holy Spirit (Acts 1:4-5). When this was fulfilled on the day of Pentecost another term was used. They were "filled with the Holy Spirit" (Acts 2:4). Peter explained that this promise of the Father was not for the 120 alone, but, he told them, for "you and your children and for all who are far off—for all whom the Lord our God will call" (Acts 2:39).

When Peter explained that the Romans at the house of Cornelius had received the same experience as the 120 at Pentecost, he said their hearts were purified by faith (Acts

15:8–9). So the two essential elements are purity and power. Outward manifestations of the Spirit may be varied or not present at all. But the essential need of each of us is purity and power.

In earlier chapters I have written much about the empowering, anointing, and enabling ministry of the Spirit which are essential to our leadership. Perhaps you may sigh inwardly as you regretfully admit that this constant empowering, this dynamic presence of the Spirit has not been characteristic of your life and ministry thus far. Do not be discouraged. God's promise is as surely for you as it was for Peter and Paul. God is neither a respecter of persons nor of periods of Christian history. God is as delighted to pour out His Spirit today as He ever was.

J. Gregory Mantle asks, "It is one thing to have the Spirit, it is quite another to be 'filled' with the Spirit. You may be full, as the tree in the springtime is full of sap; full in the stem; full in the leaf. You may be full of the Spirit as the white-hot iron is full of fire. You take the iron; it is cold and hard and black. You put it in the fire, and the fire enters into it, and soon the fire changes its color. That white-hot iron is now possessed, interpenetrated by the fire within it. Are we thus filled?"

Dr. A. J. Gordon, founder of what is now Gordon College and for whom Gordon-Conwell Theological Seminary is named, quoted this elucidation from Andrew Murray:

> Just as there was a two-fold operation of the one Spirit in the Old and New Testaments, of which the state of the disciples before and after Pentecost was the striking illustration, so there may be, and in the great majority of Christians is, a corresponding difference of experience. . . . When once the distinct recognition of what the indwelling of the Spirit was meant to bring is brought home to the soul, and it is ready to give up all to be made partaker of it, the believer may ask and expect what may be termed a baptism of the Spirit [in contemporary phraseology—an infilling of the Spirit]. Praying to the Father in accordance to the two prayers in Ephesians and coming to Jesus in the renewed surrender of faith and obedience, he may

receive such an inflow of the Holy Spirit as shall consciously lift him to a different level from the one on which he hitherto lived.

It may be that you have never been truly filled with the Spirit. Every person at the moment of the new birth receives the Holy Spirit, so every true Christian is indwelt by the Spirit (Rom. 8:9). However, the Spirit does not totally fill you until you have made a total surrender of your being to Him. Paul refers to this as offering yourself as a living sacrifice (Rom. 12:1). Only a born-again Christian can do this.

The Holy Spirit does not do a work of purifying, sanctifying, filling, and empowering in anyone in rebellion against God. The sinner needs forgiveness and new life from God. First the sinner must be regenerated, made alive in Christ Jesus. Then he can present himself as a living sacrifice to be filled, cleansed, and empowered. We receive all of the Spirit at the moment of salvation, but He does not do all of His ministry within us at the same time.

TERMINOLOGY OF THE SPIRIT'S INFILLING

The Bible is not written in the form of a theological manual. Scripture writers describe God's grace at work in the soul and urge us to appropriate that grace. The Bible includes testimonies of those transformed by God's grace. Scripture uses human pictorial language, and many of the deepest theological truths are described in picture words and phrases.

No one human word or phrase can by itself adequately describe the work of God's grace in the soul. Therefore, God uses many such terms. The wholeness of Scripture truth can be understood only as we use all the terms which the Spirit inspired the writers to use. It is true that we must use spiritual discernment in using and applying these terms, but the Holy Spirit is given us to enable us to study, discern, understand, and synthesize all of Scripture into one beautiful, practical whole.

Among the Scripture terms used for the infilling of the believer are these:

> Filled with the Spirit (Acts 2:4)
> Filled to the measure of all the fullness of God (Eph. 3:19)
> Clothed with power from on high (Luke 24:49)
> Baptized with the Holy Spirit (Acts 1:4–5)
> Baptized with the Holy Spirit and fire (Matt. 3:11)
> The outpouring of the Spirit on a person (Acts 2:17, 33)

Other terms often used in Christian testimony include the empowering of the Spirit and the anointing of the Spirit. These last two terms, however, are more wisely used for the many forms of divine enablement through the Holy Spirit. These have been used both for the initial infilling of the Spirit and also for subsequent new empowerings and infillings.

DEFINITENESS OF THE INFILLING

To be filled with the Spirit is more than to be spiritually inclined. Even some unsaved people are spiritually hungry and "spiritually inclined." They are reaching out to God, perhaps, as fully as they have light. But like Apollos they need to be taught the way of God more adequately (Acts 18:26).

We do not live a Christian life until we are born of God. We do not live a Spirit-filled life until we are filled with the Spirit. However, having made the total surrender of self, the complete consecration of ourselves as children of God, we can be filled with the Spirit as we appropriate His fullness by faith. Then as long as we keep open to the Spirit by obedience and appropriating faith, we can receive new infillings of the Spirit, new outpourings, new floodings of our innermost being from time to time as we need it and as we ask God.

The important decisive first step is that of obediently putting away all that might hinder the Spirit's working, separating ourselves from all of which the Spirit convicts us by His searching light, yielding ourselves in a totality of surrender that yearns for all that God's grace can do in our lives, and joyfully claiming by faith all God's gracious promises. We must be emptied of self before we can be filled with the Spirit. Our carnal self-will must be crucified with Christ. Then we will enter into that new victoriousness of Christian experience which has been described in so many ways: the deeper life, the higher life, the crucified life, the victorious life, the holy life, or the life of rest.

This gracious and definite experience is related to growth. But it is not simply a matter of growth. We often do not sense our need of the total commitment, the deeper cleansing, the mightier infilling of the Spirit until we have walked humbly with God for some time. Yet we feel through the Spirit's guidance, the need of something more and deeper from God.

Praising God for all He has already done for us, we may be conscious of weaknesses which we know God can change by His power, defeats which we know He can transform into victory, and perhaps defilements which we know Christ can cleanse by His blood. We know we are indwelt by the Spirit, but we realize the Spirit could and should possess us more completely. We now understand what Christ implied in John 14:17 regarding the Holy Spirit. Before the disciples had their Pentecost, He contrasted the relationship they presently had with the Spirit with that which they should have after Pentecost: "He lives with you and will be in you."

Be encouraged. The Spirit is leading you to a new step and degree of consecration so that the lordship of Christ within you may be more nearly total than you ever dreamed possible. The Spirit is making you hungry for what He longs to do within you.

TESTIMONIES OF THE INFILLING

George Fox, founder of the Society of Friends, was born again at the age of eleven. But when he was twenty-three and after hungering and thirsting for a deeper experience, a new enduement of power came upon him. From that time on he was mightily used of God as again and again he described the power of the Lord on him and through him. The Spirit's power clothed him wherever he went, and until his death he was a mighty instrument in the hand of God.

John Bunyan, after a tempestuous and sinful youth, was converted one evening as the Holy Spirit applied Hebrews 2:14–15 to his heart. After a joyous walk with the Lord he went through a two-year struggle with Satan. At last God used 1 John 1:7 ("the blood of Jesus Christ his Son, cleanseth us from all sin," King James Version), and he entered into his "Beulah Land" experience. Though not without trials, from then on he was overwhelmed with the sense of God's grace and power. God mightily used him as during his twelve years of imprisonment he wrote his famous books.

William Penn, the famous Quaker who founded Pennsylvania, was a great soul winner. He was born again at the age of twelve and at the age of twenty-two made a full consecration of his all and was filled with the Spirit after hearing a message by a Quaker preacher. He tells about it. "Paul prays [that the Thessalonians] might be sanctified wholly. . . . And as my faithful testimony . . . be it known to all that ever knew me, that when the unspeakable riches of God's love visited me . . . I was immediately endued with a power that gave me a dominion over them (i.e., over worldly conversation and habits)."

John Wesley, after years as an earnest but only nominal Christian, including ministry both in his homeland and in America, was wonderfully born again with a clear assurance of salvation on May 24, 1738, in a Moravian service on Aldersgate Street in London. After ten years of struggle he had found peace. Later in the year he began to long for a still deeper experience. On January 1, 1739, as I have already mentioned, he, his brother Charles, George Whitefield, and some sixty others were continuing in prayer. About three o'clock in the morning God poured out His Spirit on them in a mighty way in a tremendous empowering, anointing, and infilling of the Spirit that sent the Wesleys and Whitefield to blaze a trail of salvation and revival across the British Isles and in the American colonies. The Holy Spirit continued to manifest His power through John Wesley until his triumphant death on March 2, 1791.

George Whitefield, for some time a co-worker of the Wesleys, had a clear experience of the new birth before the Wesleys did. His old friends thought him insane because he was so zealous for Christ. Later he spent days and nights in prayer and fasting because of his battle with pride and other inner defeats. But God greatly blessed him and he wrote, "Oh! with what joy, joy unspeakable, even joy that was full of and big with glory, was my soul filled, when the weight of sin went off; and an abiding sense of the pardoning love of God, and a full assurance of faith broke in upon my disconsolate soul!"

Later at his ordination on June 20, 1736, he was mightily filled with the Holy Spirit. He had spent all of Saturday fasting and praying and in the evening had gone to a hill outside town where he prayed for another two hours. Sunday he rose early to pray in further preparation for his ordination at the altar of the church. "When the bishop laid his hands upon my head," he later testified, "my heart was melted down, and I offered my whole spirit, soul, and body to the service of God's sanctuary."

Dr. Lloyd-Jones writes:

> Whitefield tells us that he was aware, actually in his Ordination Service, of the power coming down upon him. He knew it. He was thrilled with the sense of power. The very first Sunday after his ordination he preached in his home town . . . and it was an amazing service (15 were convicted powerfully and converted) . . . . The subsequent Journals of Whitefield, and the various biographies of him, contain endless accounts of his awareness of the Spirit of God coming upon him while he preached, and also at other times.[1]

Remember that until the twentieth-century Pentecostal movement rose and adopted "baptism with the Spirit" or "baptism in the Spirit" as their terms for an experience accompanied by speaking in tongues, the designations were commonly used for the infilling of the Spirit. Moody, Torrey, Finney, and many others spoke constantly in this way. Today many Bible teachers prefer not to use the term "baptism" for the infilling to avoid confusion with teachings of the Pentecostal churches.

Charles G. Finney was a young lawyer who for two days struggled with God under deep conviction of sin. On October 10, 1821, he went to a hill outside town and spent the whole morning in prayer. He was determined to find God or die in the attempt, and finally laid hold of God's promise in Jeremiah 29:13. God lifted the burden of sin and filled him with peace. That evening he had a vision of Christ, fell at His feet, and bathed them with tears. He described what happened next:

> I received a mighty baptism of the Holy Spirit. Without any expectation of it, without ever having the thought in my mind that there was any such thing for me, without any memory of ever hearing the thing mentioned by any person in the world, the Holy Spirit descended upon me in a manner that seemed to go through me, body and soul. I could feel the impression, like a wave of electricity, going through and through me. Indeed, it seemed to come in waves of liquid love, for I could not express it in any other way. It seemed like the very breath of God. I can remember distinctly that it seemed to fan me, like immense wings.
>
> No words can express the wonderful love that was spread abroad in my heart. I wept aloud with joy and love . . . . These waves came over me, and over me, and over me, one after the other, until I remember crying out, "I shall die if these waves continue to pass over me." I said, "Lord, I cannot bear any more," yet I had no fear of death.[2]

Dwight L. Moody had already been greatly used by God in Chicago. Two humble Free Methodist women prayed faithfully for him during his Sunday services. At the close of the service they would say to him, "We have been praying for you." "Why don't you pray for the people?" Mr. Moody would ask. "Because you need the power of the Spirit," was the reply. "I need the power! Why," he said in relating the incident afterwards, "I thought I had power. I had the largest congregation in Chicago, and there were many conversions!"

One day Moody said to them, "I wish you would tell me

what you mean." And they told him about the definite infilling of the Holy Spirit. So he asked them to pray with him and not merely pray for him. Shortly thereafter their prayers were suddenly answered on Wall Street in New York. Moody's co-worker Dr. R.A. Torrey described what happened. "The power of God fell upon him as he walked up the street and he had to hurry off to the house of a friend and ask that he might have a room by himself, and in that room he stayed alone for hours; and the Holy Ghost came upon him filling his soul with such joy that at last he had to ask God to withhold His hand, lest he die on the spot from very joy. He went out from that place with the power of the Holy Ghost upon him."

Moody's own words were: "I was crying all the time that God would fill me with His Spirit. Well, one day, in the city of New York—oh, what a day!—I cannot describe it . . . I can only say that God revealed Himself to me, and I had such an experience of His love that I had to ask Him to stay His hand. I went to preaching again. The sermons were not different; I did not present any new truths; and yet hundreds were converted. I would not now be placed back where I was before that blessed experience if you should give me all the world—it would be as the small dust of the balance."

On another occasion Moody testified,

> May God forgive me if I should speak in a boastful way, but I do not know of a sermon that I have preached since but God has given me some soul. O, I would not be back where I was four years ago for all the wealth of the world. If you would roll it at my feet, I would kick it away like a football. I seem a wonder to you, but I am a greater wonder to myself than to anyone else. These are the very sermons I preached in Chicago, word for word. Then I preached and I preached, but it was as one beating the air. It is not new sermons, but the power of God. It is not a new gospel, but the old gospel with the Holy Ghost of power.

At Moody's funeral, Dr. C.I. Scofield, editor of the famed Scofield Reference Bible, gave four reasons why God used D.L. Moody. For his third reason he said, "He was baptized with the Holy Spirit and he knew that he was. It was to him as definite an experience as his conversion."

Dr. J. Wilbur Chapman was a Presbyterian evangelist, associate of Moody, and founder of the Winona Lake Bible Conference. He testified regarding the change in his life and ministry through the infilling of the Spirit: "From that moment to this [the Holy Spirit] has been a living reality. I never knew what it was to love my family before. I never knew what it was to study the Bible before. And why should I for had I not just then found the key? I never knew what it was to preach before. 'Old things have passed away' is my experience. 'Behold all things have become new.'"

Oswald Chambers was a strong Bible teacher of this experience. He testified, "Dr. F. B. Meyer came and spoke to us about the Holy Spirit. I determined to have all that was going, and went to my room and asked God simply and definitely for his Holy Spirit, whatever that meant." He said that no one he knew seemed able to help him trust God for this experience. Four years later God spoke to him through His Word: "Luke 11:13 got hold of me . . . it was borne in upon me that I had to claim the gift from God on the authority of Jesus Christ . . . this I did in dogged committal. I had no vision of heaven or of angels . . . but like a flash something happened inside me . . . the days that followed have truly been heaven on earth. Glory be to God—the last aching abyss of the human heart is filled to overflowing with the love of God. The power and tyranny of sin is gone and the radiant, unspeakable emancipation of the indwelling Christ has come."[3]

Dr. Arthur T. Pierson for several years pastored Spurgeon's Tabernacle in London. He was a leader in the Bible Conference and Student Volunteer movements, and for years lectured in Moody Bible Institute. For eighteen years of his ministry he depended largely on his literary power and oratory. Then he sought and received the infilling of the Spirit. Testifying to an assembly of ministers, he said, "Brethren, I have seen more conversions and accomplished more in the eighteen months since I received that blessing than in the eighteen years previous."

Dr. Walter L. Wilson, beloved physician-Bible teacher of Kansas City, was converted in his teens in a tent meeting. Eighteen years later Dr. James M. Gray, Reformed Episcopal clergyman and then the revered president of Moody Bible Institute, preaching on Romans 12:1, challenged all to give their bodies in total consecration to the Holy Spirit. Wilson went home and prostrated himself on the carpet in his study and made a detailed and absolute surrender of his body and whole being to be filled with the Holy Spirit. This is Dr. Wilson's testimony: "With regard to my own experience with the Holy Spirit, I may say that the transformation in my own life on Jan. 14, 1914, was greater, much greater, than the change which took place when I was saved Dec. 21, 1896." From the very next morning forward Walter Wilson became a tremendous soul-winner, whose thrilling experiences in soul-winning, as recorded in his books, have blessed thousands.[4]

This is but a small sampling of better known Christian leaders whose lives have been transformed by a definite experience of the Spirit's infilling. Thousands upon thousands of others from nearly all denominations can testify to a similar definite experience in their walk with God. Some are more dramatic than others, but all speak of the all-sufficient grace of God and lavishness of the Spirit's fullness.

The biographies of Christ's deepest servants over the centuries show these two definite stages of spiritual experience. Each one describes it differently, for God is so creative, so beautifully unique in His dealing with each person. But again and again you find a point of definite spiritual birth, and later a point of a new experience of the Spirit's fullness, power, victory, and blessing.

Augustus Toplady, Anglican hymnwriter, in "Rock of Ages" as originally written, expressed it thus:

> Let the water and the blood,
> From Thy riven side which flowed,
> Be of sin the double cure,
> Cleanse me from its guilt and power.

During the great Welsh revival of 1904–5 Evan Roberts, so tremendously used by the Holy Spirit, repeatedly stated, "You may go to heaven without being filled with the Spirit, but you will be the loser at the judgment seat of Christ . . . . Get into the habit of counting upon the Holy Ghost's indwelling as a greater fact than your own existence."

Let us take to heart the words of Hudson Taylor: "Should we not do well to suspend our present operations and give ourselves to humiliation and prayer for nothing less than to be filled with the Spirit, and made channels through which He shall work with resistless power? Souls are perishing now for lack of this power . . . . God is blessing now some who are seeking this blessing from Him in faith. All things are ready if we are ready."

Chapter 42

How to Be Filled
With the Spirit

Dr. Billy Graham in *The Holy Spirit* has a chapter entitled "How To Be Filled With the Spirit." In it he says, "It is interesting that the Bible nowhere gives us a neat, concise formula for being filled with the Spirit." He suggests that perhaps it was because the believers in the early church did not need to be told how. "They knew that the Spirit-filled life was the normal Christian life."[1]

Dr. W. Graham Scroggie, esteemed Baptist pastor and expositor from Edinburgh, cautioned seekers regarding the nature of the experience. Basing his observations on many years on the convention circuit and his own experience, he warned that "'to be filled with the Spirit' is not necessarily a drastic experience . . . a strange and strongly emotional experience. Emotions may be deeply manifest, and may not be. This may depend partly upon the temperament of the person. The genuineness is not based on the external, but on what God does deep within our nature. It is not necessarily accompanied by ecstatic joy."

Dr. Scroggie added, "In my own experience it was 'joy unspeakable and full of glory.' The joy became a pain, and as I walked up and down the streets of East London in those days . . . I had to ask Him to modify it, for it seemed as though my soul would rend my body."[2] He refers to this joy as an accompaniment rather than as an evidence. It is not something that "dehumanizes." We do not become superior people; we become full of the Spirit, not domineering or superior to others. We are still our own selves with our own personalities, but they are now purified, beautified, and empowered.

SIMPLE STEPS TO BE FILLED WITH THE SPIRIT

Steps to be filled with the Spirit have been described in many ways, but essentially they emphasize the same things. For example, The Salvation Army in its brochure, *It Can Happen*, lists seven points: Aspire, Acknowledge, Abandon, Abdicate, Ask, Appropriate, Act.

Total surrender means that we confirm Christ as Lord over every part of our being. Dr. Harold Lindsell teaches, "Before anyone can be filled with the Holy Spirit, he or she must voluntarily come under the lordship of Jesus Christ in the sense of being a slave. This choice will not be forced on anyone, but it is the . . . condition set down for those who wish to be filled with the Holy Spirit."

He adds that we cannot claim God's promise for the enablement to live our life on the highest plane unless we make Jesus Christ Lord in this way. "The norm for Christian life is to have Christ sitting on the throne of our hearts. Paradoxically, when Christ is truly Lord, this is when the believer reaches the highest point of self-fulfillment."[3]

Billy Graham writes, "It is amazing how many Christians never really face this issue of Christ's lordship."[4] He states, "I am convinced that to be filled with the Spirit is not an option, but a necessity. It is indispensable for the abundant life and for fruitful service. . . . It is intended for all, needed by all, and available to all. That is why the Scripture commands all of us, 'Be filled with the Spirit.' "[5] He suggests that the steps to being filled with the Spirit are understanding, submission, and walking by faith.

Dr. R.A. Torrey, after speaking of the new birth, lists these steps to the Spirit's fullness: obedience (which he defines as "the unconditional surrender of the will to God"); thirsting; asking; faith.[6]

Dr. Bill Bright, founder of Campus Crusade for Christ, places primary emphasis upon faith, but in his more nearly complete explanation he mentions these points: Desire, Surrender, Confess, Present, and Pray (or Ask) as the heart preparation for faith.[7]

Charles Cowman, founder of OMS International, outlined these steps to the fullness of the Spirit: Reckon yourself dead to sin, yield yourself, believe the promise, and obey.

Note the basic similarity in what these spiritual leaders say. Let us summarize and restate it in the following simple steps. Let the Holy Spirit guide and enable you to take these steps if you have not done so hitherto.

1. *Be sure everything is clear between you and God.* Have you become a child of God through the new birth? God does not fill unsaved people with His Spirit. Neither does He fill those who are living in known, willful disobedience to Him. Graham emphasizes, "We must deal completely with sin in our lives if we are to know the infilling of the Holy Spirit."[8] Anything about which the Spirit has convicted you, anything which has separated you from God's best or veiled His face from you must be abandoned. You must walk in the light if you would be filled with the Spirit (1 John 1:7).

2. *Acknowledge your need and God's provision.* Be honest with God. Confess your defeats and the areas in your life where you recognize spiritual need. Don't be in such a hurry that you make a simple blanket confession, a mere general admission of need. "Lord, whatever my need may be, meet it," or "Lord, You know how weak I am." Take time to

search your heart before the Lord and name your needs before Him. It may be helpful to make a list of things the Spirit brings to your attention and then to commit them one by one to the Lord. Ask Him to remind you of failures you have forgotten.

There is great blessing in emptying your heart of failures, defeats, prejudices, attitudes, and actions. Name them one by one and put them beneath Christ's covering, cleansing blood. The Holy Spirit will probably bring to your attention things you did not know were there.

Then rejoice in the full provision Christ made for you on the cross. Rejoice in the provision of the Holy Spirit who is already resident in your heart and who longs to fill every aspect of your being with His cleansing presence and His empowering for life and service. Rejoice that God's promise is available to you. "The promise is for you," said Peter (Acts 2:39).

3. *Hunger and thirst for the Spirit's fullness.* God is always moved by spiritual hunger and thirst and repeatedly promises to meet the needs of our soul. Jesus assures us, "Blessed are those who hunger and thirst for righteousness, for they will be filled" (Matt. 5:6). He stood in the temple and called, " 'If anyone is thirsty, let him come to me and drink. Whoever believes in me, as the Scripture has said, streams of living water will flow from within him.' By this he meant the Spirit" (John 7:37–39). Water is the symbol of the Holy Spirit. "Come, all you who are thirsty, come to the waters," God calls through Isaiah (55:1). "I will pour water on the thirsty land . . . I will pour out my Spirit" (Isa. 44:3). "Land" is not found in the Hebrew. It is a promise to the "thirsty," and the Spirit satisfies our thirst.

As long as the fullness of the Spirit is not your whole-souled desire, you will probably not be filled. As long as you treat the experience as something desirable, but are willing to continue as you are without it, you will not receive the fullness. Torrey said, "No man ever got this blessing who felt that he could get along without it."

We read of the people of Judah that, "They sought God

eagerly, and he was found by them" (2 Chron. 15:15). The literal Hebrew is "They sought God with their whole desire." God said through Jeremiah, "You will seek me and find me when you seek me with all your heart" (Jer. 29:13). Probably not desiring the Holy Spirit with all the heart and not making a total surrender of the self are the major reasons for failure to enter upon the experience.

4. *Surrender totally to Christ's lordship.* Make a total consecration of all you are, all you have, and all your future. Present yourself in the totality of your being—body, soul, and spirit. Offer up yourself as a living sacrifice to be wholly God's. This may well involve a dying to your own self-will in one or several areas. You must die to your carnal selfness, to all that is of "the world." You can now say with Paul, "I have been crucified with Christ and I no longer live, but Christ lives in me" (Gal. 2:20).

"Count yourselves dead to sin but alive to God in Christ Jesus. Therefore do not let sin reign in your mortal body . . . offer youselves to God, as those who have been brought from death to life; and offer the parts of your body to him as instruments of righteousness" (Rom. 6:11–13). Provisionally we were crucified with Christ at His cross. We now affirm it by an act of the will in self-surrender. This is the emptying of self which must precede the infilling of the Spirit. Make a total surrender of your will in advance for whatever God reveals to you in your tomorrows. Be willing to abandon your own plans, ambitions, and will if God ever reveals anything to you as contrary to His will. Henceforth you are not your own.

Think of your life as a checkbook. Absolute surrender is to fill all the blank checks by signing in advance your own name, making them out to the Holy Spirit, and permitting Him to fill the blanks as He sees best throughout your tomorrows. You have already said your eternal yes to His will as He makes it known to you. You are His. He is Lord and you lovingly and gladly obey day by day.

5. *Ask in prayer.* Christ's promise could not be more clear: "If you then, though you are evil, know how to give good gifts to your children, how much more will your Father

311

in heaven give the Holy Spirit to those who ask him!" (Luke 11:13). When our hearts are prepared by taking the previous four steps, we are ready to call out to God from the depths of our being for the fulfillment of His promise.

Asking and appropriating need not require a prolonged period of prayer, for God is always ready to fulfill His promise. Yet the biographies of many Christians describe how they hungered and thirsted and prayed for some hours or even days before their hearts seemed ready to take the last step of appropriating faith. Perhaps God uses such a period of asking and reaching out to Him to enable us to deepen our thirst for Him, or to enable us to realize new depths of spiritual need within our nature. From God's standpoint there need be no waiting. Yet He can greatly bless to our spiritual good a time of waiting before Him. During such a period the Spirit searches our hearts. Jesus tells us in such a case to stop our prayer and first make things right with the other person (Matt. 5:23–24).

God's promise of reward for our waiting in His presence in prayer is certain. Isaiah assures us: "Those who hope in the LORD will renew their strength. They will soar on wings like eagles; they will run and not grow weary, they will walk and not be faint" (Isa. 40:31). The Hebrew word for hope in this verse means "to wait with confident expectation and trust."

6. *Appropriate by simple trust.* How blessed that the infilling of the Spirit is by faith! It is by faith—so it is for whoever will. It is by faith—so it can be yours this moment. You don't have to wait to become more worthy. You don't have to prove yourself through self-discipline or through prolonged prayer and fasting. It is not by works; it is the gift of God. It is by grace through faith that we are filled with the Spirit.

When Peter described how the Spirit filled the Gentiles at the house of Cornelius and compared it to how the 120 were filled at Pentecost, he explained that God gave the Holy Spirit to Gentiles just as He had to those in the Upper Room on Pentecost. "He made no distinction between us and them, for he purified their hearts by faith" (Acts 15:9). God always purifies and empowers when He fills with His Spirit, and the appropriating means which God has ordained is faith.

Dr. A. J. Gordon writes, "It seems clear from the Scriptures that it is still the duty and privilege of believers to receive the Holy Spirit by a conscious, definite act of appropriating faith, just as they received Jesus Christ. . . . It is as sinners that we accept Christ for our justification, but it is as sons that we accept the Spirit for our sanctification."

Nothing could be more simple, yet nothing is more demanding. When electric lines are installed and connected with the electric power supply, even a child can turn on lights by touching a switch. Even so, when we have prepared our hearts by making everything clear between God and us, acknowledged our need and God's provision, hungered and thirsted for the Spirit's fullness, surrendered totally to Christ's lordship, and asked in prayer, all we need to do is to touch God in faith. It is not a question of the power of our faith; it is the greatness of God's available provision that counts.

Believe how intensely Christ longs to fill you with His Spirit. He wants you to be all He created you to be. Believe what joy it will bring to the heart of Jesus when He sees you filled with His presence and power. Believe in God's wonderful plan for you! How He desires to use your leadership and your life in ways beyond your own plans and thoughts! The full record you will not know until eternity, but God will encourage you at times with bits of news of how He has made you a blessing.

Believe and keep humble, giving God all the glory, and Christ will use you more and more as He leads you in His triumphal procession (2 Cor. 2:14). "The path of the righteous is like the first gleam of dawn, shining ever brighter till the full light of day" (Prov. 4:18).

REMEMBER THESE SPIRITUAL REALITIES:

1. *The infilling of the Spirit is instantaneous.* Faith is not a gradual process nor is the infilling of the Spirit a gradual

process. Faith instantly receives in your innermost being the
fullness of the presence and power of the Spirit. Rejoice!
When your prepared heart believes, that moment you are
filled with the Spirit.

2. *The infilling of the Spirit is not a matter of feeling.* It
is a spiritual reality through faith. Your trust is not in your
feelings, but in God and His promise. Many have testified to
an overwhelming awareness of God's presence, love, or
power. God may or may not choose to bless you that way. He
knows what is best for your future walk of faith. But power is
present whether you feel it or not. It will be manifest as you
serve and obey God.

3. *Continued infillings of the Spirit are available to you.*
Chapter 11 pointed out that the Bible records repeated
infillings of the Spirit. I also mentioned that Zechariah
presents a picture of God's flaming servants being kept aflame
by the constant inflow of the Spirit. That is why Zechariah 4:6
can be a continuing experience in the service of the Lord:
" 'Not by might nor by power, but by my Spirit,' says the LORD
Almighty."

4. *Rejoice in God's fullness and continue to pray and
obey.* You have been filled with the Spirit. Now let God use
you. He did not fill you to make life easy for you, but to
empower you for holy living and effective service. As long as
you keep the channel clear between God and you, His power
continues to flow into you. You cannot retain the fullness of
the Spirit without prayer and obedience.

Sometimes you may realize that you have grieved the
Spirit, and sense a loss of the abundance of His presence and
power. You may be aware of a depletion of the Spirit's
working because of your busy ministry, or for the other
reasons listed in chapter 13. Seek God's forgiveness and ask
Him for the renewal of His power upon you. Prayer and
obedience will again bring the renewal you desire.

Many occasions will rise in your leadership when you
will need a special manifestation of God's presence, a
renewed empowering, a fresh anointing. Praise God! He is
waiting to meet all your need. He knows your ministry and

the situations you face far better than you do. All of His resources are available to you. Pray and obey. Go through life praying and obeying. God will not fail you.

"Now to him who is able to do immeasurably more than all we ask or imagine, according to his power that is at work within us, to him be glory in the church and in Christ Jesus throughout all generations, for ever and ever! Amen" (Eph. 3:20). And to Him be glory through your life and ministry as you live and walk in the fullness of His Spirit's presence and power.

Make this beloved hymn of the church your prayer. It has been sung in prayer to the Lord for a century. May it express your heart cry today:

Fill Me Now

Hover o'er me, Holy Spirit,
Bathe my trembling heart and brow;
Fill me with Thy hallowed presence,
Come, O come and fill me now.

Chorus:
Fill me now, fill me now,
Jesus, come and fill me now;
Fill me with Thy hallowed presence,
Come, O come and fill me now.

Thou canst fill me, gracious Spirit,
Though I cannot tell Thee how;
But I need Thee, greatly need Thee,
Come, O come and fill me now.

I am weakness, full of weakness,
At Thy sacred feet I bow;
Blest, divine, eternal Spirit,
Fill with power, and fill me now.

Cleanse and comfort, bless and save me,
Bathe, O bathe my heart and brow;
Thou art comforting and saving,
Thou art sweetly filling now.

—Elwood H. Stokes

If God has made this book a blessing to you and you wish to share a testimony or word of encouragement, or if you would like the author to remember your ministry in a moment of prayer, please feel free to write:

Dr. Wesley L. Duewel
OMS International
Box A
Greenwood, Indiana 46142

Notes

Chapter 2

[1]Origen; Athanasius; Jerome; Chrysostom; Calvin; Clarke; Dunn; Jamieson, Faussett, and Brown; Liefeld; Marshall; Micklem; Farrar; Geldenhuys; Alford; G. Campbell Morgan; Ryle; Barclay; Leon Morris; *Dictionary of New Testament Theology*; etc.

[2]Lloyd-Jones, *Preaching and Preachers*, 97.

[3]Jamieson, Fausset, and Brown, *Commentary*, 888.

Chapter 6

[1]Lloyd-Jones, *Preaching and Preachers*, 95.

Chapter 7

[1]Marshall, *Pictorial Encyclopedia*, 805.

[2]Morris, *Thessalonians*, 57.

[3]Fee, *Corinthians*, 95.

Chapter 9

[1]Smith, *Passion for Souls*, 37–38.

[2]Orr, *Evangelical Awakening*, 35.

Chapter 10

[1]Woolsey, *Duncan Campbell*, 133.

[2]Ibid., 135.

[3]Ibid., 172.

[4]Ibid.

Ablaze for God

Chapter 11

¹Lloyd-Jones, *Preaching and Preachers*, 308.

Chapter 13

¹Shelhamer, *Heart-Searching Talks*, 124–27.

Chapter 16

¹Cowman, *Charles E. Cowman*, 60.
²Ibid., 260.

Chapter 17

¹Smith, *Passion for Souls*, 167–76, *passim*.

Chapter 31

¹Gordon, *Ministry of the Spirit*, 145.

Chapter 35

¹Smith, *Passion for Souls*, 170.
²Jowett, *Passion for Souls*, 33–36.
³Lloyd-Jones, *Preaching and Preachers*, 90
⁴Ibid., 94.

Chapter 36

¹Cumming, *Eternal Spirit*, 155.
²Lloyd-Jones, *Preaching and Preachers*, 305.

Chapter 37

¹*Journal of Francis Asbury*, 20–21.
²Lloyd-Jones, *Preaching and Preachers*, 325.

Chapter 38

¹Wessel, *Charles G. Finney*, 76.
²Dunning, *Samuel Chadwick*, 95–96.
³Smith, *Enduement*, 56–58.
⁴Smith, *Passion for Souls*, 35.
⁵Hogue, *Holy Spirit*, 314.
⁶Smith, *Enduement*, 50–51.
⁷Ibid., 46–47.

Chapter 39

¹Woolsey, *Campbell*, 163.

318

Chapter 41

[1]Lloyd-Jones, *Preaching and Preachers*, 320.
[2]Wessel, *Finney*, 21–22.
[3]Edman, *Secret*, 33–34.
[4]Ibid., 121.

Chapter 42

[1]Graham, *Holy Spirit*, 160.
[2]Scroggie, *Filled With the Spirit*, 16–18.
[3]Lindsell, *Holy Spirit*, 116.
[4]Graham, *Holy Spirit*, 166.
[5]Ibid., 159.
[6]Torrey, *Holy Spirit*, 154, *passim*.
[7]Bright, *Handbook*, 100–101.
[8]Graham, *Holy Spirit*, 164.

For Further Reading

Asbury, Francis. *The Journal and Letters of Francis Asbury.* Edited by Elmer T. Clark, J. Manning Potts, and Jacob S. Payton. Nashville: Abingdon Press, 1958.

Baker, Frank. *Methodism and the Love-Feast.* London: The Epworth Press, 1957.

Blanchard, Charles A. *Getting Things From God.* Chicago: The Bible Institute Colportage Association, 1915.

Bounds, Edward M. *The Essentials of Prayer.* Grand Rapids, MI: Baker Book House, 1979.

———. *The Necessity of Prayer.* New York: Fleming H. Revell Company, 1929.

———. *Power Through Prayer.* Grand Rapids, MI: Baker Book House, 1986. Eighteenth printing.

———. *Purpose in Prayer.* New York: Fleming H. Revell Company, 1920.

Bright, Bill. *Handbook of Concepts for Living.* San Bernardino, CA: Here's Life Publishers, Inc., 1971.

Carson, D.A. "Matthew." *The Expositor's Bible Commentary,* Vol. 8, Twelve Volumes. Grand Rapids, MI: Zondervan Publishing House, 1984.

Cowman, Lettie B. *Charles E. Cowman: Missionary–Warrior.* Los Angeles: The Oriental Missionary Society, 1947.

Cumming, J. Elder, *Through the Eternal Spirit*. London: Marshall, Morgan & Scott, Ltd., 1937.

Demaray, Donald E. *Preacher Aflame!* Grand Rapids, MI: Baker Book House, 1972.

Duewel, Wesley L. *Touch the World Through Prayer*. Grand Rapids, MI: Zondervan Publishing House, 1986.

Dunning, Norman G. *Samuel Chadwick*. London: Hodder and Stoughton, Ltd., 1933.

Edman, V. Raymond. *They Found the Secret*. Grand Rapids, MI: Zondervan Publishing House, 1984.

Edwards, Jonathan, ed., *The Life and Diary of David Brainerd*. Chicago: Moody Press, n.d.

Fee, Gordon D. *The First Epistle to the Corinthians*. Grand Rapids, MI: Wm. B. Eerdmans Publishing Company, 1987.

Finney, Charles G. *Memoirs of Rev. Charles G. Finney*. New York: Fleming H. Revell Company, 1876.

_____ *The Autobiography of Charles G. Finney*. Condensed and edited by Helen Wessel. Minneapolis, MN: Bethany Fellowship, Inc., 1977.

Gordon A.J. *The Ministry of the Spirit*. Minneapolis, MN: Bethany Fellowship, Inc., 1964.

Graham, Billy. *The Holy Spirit*. Waco, TX: Word Books, 1978.

Hills, Rev. A.M. *Holiness and Power*. Cincinnati: Revivalist Office, 1897.

Hogue, Wilson T. *The Holy Spirit*. Winona Lake, IN: The Free Methodist Publishing House, 1950.

Jamieson, Robert; Fausset, A.R.; Brown, David. *Commentary on the Whole Bible*. rev. ed. Grand Rapids, MI: Zondervan Publishing House, 1961.

Jowett, J.H. *The Passion for Souls*. New York: Fleming H. Revell Company, 1905.

Lawson, J. Gilchrist. *Deeper Experiences of Famous Christians*. Anderson, IN: The Warner Press, 1911.

Liefeld, Walter L. "Luke." *The Expositor's Bible Commentary*, Vol. 8. Grand Rapids, MI: Zondervan Publishing House, 1984.

Lindsell, Harold. *The Holy Spirit in the Latter Days*. Nashville, TN: Thomas Nelson, Inc., 1983.

Lloyd-Jones, D. Martyn. *Preaching and Preachers*. Grand Rapids, MI: Zondervan Publishing House, 1971.

MacIntyre, David Martin. *Hidden Life of Prayer*. Stirling, Scotland: Drummond Tract Depot, 1907.

Marshall, I. H. "Kingdom of God, of Heaven." *Zondervan Pictorial Encyclopedia of the Bible,* Vol. III. Grand Rapids, MI: Zondervan Publishing House, 1970.

McLeister, Clara. *Men and Women of Deep Piety*. Cincinnati: God's Bible School and Revivalist, 1920.

Miller, Basil. *Praying Hyde*. Grand Rapids, MI: Zondervan Publishing House, 1943.

Morris, Leon. *The Epistle of Paul to the Thessalonians*. London: Marshall, Morgan & Scott, Ltd., 1959.

Newell, William R. *The Book of The Revelation*. Chicago: Moody Press, 1935.

Orr, J. Edwin. *The Second Evangelical Awakening in Britain*. London: Marshall, Morgan, & Scott, Ltd., 1953.

Payne, Thomas. *The Greatest Force on Earth*. London: Marshall Brothers, Ltd., 7th ed., n.d.

Quayle, William A. *The Pastor-Preacher*. Edited by Warren W. Wiersbe. Grand Rapids, MI: Baker Book House, 1979.

Scroggie, W. Graham. *Filled With the Spirit*. Chicago: Moody Press, 1925.

Shelhamer, E. E. *Heart Searching Talks to Ministers*. Louisville, KY: Pentecostal Publishing Company, 1914.

Smith, Oswald J. *David Brainerd: His Message for Today*. London: Marshall, Morgan & Scott, Ltd., 1949.

_____. *The Enduement of Power*. rev. ed. London: Marshall, Morgan & Scott, 1965.

_____. *The Passion for Souls*. rev. ed. London: Marshall, Morgan & Scott, 1965.

Torrey, R. A. *The Holy Spirit*. New York: Fleming H. Revell Company, 1927.

For Further Reading

_____. *Why God Used D.L. Moody.* Chicago: Moody Press, 1963.

Wenham, G.J. "The Book of Leviticus," *The New International Commentary on the Old Testament.* Grand Rapids, MI: Wm. B. Eerdmans Publishing Company, 1979.

Wessel, Helen, ed. *The Autobiography of Charles G. Finney.* Minneapolis, MN: Bethany Fellowship, Inc., 1977.

Woolsey, Andrew. *Duncan Campbell—A Biography.* London: Hodder and Stoughton, 1974.

Index

Index

Index